Data Communications Software Design

Data Communications Software Design

Malcolm G. Lane
West Virginia University

COMPUTER SCIENCE SERIES

Boyd & Fraser Publishing Company
Boston

Editor: Tom Walker
Production manager: Erek Smith
Development editor: Sharon Cogdill
Production editors: Toni Rosenberg, Traute M. Marshall
Ancillaries editor: Donna Villanucci
Design: Prentice Crosier
Art: Len Shalansky
Cover: Carol Rose

Manufactured in the United States of America

10 9 8 7 6 5 4 3 2

Library of Congress Cataloging in Publication Data

Lane, Malcolm G., 1943-
   Data communications software design.

   Includes index.
   1. Data transmission systems.   2. Computer
networks.   3. Programming (Electronic computers)
I. Title.
TK5105.L357   1985   001.64'25   84-29293
ISBN 0-87835-145-0

To
Maureen, Melanie, and Maura

Contents

List of Tables

Preface

Just a few short years ago, data communications was a relatively new concept, and few computer professionals were familiar with data communications techniques. Today, even the smallest microcomputer provides some data communications capability, if only as a terminal to a larger computer.

In the fifties and sixties, computers required little data communications with other computer systems. As terminals were introduced as a way of accessing a computer, communications began to play a larger role in a computer center's ability to deliver service to the computer user. Most of the terminals and communications equipment of this time were hardwired to provide a very specific type of communication to a larger computer.

With the advent of minicomputers in the late sixties and the increased popularity of these systems, particularly in universities, a new way of providing data communications to larger computers evolved. Also, during this period, the ARPANET project began and ultimately provided most of the theory of networking known today. Minicomputers were programmed to "speak" the protocols of larger mainframe computers and of the new ARPANET network that was being developed.

The need to submit batch jobs from remote locations in the many IBM installations which existed at the time prompted the birth of a new industry — the remote batch terminal vendors. Many companies provided remote batch terminals by programming minicomputers of one type or another. In fact, many of these minicomputers were programmed to be strictly remote batch terminals. At the same time, minicomputers were used to develop sophisticated communications controllers. These controllers served as terminal concentrators and front-end communications controllers to larger computers.

Minicomputer vendors realized that this remote batch communications capability could be provided on the already popular minicomputer. It was difficult for the specialized remote batch terminal vendors to turn their remote batch systems into stand-alone minicomputers complete with operating systems. The remote batch terminal vendors began to suffer the fate of technological obsolescence. The minicomputers of the seventies were crucial to the evolution of data communications.

When the microcomputer was introduced, one of its early capabilities was communication via serial asynchronous communications interfaces. Many microcomputers were capable of communicating in synchronous mode to other computer systems at a cost far below what had previously been possible. Point-to-point communications between computers using microcomputers was introduced early in the microcomputer's development and has become very commonplace.

It is interesting to note that the text of this book has been transmitted on many occasions from one computer to another using terminal emulators described in Chapter 19. Data communications hardware and software made possible the writing, editing, and transmission of this book: the text was initially entered on a battery-operated portable; it was transferred to several different personal computers for word processing; it was transferred back to a battery-operated portable for editing while traveling; and it was finally transferred to a Digital Equipment Corporation VAX, running UNIX, so that a magnetic tape could be provided for the typesetting.

Today the concepts of networking, systems network architectures, and local area networks dominate much of the published literature. Seminar after seminar provides information about these topics. Yet a basic understanding of *how* computers communicate is often lacking. This text describes how computers communicate, the language of communications (the "protocol"), hardware interfaces used to communicate, and most important, the software which controls a computer's communications. The primary goal of this book is to provide the reader with a complete understanding of data link control protocols, timing considerations, error recovery, communications software design, and communications testing and debugging techniques.

This book is appropriate for a course on data communications or data communications software design. The student should have a background in basic concepts in computer science and be familiar with such operating concepts as interrupts. A chapter describing the concepts of interrupts is included, but it may be skipped by those who are already familiar with such topics.

There is a distinct practical orientation in the book, with a presentation of software design concepts that have been successful in actual communications projects. To thoroughly understand data communications, it is necessary to get one's hands "dirty" with data communications software design, implementation, testing, and debugging. Hence, this book was designed for use in a laboratory-oriented course. Three simple data communications projects are described in Appendixes E, F, and G.

The book is divided into two parts. Part I deals with basic data communications concepts required to be able to implement data communications software. It includes chapters on network architectures and local area networks so that students will be familiar with all areas in which data communications software is required. Part II deals with data communications software and emphasizes how to control communications hardware, the structure of data link control communications software, and implementation techniques for communications software.

This book can be used sequentially, by covering each chapter in order. This may be most appropriate if a laboratory for projects is not available for the course. However, in order to have the students work on data communications software projects throughout the course, it would be best if Part I and Part II were used together; for example, after covering certain chapters in Part I, students could be assigned material in Part II which would allow them to do software projects related to the material in Part I. The following is a recommended ordering of chapters which allows software projects to be assigned throughout the course:

Chapters 1 through 5	Basic Communications Concepts
Chapters 14 through 15	Introduction to Software Design
Chapter 16	Error Detection Software Projects
Chapters 17 through 18	Asynchronous Communications Software Project (Appendix E)
Chapter 19	Asynchronous Terminal Emulators and XON/ XOFF Control
Chapters 6 through 12	Networks and Protocols
Chapters 20 through 23	Software Design Principles
Appendix F Protocol Project	Uses Project from Appendix E to Implement Data Link Control Protocol
or Appendix G Protocol Project	Implementation of Data Link Control Protocol using Synchronous Communications
Chapters 24 and 25	Review; Testing and Debugging Techniques
Chapter 13	Overview of Local Area Networks

This ordering of the chapters has been used very successsfully since 1979 in a course in data communications software engineering at West Virginia University.

Appendix A enables instructors to show students why CRC algorithms are more effective than parity techniques in detecting errors. It can be assigned as reading and discussion material at the end of Chapter 4. Appendix B is the formal grammar of the DDCMP protocol and provides the student with a more detailed description of a data link control protocol than is contained in the text itself. Appendix B is very important in the implementation of the project presented in Appendix G.

Appendixes C and D are included so that various implementations of finite state machine software in different languages can be studied. Appendix C is an implementation in the "C" programming language, while Appendix D is an implementation in Pascal.

Many of the communications projects described in this book are often implemented in whole or in part using assembler language because of the requirement to control communications hardware. The pseudocode illustrations of logic listed in Part II are general and are included to provide the student with an understanding of what communications software must do. It is difficult to describe data structures which represent implementations in both assembler language and high-level languages. Hence, it is pointed out that how information in the data structures is referenced is very language-dependent, but the basic ideas are the same. Differences which occur because of the use of assembler language are pointed out where possible.

The figures and tables in this book reflect its practical orientation. Tables of codes generally include decimal, octal, and hexadecimal values because various laboratories will require different representations. A table listing parity codes for ASCII with octal and hexadecimal values is included to illustrate parity more fully. Computation of CRC-16 error check characters is illustrated in great detail using both polynomial division and exclusive OR/shifts.

Message traffic in figures is usually shown moving from left to right so that the low order bits of characters, which are transmitted first, indeed appear to arrive first at the destination station. This is extremely important in illustrating asynchronous communications and synchronization in synchronous communications. Hence, characters in messages to be transmitted are shown in the reverse order of the normal representation in a buffer when they are shown as being transmitted from left to right, but are in the normal order when shown being transmitted from right to left. This happens in figures illustrating message traffic between two or more stations.

While many books have used the word *datum* as the singular of the word *data,* *data* is most commonly used in the singular in presentations, discussions and documentation. I have chosen to use the word *data* to mean a collection of information and have used this word in the singular throughout the book.

Giving students the opportunity to design and implement data communications software is the real key to the successful use of this book. The application of these techniques in the past few years has shown the great value of this experience for achieving a true understanding of data communications concepts and software design principles.

Malcolm G. Lane
Morgantown, WV
1985

Preface to the Student

This book is oriented towards laboratory projects which will help you thoroughly understand the principles of data communications and data communications software design. At the end of each chapter are Terminology and Review Questions to help you review what you have learned. Each term in the Terminology list appears in boldface type in the chapter and is defined in the Dictionary. Answers to selected Review Questions are given in the Answer Section at the back of the book so that you can check your understanding of the material presented.

Assignments, listed at the end of appropriate chapters, are mostly programming assignments, although some require application of the theory presented in the chapter and not programming. The Assignments are perhaps the most important part of the book; they are necessary to master the subject matter. Appendixes E, F, and G describe projects which are assigned in the Assignments sections of various chapters.

Appendixes A through D are included to provide more detailed information than is practical to include in the text itself on CRC error check algorithms, on the DDCMP protocol, and on finite state machine data link control protocol implementations. Appropriate references to these Appendixes are indicated in the text.

References to other works are cited where appropriate within chapters, and are listed in full at the end of each chapter. Use these References and your library to learn more about subjects in this book that particularly interest you. Some References cite specific page numbers. When page numbers are not cited, go to the table of contents and the index of the referenced work for the information you want.

Many figures in the book illustrate data communications message traffic. After many experiments in the classroom, it has been found that message traffic in a figure is best illustrated moving from left to right so that the low order bits of characters, which are transmitted first, indeed appear to arrive first at a destination station. This is extremely important in illustrating asynchronous communications and synchronization in synchronous communications. Hence, when characters in messages to be transmitted are shown being transmitted from left to right, they are shown in the reverse order of the normal representation in a buffer. In figures showing two-way traffic, message traffic must also be illustrated moving from right to left in which case the characters in the message appear in the order you would normally expect, that is, the beginning of a message is on the left and the end of a message is on the right. It is important to remember why the illustrations of message traffic appear as they do as you study the figures dealing with message traffic.

You are encouraged to read the Preface to learn more about the organization and goals of this book and the projects assigned in it.

Acknowledgements

I am grateful to the many students who used preliminary versions of much of this book for the course Software Engineering for Data Communications Systems in the Department of Statistics and Computer Science at West Virginia University. Their valuable suggestions and their willingness to consider various ideas in the many figures in the book are greatly appreciated. I wish to thank Bill Duggan of Idaho State University, Kenneth P. Johnson of Grand Valley State College, Rayno Niemi of the Rochester Institute of Technology, C. Andrew Belew of Ferris State College, Dennis Lee Brown of Morgan State University, H. Doug Ponder of Gadsden State Junior College, Greg Hodge of Northwest Michigan College, Paul W. Ross of Millersville State University, and James A. Metzler of Bently College who reviewed preliminary versions of the manuscript for their valuable suggestions and comments.

Many of the ideas in Part II of the book are based on ideas of mine published by John Wiley & Sons as two chapters in *Advances in Data Communications Management: Volume 2*. Chapter 20 contains material from Chapter 1 of this book. Chapters 22 and 25 are extensions and revisions of some of the material in this same book.

The ideas on software structure were tested and verified by several of my graduate students over the past six years. I am grateful to Daniel Omer, who first applied the modular structure and finite state machine implementations in assembler language after I had first tested the ideas in a commercial setting. His suggestions for formatting figures were most useful in Chapter 12. John Wack used the modular structure to implement a prototype DDCMP software system, which can be used to test the DDCMP protocol project described in Appendix G. Kenneth Jones and Paul Gesalman applied the ideas of modular structures and finite state machines in high level languages, mainly "C" and Pascal, respectively. Parts of their work appear as Appendixes C and D in this book. Mark Osborne provided background work and Figure 19-2 for Chapter 19, on terminal emulators.

Digital Equipment Corporation's DDCMP protocol definition provides a very nice illustration of formal grammars describing protocol syntax and of state tables describing procedural rules. Appendix B of this book is a reprint of Appendix B of the DDCMP specification.

Without the support of the Department of Statistics and Computer Science, in particular Donald F. Butcher, who encouraged me to pursue this project, this book would have never been written. I am most grateful to Louise Tudor of the Department for her word-processing knowledge, accurate and professional work, long hours, and patience in the final revisions to the manuscript. Thanks to James Foltz, who was ready when required to help in the necessary transfers of machine-readable text to magnetic tape using UNIX. It was in fact, data communications which allowed such transfers to be accomplished easily and quickly!

The staff of Boyd & Fraser has been outstanding to work with in the production of this book. I am grateful to Tom Walker, Editor-in-Chief, and Donna Villanucci, Ancillaries Editor, for their work and support. And to Sharon Cogdill, Development Editor, who worked with me side by side in the final editing of the manuscript, I am extremely grateful. Her excellent suggestions in improving the manuscript are reflected in the final product. In spite of working long hours editing the manuscript, she never lost her sense of humor and pleasant personality.

My mother and late father taught me that every task should be given my best. I am grateful to them for that and for the love, support, and encouragement they gave me as I pursued my education, which ultimately enabled me to work as a university faculty member in computer science.

My wife, Maureen, and my two lovely daughters, Melanie and Maura, deserve the most thanks. Without their infinite patience, love, and understanding, this book would have been impossible. Finally, I thank the Lord for the talents and abilities I was given which allowed me to write a book such as this.

Part 1

Principles of
Data Communications

1

Introduction

Introduction • Background • Early Days of Data Communications

Introduction

As young as computer science is as a field, the area of data communications software design is even younger. Yet the field of data communications software is and will continue to be extremely important to computer technology.

From the smallest microcomputer to the largest mainframe computer, data communications capabilities are and will be a major factor in the success and usefulness of the computer system. No longer are users willing to work with their data isolated on one computer system. The need for larger systems to process data created on small computers, the need to move subsets of data to small computers from larger computers for local processing, the need to access larger computers for other capabilities (via terminal emulation), and the need for growth in hardware capability are all major reasons that data communications is so important to today's technology.

In spite of attempts at standardization in many areas of data processing, computer systems are not fully compatible with one another. Data communications can help bridge the gap between computers, particularly in the transfer of user data from one system to another. Whether it is with a specific **protocol** (rules for communicating between computers) or with **terminal emulation** (in which the computer "looks like a terminal"), the communications capabilities available for a given computer ultimately determine its flexibility and power. Problems which cannot be solved *on a particular computer* can often be solved "through" the computer by utilizing its data communications capability to gain access to a computer system that does provide sufficient power.

The approach this book takes is to present the concepts of data communications (Part I) and then the software design considerations in implementing software which provides data communications capability (Part II). It is the emphasis on software that makes this book unique, and, upon completing it, a reader should be able to understand and implement simple data communications software.

The inclusion of prototype projects, along with software prototypes and design ideas, should make the processes of data communications software design, implementation, and debugging easier to understand.

Both asynchronous serial communications interfaces and synchronous communications interfaces will be studied. Even the smallest microcomputer systems have asynchronous communications capability (RS–232 serial interface) and most have synchronous capability, although many of these systems do not provide software to drive the synchronous interface.

Probably one of the most popular and most common communications programs is the asynchronous terminal emulator which is available for virtually all microcomputers. Because of the popularity of such programs and the potential need by a user either to implement or modify such a program, a chapter has been included which outlines the capabilities and operation of asynchronous terminal emulators.

Because most communications software tends to be **event-driven** (for example, receiving or transmitting a character or buffer) and because the interrupt hardware capability is most often utilized to implement such software, the concepts of interrupts and the design of interrupt handlers is presented. Readers already familiar with these concepts may choose to skip Chapter 15.

Software engineering, modular programming, and structured programming have been popular ideals within the computer industry for a long time. While many programmers claim that they apply the principles of all three, there is some disagreement about what each is. Communications software design can be quite complex, and the application of rigorous software design principles is critical to the design and debugging processes. The modular **data link control protocol** software structure presented in this book isolates the functions required within data communications software. This structure has been used in many implementations by the author and his colleagues and has been quite successful, particularly for simplifying debugging and maintenance.

Finally, debugging problems and debugging techniques are presented to help completely implement operational data communications software. One valuable part of the chapter on debugging is the table which presents certain symptoms of failures during debugging (and sometimes after production begins), the possible causes, and the possible corrections to these problems.

This book should serve both as a reference book for those familiar with data communications concepts but unfamiliar with the implementation of data communications software and as a text to those who have never been exposed to data communications concepts.

Background

There are many similarities in the evolution of communication between people and the evolution of communication between computers. Early in human history, communication was very primitive. Writing was an advance that allowed the thoughts and ideas of a person to be moved from one place to another; the person whose ideas were preserved did not have to be present when the ideas were communicated to another. In this case, data moves in one direction only.

This dramatizes precisely how information was communicated in the early days of computing. Probably the simplest method of communicating between one computer and another was to rekey the information produced on paper by one computer into a medium which could be read by another computer. Another common method was to physically carry computer-produced media like punched cards, paper tape, or magnetic tape from one computer system to another. This direct reading of a computer medium is a one-way transfer of information between computers.

Telephone revolutionized the way people communicate; timely information could be conveyed from one person to another with minimal effort. Similarly, the early links between computers using telephone media allowed data to be moved from one computer to another in a more timely manner. Just as a telephone receiver has two parts, which correspond to a microphone into which one speaks and an earpiece from which one hears a conversation, a computer must be able to make use of both the transmission and receiving functions on a telephone line. This means that there must be hardware which provides both transmitting and receiving functions.

There are many useful analogies between human and computer communication which will appear later, in the discussion of particular communications concepts. One thing is certain: both need three components to communicate:

a transmitter (voice)

a receiver (ear)

a medium (phone line, air)

Figure 1–1 illustrates this analogy with the three components.

In order for actual communication to occur, these three components must exist along with an understanding of what is being received - there must be language (or protocol). Without such a language, information is "heard" but not understood. In spite of the appearance of the simplicity of this model, it should also be noted that real communication on these components is only truly effective if it is two-way communication.

Early Days of Data Communications

Perhaps the telegraph gave us the first data communications capability. Certainly, the punching and reading of paper tapes during receipt and transmission produced a computer medium. In fact, the early torn tape centers consisted of many teletypes connected remotely via telegraph lines to different geographic locations (see Figure 1–2). Each teletype had a specific address (like A, B, and C in Figure 1–2). A tape which was produced on one teletype could be removed and read in another to be relayed to another location. This is analogous to the **store and forward** techniques used in many computer networks today. [Sherman 1981]

Note that the operation of a torn tape center provided queue management (storing the tape in proper place), buffer management (having tape to punch), routing (moving a tape from one unit to another), priority control (determining the most important messages to be forwarded and reading them first), and validation control (making sure tapes make sense and will read). None of these functions were automated; they were all manual operations performed by people. Typically, these functions must be provided today by data communications software.

It should be noted that it was not until the early 1950s that terminals were used to communicate to and from computers. In fact, the teletype units themselves were the first terminals. One problem caused by these terminals was that they used five-bit **Baudot code**. This code was not adequate for computer use, particularly since it provided no error checking for data being sent on a medium which was often noisy. Also,

FIGURE 1–1   Three Components Necessary for Communication

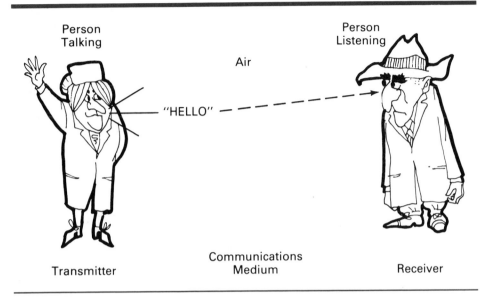

FIGURE 1–2   Teletype Torn Tape Center

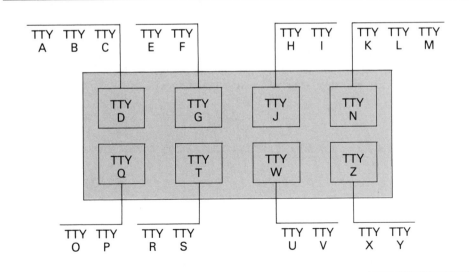

only 32 different codes can be transmitted using five bits and it was necessary to shift from one code interpretation to another in order to be able to represent all necessary characters. Hence, special modes were introduced so that information which required more than 32 distinct characters could be transmitted and received with a five-bit code (see Chapter 4).

New codes (**ASCII** and **EBCDIC**) evolved during the 1960s. It was not until the middle 1960s that communications interfaces became of real importance to computer manufacturers.

The early to middle 1960s was the era of the stand-alone computer. IBM dominated the computer market with many computers, among them the 1401, 1620, and the 7040 computer systems. Data was moved from one system to another either on cards or magnetic tape.

The advent of the IBM 360 series computer introduced a more powerful commercial computer. Concepts which had already been proved by the Atlas Project at the University of Manchester, England, found their way into a commercial operating system (OS–360) — most notably **multiprogramming**. Because the power of such a large system could not always be made use of by on-site users, a need for data communications arose, particularly for remote job entry via cards.

Early communications controllers such as the IBM 2701, 2702, and 2703 series were **hardwired**, that is, they were not at all programmable. Today, almost all communications controllers are programmable, making the support of different protocols possible, often at the same time.

Communications front-end processors have emerged to ease the workload on mainframe computers. In addition, communications software is used in terminal concentrators or multiplexers, remote batch terminals, microcomputers, and minicomputers. In fact, the functions of front-end processor, remote batch terminal, and multiplexer are now performed by minicomputers and microcomputers running appropriate data communications software.

The need for an understanding of data communications and data communications software is obvious. In order to fully comprehend data communications design, however, it is necessary to master many basic concepts. Part I of this book (Chapters 1 through 13) deals with this required background material.

═══ Terminology ═══

ASCII	hardwired
Baudot Code	multiprogramming
data link control protocol	protocol
EBCDIC	store and forward
event-driven	terminal emulation

≡ Review Questions ≡

1. Three components necessary for communication between people or computers are _____ , _____ , and _____ .

2. The rules for communicating between computers are called a _____ .

3. Early teletype systems used techniques which are analogous to
    a. multiprogramming techniques
    b. terminal emulation techniques
    c. store and forward techniques

4. Why is data communications so important in modern computer systems?

Reference

Sherman, Kenneth. 1981. *Data Communications: A Users Guide*. Reston, Virginia: Reston.

2

Basic Communications Concepts

Signalling Techniques • Noise • Media • Microwave • Fiber Optics • Satellite • Summary of Media Choices • Limitations of Transmission Rates • Modes • Types of Communications Lines • Multiplexing

Signalling Techniques

An electronic signal is used to move information from one computer system to another or from a computer to a terminal device. Different states, often two, can be represented by the modification of a particular signal; these modified signals are then interpreted as a zero or one, which correspond to the binary bits within a computer system. Representing two or more states using an electronic signal provides the means for moving information (data) from one computer system to another. Data communications takes place when information is first processed via hardware and software, so that it is represented by this modified electronic signal, and then reassembled in the destination computer or terminal.

The **frequency** of signal (its cycles per second) is represented by a **sine wave**, which is shown in Figure 2–1. This sine wave begins at zero, goes through a positive direction, back to zero, through a negative direction, and returns to zero for a complete cycle. A frequency of 1100 **herz** has 1100 such cycles occuring in a period of one second.

Information within a computer is stored using discrete states (1 = on, and 0 = off) which are represented by a **square wave**. The square wave is similar to a sine wave, except that it reaches its maximum positive and negative values almost instantly. Figure 2–2 represents a square wave.

The square wave is a **digital signal** and the sine wave is an **analog signal**. In order for information to be successfully transmitted and received over typical communications media like a telephone line or four copper wires, it must be processed from its

FIGURE 2–1   A Sine Wave

FIGURE 2–2   Square Wave

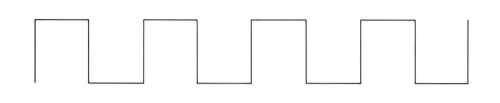

digital form as stored in a computer into the discrete states represented by the modification of the analog signal shown in Figure 2–1 [Sherman 1981, pp. 25–28].

This "imprinting" of a digital signal on an analog signal (a **carrier signal**) is **modulation**. The re-creation of the digital form of the signal is **demodulation**. The devices which perform this are **modems** (**mo**dulation/**dem**odulation) and are covered in Chapter 7.

Noise

Problems arise during the process of modulation and demodulation, in which digital information is transferred from one computer system to another. One of these problems is **noise**, unwanted electronic signals which exist on the communications media. Noise can be inherent in the equipment or caused by outside sources (e.g., lightning). Noise prevents the correct interpretation of received signals; they cannot be interpreted as the original digital signals because the modulated signal has been changed by the noise.

Users of telephone systems are usually familiar with noise problems, like static and clicks on a line during a voice conversation. At a transmission rate of 150 eight-bit characters per second, 15 characters are affected by a 0.1-second click on a line. Without some type of error detection, erroneous information would be stored in the receiving system. Methods of error detection and error recovery are covered in Chapter 4.

One other problem which must be recognized is that of **distortion**. Essentially, distortion results from the characteristics and transmission capabilities of the communications medium itself and is an unwanted change of a signal from its true form. A good example of distortion is a digital signal which, when put onto a transmission medium without modulation/demodulation, will begin to lose its square edges. Eventually, a distorted digital signal will be interpreted incorrectly. Figure 2–3 illustrates the distortion of a digital signal over distance.

Of most interest in data communications are two types of distortion — **attenuation** and **delay**. Attenuation is the loss of signal power as it travels over a distance [Loomis 1983, p. 73; Sherman 1981, p. 323]. The signal loses strength because the power is absorbed by the communications medium itself. In order to overcome this signal loss, amplifiers are placed at certain intervals. Attenuation is, in fact, frequency dependent: some frequencies, mainly the higher and lower frequencies, lose power

FIGURE 2–3   Distortion of a Digital Signal

more quickly than the frequencies in the middle. An attenuation equalizer evens out the attenuation differences of various frequencies [Loomis 1983, p. 73].

Delay distortion occurs on communications media because signals have different propogation speeds at different frequencies. This means that certain frequencies travel more slowly than others and arrive at a given location at a different time. Delay distortion is not noticeable in voice transmission but can result in errors in receiving data, because of the preciseness of measurement required in demodulation.

Attenuation and delay distortion are overcome by the use of **equalizers** on the line, which compensate for the distortion. Frequencies which lose power are boosted; frequencies which do not suffer delay are delayed. The net effect is to equalize the distortion so that the signal arrives basically in the proper form. A line which has equalizers is said to be **conditioned** and is only available on leased lines. [Loomis 1983, p. 74; Sherman 1981, p. 330]

Media

It is axiomatic that in order for communication to take place, a receiver, a transmitter, and a communications medium are necessary. For data communications, the following are among the media possibilities:

> wire communications paths
>
>> open wire
>> twisted pair cable
>> coaxial cable
>
> microwave
>
> fiber optic cable
>
> satellite

Open wires attached to ceramic or glass insulators may at first seem obsolete. They are still in use in parts of the U.S. and in other parts of the world, however, particularly when traffic is low [Sherman 1981, p. 29].

Twisted wire pair cables consist of copper wires insulated by plastic or other material and twisted into pairs. There are often multiple twisted pairs in units, and these units are twisted into a cable. There are many considerations in the construction of such cables; it is important, for instance, to minimize **cross talk** (the undesirable detection of a signal from one pair on another). The need to overcome cross talk resulted in the development of coaxial cable, a cable with a grounded shield around a copper conductor or around twisted pairs of conductors, separated by an insulating material. These coaxial cables are capable of transmitting much higher frequencies than a twisted wire pair. Coaxial cable is a medium which is very common in the implementation of local area networks (see Chapter 13).

Microwave

Much of the circuitry of the telephone system depends on **microwave** technology, which uses very high frequency radio waves in the range of 4.6 to 12 **gigahertz (GHz,** one billion cycles per second). This broadband facility provides line-of-site transmission capability, so there must be **repeaters** installed at approximately 30-mile intervals. These repeaters retransmit the signal to the next receiving microwave station. When geographic and other obstructions prevent 30-mile line-of-site transmission, repeaters must be placed at closer intervals. [Housley 1979, pp. 191–193] Figure 2–4 illustrates microwave transmission.

Fiber Optics

Optical fibers consisting of a strand of glass about the same thickness as a human hair provide a most attractive medium for data transmission. The fibers are flexible, carry high-band width signals (light), and are practically immune from distortion and noise. A light source consisting of either a laser diode or a light-emitting diode allows modulation of data at extremely high transmission rates. One added advantage of **fiber optics** is

FIGURE 2–4   Microwave Transmission

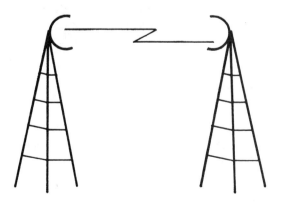

that it is not possible to tap the transmission medium without disturbing it, making it a very secure medium for transmission. Because it is difficult to tap, this very feature is a disadvantage in using the medium in a local area network with a bus topology (see Chapter 13). [Loomis 1983, p. 67; Housley 1979, p. 191]

Satellite

Extending the range of microwave transmission, made possible by the use of **satellites** acting as relay stations, as illustrated in Figure 2–5, opened a new era of communications for the world. Using satellites, countries like Indonesia, with its thousands of islands, and Australia, with its vast open areas, can provide communications to remote areas without ground facilities other than the sending and receiving stations needed for the satellite systems. Satellites receive a signal in one frequency and transmit it in another so as to not interfere with the signals being received. This is done by what is called a **transponder** [Loomis 1983, pp. 67–68]. Satellites tend to have longer propagation delays (250 to 300 milliseconds) in data transmission than ground links (approximately 6 microseconds). The increased speed of satellite transmission, however, tends to minimize the effect of the propogation delay as it relates to data throughput. [Loomis 1983, p. 68; Tanenbaum 1981, pp. 110–114]

Summary of Media Choices

There are many media possibilities for data transmission. Dial-up voice-grade lines are still the most common media of all those mentioned. In choosing the best medium for data transmission, the cost, error rate, security, and speed requirements for data communications must be taken into account.

Limitations of Transmission Rates

The discussion of media types implied that limitations on line speed exist on various media. Voice-grade lines generally operate at speeds no higher than 9600 bps. Yet for light link transmission, data rates magnitudes of order greater than 9600 bps are possible. The reason for this is that there is a theoretical limit on the maximum data rate of a

FIGURE 2–5   Use of Satellites for Communication

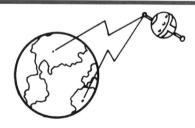

given transmission medium, which is proportional to the bandwidth of the signal used on the medium.

H. Nyquist proved in the 1920s that such a fundamental limit exists, but his work was limited to a channel with no noise [Nyquist 1924; Nyquist 1928]. In 1948, C. Shannon extended Nyquist's work to a channel which was subject to random (thermal) noise [Shannon 1948]. It is useful to be aware of the results of Shannon's work in order to understand the limitations on transmission speed.

Shannon proved that in the presence of noise on a channel with a **bandwidth** of W Hz and **signal-to-noise ratio** of S/N that maximum transmission rate is

$$\text{Maximum Number of Bits/Second} = W \log_2 (1 + S/N)$$

This is **Shannon's law**. The signal-to-noise ratio is usually stated in **decibels**, which is $10 \log_{10}$ S/N. Hence, a 30-decibel (dB) noise ratio yields a signal-to-noise ratio of 1000, because

$$30 = 10 \log_{10} (S/N)$$

so that

$$\log_{10} (S/N) = 3$$

Using this, we have that

$$S/N = 10^3 = 1000$$

Applying Shannon's law, a voice-grade channel with 3000 Hz bandwidth and typical signal to noise ratio of 30 dB yields

$$
\begin{aligned}
\text{Maximum Number of Bits/Second} &= 3000 \log_2 (1 + 1000) \\
&= 3000 \log_2 (1001) \\
&= 3000 \times 9.967 \\
&= 29,901
\end{aligned}
$$

Hence, a voice-grade line cannot transmit at a speed greater than 30,000 bits per second, no matter how many signal levels are used and no matter how often samples are taken.

Trying to reach the maximum limit given by Shannon's law is extremely difficult. Data rates of 9600 bits per second on a voice-grade line are achieved when multiple bits per state are sent; such rates are considered to be quite good. [Tanenbaum 1981, pp. 95–96] Chapter 7 provides more detail on sending multiple bits (dibits).

Modes

There are three modes of data transmission: simplex, half-duplex, and full-duplex. **Simplex** transmission provides for data transmission in one direction only. There can be no response from the receiving system or device. The use of a doorbell in a home, as shown in Figure 2–6, illustrates a type of simplex communication. A person pressing the doorbell communicates to people inside the house that someone is at the door.

FIGURE 2–6   Illustration of Simplex Communication

FIGURE 2–7   Illustration of Half-Duplex Communication

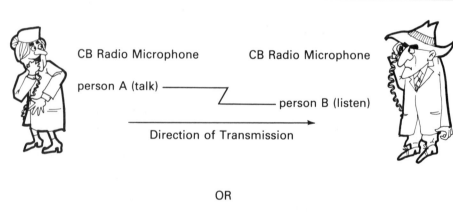

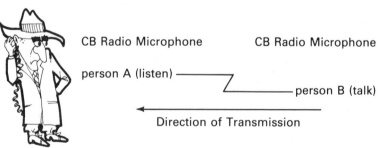

However, there is no electronic mechanism to acknowledge to the person at the door that the doorbell has been heard, unless a two-way intercom is present.

Half-duplex transmission allows the transmission of information in either direction, but not simultaneously. This type of transmission of information involves the alternating of transmission and receiving by two stations. Citizen's Band (CB) radios provide an excellent illustration of half-duplex transmission. A person speaking on a CB radio pushes a "press to talk" button while speaking. If another receiver presses the "press to talk" button at the same time, neither party receives the other's message. The receiving and transmission must alternate to be successful (see Figure 2–7).

"Press to talk" radios utilize an explicit and implicit protocol to allow a person receiving a message to know when it is his turn to transmit. Implicit rules include voice intonation and pauses. Explicit rules include such words as "over." As will be seen later, computer communications in half-duplex modes require rules called **data link control protocol** to specify when it is a particular station's turn to transmit.

Full-duplex transmission allows transmission in both directions at the same time. In the example of the "press to talk" radio, transmission had to wait until receipt of a message was completed. Telephone conversations provide an excellent illustration of full-duplex capability. As depicted in Figure 2–8, a person can speak on a telephone even though the other party has not yet finished speaking. While the other party may not know exactly what was said because of difficulty listening and talking at the same time, the information can be heard by that party.

Hence, the telephone can be used in full-duplex mode, but our rules of etiquette say that one should wait until another person finishes before beginning to speak. The same is true of computer-to-computer communications. A particular link may be capable of full-duplex operation, but the rules or protocol being utilized may not allow full-duplex operation.

FIGURE 2–8   Illustration of Full-Duplex Communication

Person A

talking and listening

Person B

talking and listening

FIGURE 2–9   Point-to-Point Communication Line

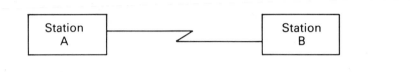

Types of Communications Lines

There is a variety of ways for lines to communicate in a network. The lines connecting stations in a network can be very simple or quite complex. The simplest and most fundamental component of a communications network is the **point-to-point** line. A point-to-point line connects two communicating stations using simplex, half-duplex, or full-duplex mode of operation, as shown in Figure 2–9. Early networks used point-to-point lines in a **star configuration**, as shown in Figure 2–10. Such networks transmitted on multipoint lines from remote "slave" stations to a host "master" station and were typically used for remote job entry.

Multidrop lines allow for the connection of more than one terminal or remote computer on a line attached to a central computer system. This configuration is particularly attractive when the terminals or remote computers do not constantly need the line for data transmission. Multidrop lines are more cost-effective than multiple point-to-

FIGURE 2–10   Star Network Using Point-to-Point Lines

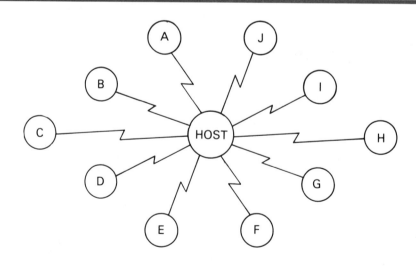

point lines, because more than one slave station shares the same line. Figure 2–11 illustrates a multidrop configuration. Obviously, it is not possible for data transmission by two remote stations to take place simultaneously, since the data would "collide" on the multidrop line and become garbled [Housley 1979, p. 43]. Hence, as will be seen later, it is necessary that the protocol for communications provide for the polling of a specific station on the multidrop line to allow it to send if it has data to transmit. This polling mechanism must be part of the data link control protocol used to move information on the communications line.

Multiplexing

The concepts of simplex, half-duplex, and full-duplex imply that a given communications line is capable of transmitting and receiving one "stream" of information. However, it is possible to support multiple "streams" of data on a single communications line using what is known as **multiplexing**. Essentially, a multiplexer divides the line transmission capacity into pieces using one of two techniques: **time division multiplexing (TDM)** and **frequency division multiplexing (FDM)**.

When a multiplexer is used at each end of a point-to-point line, information from several stations on one end can be transmitted to a central computer (or other system) over a single communications line and be directed to the correct port or interface at the central computer by the receiving multiplexer. Similarly, information which is to be transmitted from the central computer to remote stations will be sent using the multiplexer at the central computer site to the multiplexer at the remote site and will be directed to the correct station by the receiving multiplexer. This is illustrated in Figure 2–12.

The transfer of information using multiplexing can greatly reduce communications line costs, since leased lines can be shared by several "data streams" to and from multiple remote stations. Multiplexers and the techniques used in multiplexing will be discussed further in Chapter 3.

FIGURE 2–11   Multidrop Communications Lines

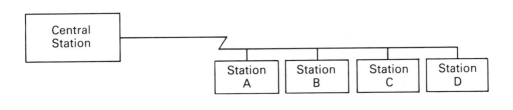

FIGURE 2–12   Multiplexing Data from Multiple Stations on a Single
Communications Line

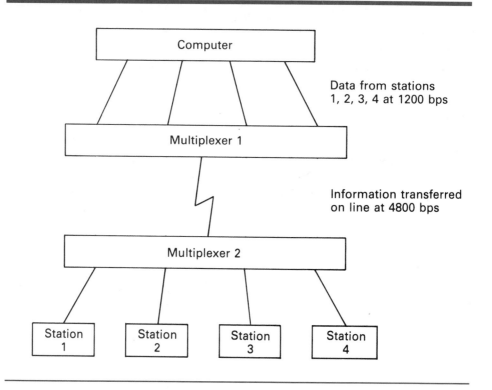

Data from stations
1, 2, 3, 4 at 1200 bps

Information transferred
on line at 4800 bps

≡ **Terminology** ≡

analog signal	distortion
attenuation	equalizer
bandwidth	FDM
carrier signal	fiber optics
conditioned	frequency
cross talk	frequency division multiplexer
data link control protocol	full-duplex
decibel	GHz
delay	gigahertz
demodulation	half-duplex
digital signal	herz

microwave	Shannon's law
modem	signal-to-noise ratio
modulation	simplex
multidrop lines	sine wave
multiplexing	square wave
noise	star configuration
open wires	TDM
point-to-point	time division multiplexing
repeater	transponder
satellite	twisted wire pair cables

≡ Review Questions ≡

1. The basic problem of transmitting digital signals over long distances is due to _____ .

2. True or False:
   a. The speed of data being transmitted on a voice-grade communications line can be arbitrarily large, provided that one is willing to pay the increase costs for the modems.
   b. In a full-duplex multidrop environment, two slave stations can transmit data at the same time.
   c. Multiplexing techniques provide for communications of data from several lines to be sent on just one line.
   d. Open wires are still used in parts of the world today.

3. Two types of multiplexing are _____ and _____ .

4. A _____ is used by a satellite to retransmit a received signal.

5. The limitation for the speed of data transmission over a communications line in the presence of noise is given by _____ .

6. Match the term on the right to the type of data transfer which each describes:
   a. full-duplex   one-way transfer
   b. simplex   two-directional alternating transfer
   c. half-duplex   simultaneous two-directional transfer

≡ Assignment ≡

Given that a communications line has a signal-to-noise ratio of 20 dB and a bandwidth of 4500 Hz, what is the theoretical maximum number of bits per second which can be realized?

References

Housley, Trevor. 1979. *Data Communications and Teleprocessing Systems*. Englewood Cliffs, New Jersey: Prentice-Hall.

Loomis, Mary E. S. 1983. *Data Communications*. Englewood Cliffs, New Jersey: Prentice-Hall.

Nyquist, H. 1924. "Certain Factors Affecting Telegraph Speed." *Transactions A.I.E.E.*

— — —. 1928. "Certain Topics in Telegraph Transmission Theory." *Transactions A.E.E.E.*

Shannon, Claude E. 1948. "Mathematical Theory of Communication." *Bell System Technical Journal* (July and October).

Sherman, Kenneth. 1981. *Data Communications: A Users Guide*. Reston, Virginia: Reston.

Tanenbaum, Andrew S. 1981. *Computer Networks*. Englewood Cliffs, New Jersey: Prentice-Hall.

3

Overview of Communications Hardware

Introduction

Data Communications require many types of hardware. Figure 3–1 illustrates some of the possibilities of such hardware. The hardware illustrated includes **Front-End Processors (FEP)**, modems, multiplexers (MPX), concentrators, interactive terminals, and remote job entry terminals (RJE).

Interactive Terminals

One of the most common types of communications hardware is the **interactive terminal**. An interactive terminal consists of a keyboard and some type of display, either hardcopy (printer) or other display (**CRT** — cathode ray tube, or **LCD** — liquid crystal display). Figure 3–2 illustrates the keyboard and display of an interactive terminal.

The earliest interactive terminals were teletype units **(ASR 33)**, illustrated in Figure 3–3. These original terminals were quite cumbersome to use because of the types of keys that the terminals had and the amount of pressure required to strike a key, but they were adequate for their intended purpose — entering the message of a telegram.

Today the name **TTY** is still used in many system environments as the symbolic name of any interactive terminal attached to the system. Today's interactive terminals are far more sophisticated than the early teletypes. The operating characteristics of early interactive terminals could only be changed by wire jumpers or switches. Most recent interactive terminals contain microprocessors which control and allow the changing of their operating characteristics. Characteristics most often changed are:

speed

number of bits per character

parity (error checking)

duplex (whether terminal can send and receive at same time)

Today's terminals provide far more flexibility than early terminals could. Using a terminal's own keyboard and display in "setup" mode, other capabilities can be changed besides speed, number of bits per character, parity, and duplex. Programmable capa-

FIGURE 3–1   Illustration of Data Communications Hardware

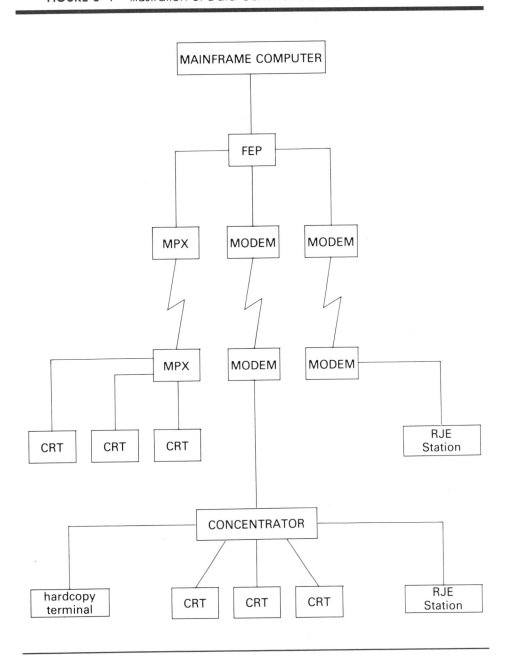

FIGURE 3–2   Keyboard and Display of an Interactive Terminal (Courtesy Burroughs Corporation)

FIGURE 3–3   ASR 33 Teletype (Courtesy AT&T Teletype Corporation)

FIGURE 3–4   Typical "Hardcopy" Terminal (DEC Correspondent)
(Courtesy Digital Equipment Corporation)

bilities of most interactive terminals today include:

CRT display (light on dark, dark on light, etc.)

CRT brightness

type of terminal (terminals can be set to emulate other types)

protocol (rules for communicating with a terminal)

function key definition

As will be seen later, different terminals utilize different control characters. These control characters determine such things as location of display, reverse video, and half-intensity on CRT terminals and density of print, number of characters per inch, and margins on **hardcopy** terminals. Being able to set one terminal to operate like another is very important if the terminal is not supported in its **native mode** of operation. Manufacturers provide this **emulation** to make terminals more flexible.

Programming different terminals to operate in an identical manner can be quite difficult. Now available even for microcomputers is software which allows descriptions of terminal control characters to be maintained in control files [Digital Research 1983]. When terminal characteristics are defined, programs can be implemented which will operate correctly on different terminals and require no software changes to the application programs. This will be considered in more detail in Chapter 18.

Today's wide variety of hardcopy, CRT and other type display terminals gives users almost unlimited flexibility in the interactive terminal environment. Figures 3–4,

FIGURE 3–5   Typical "CRT" Terminal (DEC VT100) (Courtesy Digital
Equipment Corporation)

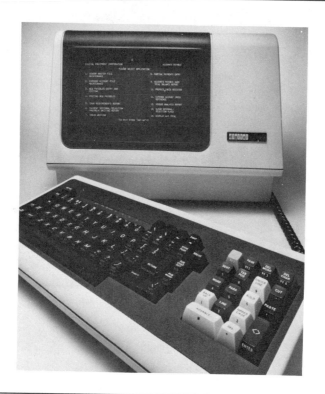

3–5, and 3–6 illustrate several types of hardcopy, CRT, and LCD display interactive
terminals. In most cases, flexibility and cost are the deciding factors in the selection of
a particular terminal for a particular application.

Remote Batch Terminals

In the period from 1960 to 1965, computers became more and more powerful. In order
to fully utilize the capabilities of these more powerful computers, it was necessary that
more and more users were allowed access to them. Since IBM provided the majority of
these mainframe computers, and since IBM provided what was known as a **batch
environment** using a control language known as **JCL** to run **jobs**, a capability known
as **Remote Job Entry (RJE)** was developed. Also known as **Remote Batch Entry**,
the RJE terminals provided for reading a job on cards (later, on other media in "80
column image") and transmitting the information on these cards to the mainframe computer. These jobs were run by the mainframe computer and the printed output trans-

FIGURE 3–6   Typical "LCD" Terminal (Radio Shack Model 100) (Courtesy Tandy Corporation)

mitted to the RJE terminal and printed on the RJE terminal's printer. Figure 3–7 illustrates the components of an RJE terminal, and Figure 3–8 is a photograph of a Data 100 RJE terminal.

Between 1968 and 1974, a new industry developed, the RJE vendors. These vendors provided more and more features in IBM-compatible RJE terminals. Users wanted more and more power in their RJE terminals. RJE vendors expanded the terminals with such capabilities as multiple printer support, local buffering of jobs before transmission, local data editing on disk, and tape support. As the decade of the minicomputer (1970–80) progressed, the specialized minicomputers which provided RJE capability replaced specialized RJE vendors. Since it was generally easier to add RJE capability to a minicomputer than it was to turn a specialized RJE terminal into a minicomputer, the RJE vendor industry began to fade away.

Today, both minicomputers and microcomputers attached to large mainframe computers show RJE capability. It is likely that RJE terminals will continue to exist as long as powerful batch capabilities are required by mainframe users. In many installations, however, the use of interactive terminals to edit "jobs" on the mainframe's disk and to submit these jobs to the batch system has eliminated the need for RJE terminals.

UARTs/USARTs

Data being received or transmitted over a communications medium through a modem must ultimately be read or written by some interface in a front-end processor, concentrator, RJE terminal (computer), minicomputer, or microcomputer. This is done by the communications interface.

Most computer users today use microcomputers at one point or another in their work. The interfaces utilized on most microcomputers are either UARTs or USARTs.

The **UART** (Universal **A**synchronous **R**eceiver/**T**ransmitter) processes characters using what is known as asynchronous communications, as described in Chapter 5. **Asynchronous communications** involves character-by-character transfers with arbitrary time intervals between characters.

USARTs (Universal **S**ynchronous/**A**synchronous **R**eceiver/**T**ransmitter) provide for both asynchronous and synchronous communications, which are described in Chapter 6. In **synchronous communications**, no time intervals are permitted between

FIGURE 3-7   Components of an RJE Terminal

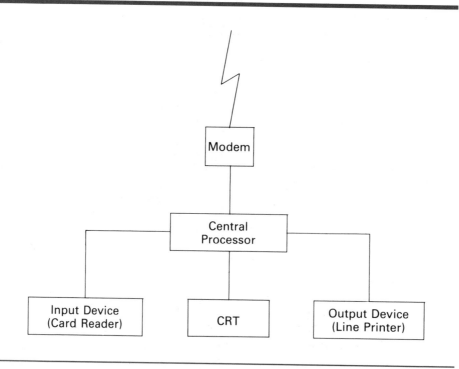

FIGURE 3—8   Data 100 RJE Terminal (c. 1975) (Courtesy Northern
Telecom, Inc.)

characters or bits in the blocks of data being received and transmitted. Time intervals are permitted between blocks.

While there is a wide variety of communications interfaces, some of which are very powerful, the UART and USART provide excellent examples of communication interface requirements. The UART and USART interfaces are relatively inexpensive. Sophisticated interfaces for minicomputers, super minicomputers, front-end concentrators, and even concentrators can get relatively expensive.

Front-End Processors

In the late 60s, both interactive and RJE terminals interfaced to mainframes using "hardwired" communications controllers (e.g., IBM 2701s, 2702s, etc. See Figure 3–9). These hardwired controllers provided little processing capability, which meant that the mainframe computer had to do quite a bit of processing of the data being received and transmitted.

FIGURE 3–9   IBM 2701 Communications Controller (c. 1971) (Courtesy of
International Business Machines Corporation)

Eventually, the functions of the these hardwired communications controllers began
to be placed into programmable **front-end processors**, like the **IBM 3705** shown in
Figure 3–10. These front-end processors were designed specifically to process a high
volume of data from many communications lines and transfer information to and from
the mainframe computer in an efficient manner.

The early front-end processors merely emulated IBM 2701s, 2702s and 2703s and
provided simple interactive terminal control as well as the protocol (e.g., Binary Synchronous Communications — BSC) used to "talk" to RJE terminals. As the concept of
networking evolved, these communications controllers provided more and more capabilities. IBM developed what is known as the **Network Control Program** for the
IBM 3705, which is today used in a **Systems Network Architecture (SNA)** environment, described in Chapter 8.

FIGURE 3–10   IBM 3705 Communications Controller (Courtesy of International Business Machines Corporation)

Modems

In order to communicate with interactive or RJE terminals, it is necessary to modify the discrete digital signals (in the computer system or terminal) into an analog format which can be used on a communications medium. This is accomplished by a modem (modulator/demodulator). Chapter 7 describes the processes of modulation and demodulation as well as modems in great detail. Figure 3–1 illustrates where modems are used in a data communications environment.

Multiplexers

Another way to reduce communications costs is to use multiplexers. When multiplexers are used, the data is manipulated so the line can be "shared."

The two basic techniques of multiplexing are **time division** and **frequency division multiplexing**. Time division multiplexing allocates a certain time period in each transmission to a given terminal or line. The data is represented in an appropriate electronic manner in this time period. In frequency division multiplexing, data "co-exists" on the line as different frequency bandwidths are used to represent the flow of information for different terminals. This is similar to the technique used to multiplex voice lines over one cable. The electronic signals are divided into bandwidths which all share one wider bandwidth. Figure 3–11 illustrates the concept of time division multiplexing, and Figure 3–12 illustrates frequency division multiplexing.

Multistream Modems

There are modems available today which provide more than one stream of data transfer on a single line. Also known as **split stream modems**, these **multistream modems** operate using time division multiplexing to split a single line into multiple streams. The most common split stream modems split a 9600 bps line into four 2400 bps streams or perhaps two 2400 bps and one 4800 bps stream. Other combinations of multiple streams are possible, but the general idea of multistream modems is more important here than particular splits. Figure 3–13 depicts multistream modems splitting a single line into three streams, one 4800 bps and two 2400 bps streams.

Concentrators

While it is relatively easy and inexpensive to attach multiple interactive terminals locally — e.g., within 1,000 feet — to a communications controller, the cost goes up considerably when telephone lines with modems must be relied upon. Concentrators have been used to reduce the cost of communications per interactive terminal (asynchronous or synchronous) and per RJE terminal (synchronous). These concentrators process information received from terminals, placing it into a common buffer and appropriately identifying the origin of the data (e.g., terminal number). This common buffer is then sent using a high-speed line (usually via synchronous communications) and a protocol to a hardware concentrator on the other end, which passes the information on to the communications controller on a line-by-line basis. Information to be sent by the mainframe is sent back through the concentrator at the mainframe site to the remote concentrator using the same principle.

FIGURE 3–11   Multiplexing "Multiple" Streams on a Single
Communications Line Using Time Division Multiplexing

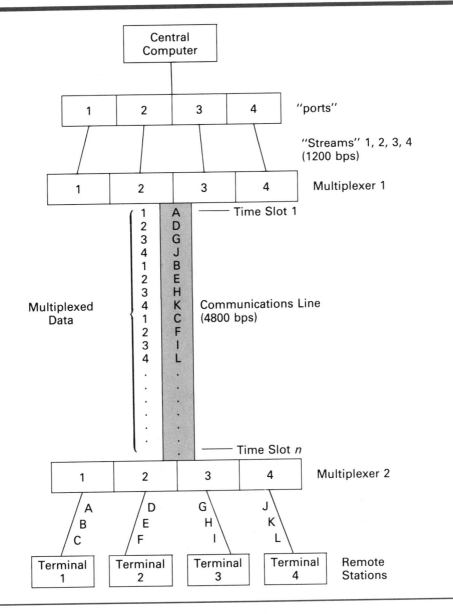

FIGURE 3–12   Multiplexing "Multiple" Streams on a Single
Communications Line Using Frequency Division
Multiplexing

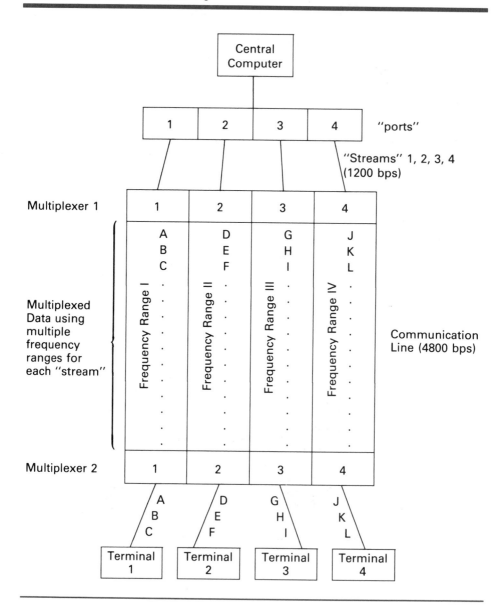

FIGURE 3–13   Multistream Modem Operation

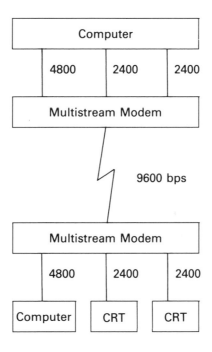

Figure 3–14 depicts a concentrator's operation. In this example the host system sends a buffer of characters for terminals 1 through 5 at 9600 bps. As you can see in this example, the terminal ID is used to identify which terminal is to receive the character or characters that follow the ID. Terminal IDs and data characters are placed into the concentrator buffer on a first-in/first-out basis. The rate at which data characters are received from and transmitted to terminals is unpredictable, so the ordering of IDs and characters in the concentrator buffer is somewhat random. Figure 3–15 illustrates the layout of a concentrator buffer containing terminal IDs and data characters.

FIGURE 3–14   Typical Concentrator Configuration

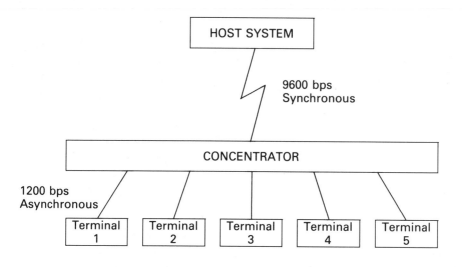

FIGURE 3–15   Buffer Structure for Data Being Transmitted and Received
Via a Concentrator

ID1	CHAR	ID2	CHAR	ID3	CHAR	ID1	CHAR	ID4	CHAR	ID2	CHAR

IDn = Identification (Byte or Bits) of Terminal
with Character(s) CHAR Following.

≡ Terminology ≡

ASR 33	front-end processors
asynchronous communications	hardcopy
batch environment	IBM 3705
CRT	interactive terminal
emulation	JCL
FEP	job
frequency division multiplexing	LCD

multistream modem	time division
native mode	TTY
Network Control Program	UART
remote batch entry	universal asynchronous receiver
remote job entry	transmitter
RJE	universal synchronous/
SNA	asynchronous receiver
split stream modem	transmitter
synchronous communications	USART
Systems Network Architecture	

Review Questions

1. Two ways by which the effective cost of a communications line can be decreased are _____ and _____ .

2. Modems used for short distances are called _____ .

3. True or False:
   a. Remote Batch Terminals are most often found in timesharing systems.
   b. Front-end processors reduce the communications workload on mainframe computers.
   c. A split stream modem is another name for a multistream modem.

4. List four characteristics which can be changed for today's CRT terminals.

5. Match the descriptions on the right to the terms on the left:
   a. asynchronous transmission   character-by-character transfer
   b. synchronous transmission   block transfer

Reference

Digital Research, Inc. 1983. *Display Manager Productivity Tool Programmer's Guide for the CP/M-86 Family of Operating Systems*. Pacific Grove, California: Digital Research, Inc.

4

Data Codes and Error Detection

Data Codes • Baudot Code • Binary Coded Decimal • ASCII • EBCDIC •
Code Conversion • Error Detection • Parity • Cyclic Redundancy Check •
Method for Computing CRC • Summary of Error Detection of CRC–16 •
Computation of CRC–16

Data Codes

Data which is transmitted using communications usually originates in a computer system or in a computer terminal. Since information stored in a computer system is based on the binary system and since codes representing letters, numbers and symbols which are to be entered, displayed, or printed, data codes are the basis of information which is transmitted. In some cases, control codes are used to control how data is transmitted, but these codes are dependent upon the protocol being used to transmit and receive data.

Several **data codes** are important in data communications: Baudot code, Binary Coded Decimal, ASCII, and EBCDIC. These will now be discussed.

Baudot Code

From the early days of teletype terminals, codes represented information, like alphabetic characters, numbers, and symbols. Codes could also be punched on paper tape in the form of small round holes. When information was read into a computer from a teletype or a teletype paper tape, punched holes were translated to ones and "no holes" to zeroes, i.e., to binary format. Similar techniques were used for punched cards as well but the binary code on a punched card is not the same as the binary code internal to a computer. For punched cards, holes are not translated directly to 1 bits in corresponding bit positions in characters. Instead, the bit patterns are translated to the appropriate seven- or eight-bit code, usually by the card reader interface. The early teletype five-bit codes, called **Baudot code**, could represent 32 different characters. The code was named after a French postal engineer who worked on telegraphy in the 1870s [Housley 1979, p. 12]. Also referred to as **CCITT International Alphabet Number 2** (named for the International Telegraph and Telephone Consultative Committee — an international body concerned with communications standards), this code is the basis of a wide number of Telex stations throughout the world.

It is obvious that a five-bit code cannot represent more than 32 unique codes. To represent the needed information in Baudot code, two of the codes are used to extend the code. The Letter Shift Character (11111) causes subsequent codes to be interpreted as Letter Characters, as shown in Table 4–1, unless a Figure Shift Character

(11011) is received. Once a Figure Shift Character is detected, subsequent received characters are interpreted as Figure Characters, as shown in column 4 of Table 4–1, until a Letter Shift Character is detected.

TABLE 4–1   Baudot Code Representations

Decimal	Binary	Letter Characters	Figure Characters
0	00000	blank	blank
1	00001	E	3
2	00010		Line Feed
3	00011	A	—
4	00100	SP	SP space
5	00101	S	'
6	00110	I	8
7	00111	U	7
8	01000	‹	‹ Carriage Return
9	01001	D	Who Are You?
10	01010	R	4
11	01011	J	Bell
12	01100	N	,
13	01101	F	%
14	01110	C	:
15	01111	K	(
16	10000	T	5
17	10001	Z	+
18	10010	L	)
19	10011	"	2
20	10100	H	£ British pound
21	10101	Y	6
22	10110	P	0
23	10111	Q	1
24	11000	O	9
25	11001	B	?
26	11010	G	$
27	11011		Figure Shift
28	11100	M	.
29	11101	X	/
30	11110	V	=
31	11111		Letter Shift

Baudot Code is certainly cumbersome for the types of data communications required today. However, it served its purpose in the early days of data transmission and, in fact, is still in use today.

Binary Coded Decimal

Early IBM codes represented information in a 6-bit code called Binary Coded Decimal (BCD). These IBM systems and other vendors' systems utilized this code, particularly when processing cards.

ASCII

ASCII (American Standard Code for Information Interchange) provides a seven-bit code which is used to represent letters, including upper and lower case, numbers, and special symbols. Table 4–2 lists the 128 ASCII codes and the symbols associated with them.

TABLE 4–2   ASCII Code Table [IBM]

Decimal	Binary	Hex	Octal	Character
0	0000000	00	000	NUL
1	0000001	01	001	SOH
2	0000010	02	002	STX
3	0000011	03	003	ETX
4	0000100	04	004	EOT
5	0000101	05	005	ENQ
6	0000110	06	006	ACK
7	0000111	07	007	BEL
8	0001000	08	010	BS
9	0001001	09	011	HT
10	0001010	0A	012	LF
11	0001011	0B	013	VT
12	0001100	0C	014	FF
13	0001101	0D	015	CR
14	0001110	0E	016	SO
15	0001111	0F	017	SI
16	0010000	10	020	DLE
17	0010001	11	021	DC1
18	0010010	12	022	DC2
19	0010011	13	023	DC3
20	0010100	14	024	DC4
21	0010101	15	025	NAK
22	0010110	16	026	SYN
23	0010111	17	027	ETB
24	0011000	18	030	CAN
25	0011001	19	031	EM
26	0011010	1A	032	SUB
27	0011011	1B	033	ESC
28	0011100	1C	034	FS
29	0011101	1D	035	GS
30	0011110	1E	036	RS
31	0011111	1F	037	US
32	0100000	20	040	SP
33	0100001	21	041	!
34	0100010	22	042	"
35	0100011	23	043	#

TABLE 4–2   ASCII Code Table [IBM] Continued

Decimal	Binary	Hex	Octal	Character
36	0100100	24	044	$
37	0100101	25	045	%
38	0100110	26	046	&
39	0100111	27	047	'
40	0101000	28	050	(
41	0101001	29	051	)
42	0101010	2A	052	*
43	0101011	2B	053	+
44	0101100	2C	054	,
45	0101101	2D	055	−
46	0101110	2E	056	.
47	0101111	2F	057	/
48	0110000	30	060	0
49	0110001	31	061	1
50	0110010	32	062	2
51	0110011	33	063	3
52	0110100	34	064	4
53	0110101	35	065	5
54	0110110	36	066	6
55	0110111	37	067	7
56	0111000	38	070	8
57	0111001	39	071	9
58	0111010	3A	072	:
59	0111011	3B	073	;
60	0111100	3C	074	<
61	0111101	3D	075	=
62	0111110	3E	076	>
63	0111111	3F	077	?
64	1000000	40	100	@
65	1000001	41	101	A
66	1000010	42	102	B
67	1000011	43	103	C
68	1000100	44	104	D
69	1000101	45	105	E
70	1000110	46	106	F
71	1000111	47	107	G
72	1001000	48	110	H
73	1001001	49	111	I
74	1001010	4A	112	J
75	1001011	4B	113	K
76	1001100	4C	114	L
77	1001101	4D	115	M
78	1001110	4E	116	N
79	1001111	4F	117	O
80	1010000	50	120	P
81	1010001	51	121	Q
82	1010010	52	122	R
83	1010011	53	123	S
84	1010100	54	124	T
85	1010101	55	125	U
86	1010110	56	126	V
87	1010111	57	127	W
88	1011000	58	130	X
89	1011001	59	131	Y
90	1011010	5A	132	Z
91	1011011	5B	133	[
92	1011100	5C	134	\
93	1011101	5D	135	]
94	1011110	5E	136	^
95	1011111	5F	137	_
96	1100000	60	140	`
97	1100001	61	141	a

TABLE 4–2   ASCII Code Table [IBM] Continued

Decimal	Binary	Hex	Octal	Character
98	1100010	62	142	b
99	1100011	63	143	c
100	1100100	64	144	d
101	1100101	65	145	e
102	1100110	66	146	f
103	1100111	67	147	g
104	1101000	68	150	h
105	1101001	69	151	i
106	1101010	6A	152	j
107	1101011	6B	153	k
108	1101100	6C	154	l
109	1101101	6D	155	m
110	1101110	6E	156	n
111	1101111	6F	157	o
112	1110000	70	160	p
113	1110001	71	161	q
114	1110010	72	162	r
115	1110011	73	163	s
116	1110100	74	164	t
117	1110101	75	165	u
118	1110110	76	166	v
119	1110111	77	167	w
120	1111000	78	170	x
121	1111001	79	171	y
122	1111010	7A	172	z
123	1111011	7B	173	{
124	1111100	7C	174		
125	1111101	7D	175	}
126	1111110	7E	176	~
127	1111111	7F	177	DEL

ASCII is the code used by most microcomputers and minicomputers. It permits information interchange between these computers with no need for code conversion. With the addition of a parity bit, discussed later in this chapter, ASCII becomes an eight-bit code. A table with even and odd parity values for ASCII is included in Chapter 16.

EBCDIC

The current data code used by large- and medium-scale IBM computers is Extended Binary Coded Decimal Interchange Code (**EBCDIC**). This eight-bit code provides for 256 different characters. Punched card (**Hollerith**) representations are also defined by this standard. Table 4–3 contains the 256 EBCDIC codes and their symbols.

TABLE 4–3   EBCDIC Code Table [IBM]

Decimal	Binary	Hex	Octal	Character or Symbol
0	00000000	00	000	NUL
1	00000001	01	001	SOH
2	00000010	02	002	STX
3	00000011	03	003	ETX
4	00000100	04	004	SEL
5	00000101	05	005	HT
6	00000110	06	006	RNL
7	00000111	07	007	DEL
8	00001000	08	010	GE
9	00001001	09	011	SPS
10	00001010	0A	012	RPT
11	00001011	0B	013	VT
12	00001100	0C	014	FF
13	00001101	0D	015	CR
14	00001110	0E	016	SO
15	00001111	0F	017	SI
16	00010000	10	020	DLE
17	00010001	11	021	DC1
18	00010010	12	022	DC2
19	00010011	13	023	DC3
20	00010100	14	024	RES/ENP
21	00010101	15	025	NL
22	00010110	16	026	BS
23	00010111	17	027	POC
24	00011000	18	030	CAN
25	00011001	19	031	EM
26	00011010	1A	032	UBS
27	00011011	1B	033	CU1
28	00011100	1C	034	IFS
29	00011101	1D	035	IGS
30	00011110	1E	036	IRS
31	00011111	1F	037	ITB/IUS
32	00100000	20	040	DS
33	00100001	21	041	SOS
34	00100010	22	042	FS
35	00100011	23	043	WUS
36	00100100	24	044	BYP/IMP
37	00100101	25	045	LF
38	00100110	26	046	ETB
39	00100111	27	047	ESC
40	00101000	28	050	SA
41	00101001	29	051	SFE
42	00101010	2A	052	SM/SW
43	00101011	2B	053	CSP
44	00101100	2C	054	MFA
45	00101101	2D	055	ENQ
46	00101110	2E	056	ACK
47	00101111	2F	057	BEL
48	00110000	30	060	
49	00110001	31	061	
50	00110010	32	062	SYN
51	00110011	33	063	IR
52	00110100	34	064	PP
53	00110101	35	065	TRN
54	00110110	36	066	NBS
55	00110111	37	067	EOT
56	00111000	38	070	SBS
57	00111001	39	071	IT
58	00111010	3A	072	RFF
59	00111011	3B	073	CU3
60	00111100	3C	074	DC4
61	00111101	3D	075	NAK
62	00111110	3E	076	
63	00111111	3F	077	SUB
64	01000000	40	100	Sp

TABLE 4–3   EBCDIC Code Table [IBM] Continued

Decimal	Binary	Hex	Octal	Character or Symbol
65	01000001	41	101	
66	01000010	42	102	
67	01000011	43	103	
68	01000100	44	104	
69	01000101	45	105	
70	01000110	46	106	
71	01000111	47	107	
72	01001000	48	110	
73	01001001	49	111	
74	01001010	4A	112	¢
75	01001011	4B	113	.
76	01001100	4C	114	<
77	01001101	4D	115	(
78	01001110	4E	116	+
79	01001111	4F	117	|
80	01010000	50	120	&
81	01010001	51	121	
82	01010010	52	122	
83	01010011	53	123	
84	01010100	54	124	
85	01010101	55	125	
86	01010110	56	126	
87	01010111	57	127	
88	01011000	58	130	
89	01011001	59	131	
90	01011010	5A	132	!
91	01011011	5B	133	$
92	01011100	5C	134	*
93	01011101	5D	135	)
94	01011110	5E	136	;
95	01011111	5F	137	¬
96	01100000	60	140	−
97	01100001	61	141	/
98	01100010	62	142	
99	01100011	63	143	
100	01100100	64	144	
101	01100101	65	145	
102	01100110	66	146	
103	01100111	67	147	
104	01101000	68	150	
105	01101001	69	151	|
106	01101010	6A	152	|
107	01101011	6B	153	,
108	01101100	6C	154	%
109	01101101	6D	155	_
110	01101110	6E	156	>
111	01101111	6F	157	?
112	01110000	70	160	
113	01110001	71	161	
114	01110010	72	162	
115	01110011	73	163	
116	01110100	74	164	
117	01110101	75	165	
118	01110110	76	166	
119	01110111	77	167	
120	01111000	78	170	
121	01111001	79	171	`
122	01111010	7A	172	:
123	01111011	7B	173	#
124	01111100	7C	174	@
125	01111101	7D	175	'
126	01111110	7E	176	=
127	01111111	7F	177	"
128	10000000	80	200	
129	10000001	81	201	a

TABLE 4–3   EBCDIC Code Table [IBM] Continued

Decimal	Binary	Hex	Octal	Character or Symbol
130	10000010	82	202	b
131	10000011	83	203	c
132	10000100	84	204	d
133	10000101	85	205	e
134	10000110	86	206	f
135	10000111	87	207	g
136	10001000	88	210	h
137	10001001	89	211	i
138	10001010	8A	212	
139	10001011	8B	213	
140	10001100	8C	214	
141	10001101	8D	215	
142	10001110	8E	216	
143	10001111	8F	217	
144	10010000	90	220	
145	10010001	91	221	
146	10010010	92	222	j
147	10010011	93	223	k
148	10010100	94	224	l
149	10010101	95	225	m
150	10010110	96	226	n
151	10010111	97	227	o
152	10011000	98	230	p
153	10011001	99	231	q
154	10011010	9A	232	r
155	10011011	9B	233	
156	10011100	9C	234	
157	10011101	9D	235	
158	10011110	9E	236	
159	10011111	9F	237	
160	10100000	A0	240	
161	10100001	A1	241	~
162	10100010	A2	242	s
163	10100011	A3	243	t
164	10100100	A4	244	u
165	10100101	A5	245	v
166	10100110	A6	246	w
167	10100111	A7	247	x
168	10101000	A8	250	y
169	10101001	A9	251	z
170	10101010	AA	252	
171	10101011	AB	253	
172	10101100	AC	254	
173	10101101	AD	255	
174	10101110	AE	256	
175	10101111	AF	257	
176	10110000	B0	260	
177	10110001	B1	261	
178	10110010	B2	262	
179	10110011	B3	263	
180	10110100	B4	264	
181	10110101	B5	265	
182	10110110	B6	266	
183	10110111	B7	267	
184	10111000	B8	270	
185	10111001	B9	271	
186	10111010	BA	272	
187	10111011	BB	273	
188	10111100	BC	274	
189	10111101	BD	275	
190	10111110	BE	276	
191	10111111	BF	277	
192	11000000	C0	300	{
193	11000001	C1	301	A
194	11000010	C2	302	B

TABLE 4–3　EBCDIC Code Table [IBM] Continued

Decimal	Binary	Hex	Octal	Character or Symbol
195	11000011	C3	303	C
196	11000100	C4	304	D
197	11000101	C5	305	E
198	11000110	C6	306	F
199	11000111	C7	307	G
200	11001000	C8	310	H
201	11001001	C9	311	I
202	11001010	CA	312	
203	11001011	CB	313	
204	11001100	CC	314	
205	11001101	CD	315	
206	11001110	CE	316	
207	11001111	CF	317	
208	11010000	D0	320	}
209	11010001	D1	321	J
210	11010010	D2	322	K
211	11010011	D3	323	L
212	11010100	D4	324	M
213	11010101	D5	325	N
214	11010110	D6	326	O
215	11010111	D7	327	P
216	11011000	D8	330	Q
217	11011001	D9	331	R
218	11011010	DA	332	
219	11011011	DB	333	
220	11011100	DC	334	
221	11011101	DD	335	
222	11011110	DE	336	
223	11011111	DF	337	
224	11100000	E0	340	\
225	11100001	E1	341	
226	11100010	E2	342	S
227	11100011	E3	343	T
228	11100100	E4	344	U
229	11100101	E5	345	V
230	11100110	E6	346	W
231	11100111	E7	347	X
232	11101000	E8	350	Y
233	11101001	E9	351	Z
234	11101010	EA	352	
235	11101011	EB	353	
236	11101100	EC	354	
237	11101101	ED	355	
238	11101110	EE	356	
239	11101111	EF	357	
240	11110000	F0	360	0
241	11110001	F1	361	1
242	11110010	F2	362	2
243	11110011	F3	363	3
244	11110100	F4	364	4
245	11110101	F5	365	5
246	11110110	F6	366	6
247	11110111	F7	367	7
248	11111000	F8	370	8
249	11111001	F9	371	9
250	11111010	FA	372	
251	11111011	FB	373	
252	11111100	FC	374	
253	11111101	FD	375	
254	11111110	FE	376	
255	11111111	FF	377	

Code Conversion

There have been other codes used in data processing and data communications, like Univac's Field Data, 4-out-of-8 code but they have only historical interest [Martin 1970]. However, with all the different codes which have been and will be used, it is obvious that there will continue to be a great need for data code conversion in many environments.

Data code conversion is often embedded somewhere in a data communications system. Most code conversion incorporates a translation technique that uses two tables: the code being converted and the target code. For example, seven bit ASCII can be converted by using the code itself as an "index" into a table with the EBCDIC equivalents. In this case the ASCII source table is merely the ASCII code itself and is not as such represented in a table in memory. Notice that, in this example, converting 128 ASCII codes into EBCDIC is easy, since there are more EBCDIC codes than there are ASCII. However, conversion in the other direction results in many characters which are represented in EBCDIC but are not represented in ASCII. Some of these codes cannot be converted and must be taken to an "unknown" code value (often 000_8 or 177_8). In some cases, codes with no equivalents in ASCII are taken into two-character "special sequences" of two characters; for example, #T might represent a special tab on a word processor [Lane and Mooney 1983]. In this case, the character used to start this two-character sequence must be represented by two occurrences of this character in the ASCII data, e.g., ## instead of #.

Conversion techniques often take into account the instruction set available, e.g., a translate instruction. Figure 4–1 illustrates a simple table lookup conversion using a conversion table from ASCII to EBCDIC.

Error Detection

As has been mentioned before, the effects of noise on data communications can be disastrous. When people talk on the telephone, they make a judgment about whether

FIGURE 4–1   Simple Translation Technique for Code Conversion (ASCII "A" [101_8] to EBCDIC "A" [$C1_{16}$])

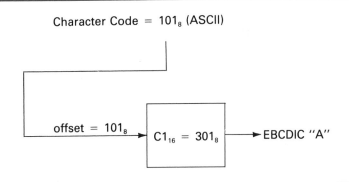

Character Code = 101_8 (ASCII)

offset = 101_8 $C1_{16} = 301_8$ ► EBCDIC "A"

or not what they heard was intelligible. If not, they can ask the person speaking to repeat what was said. Computer communications software for line control protocols must also be able to detect errors on a communications line, but, without the human reasoning capability, there must be some type of **error detection** mechanism.

When speaking on a telephone, you often hear a click on the line. Such clicks are noise bursts lasting up to .01 second. At 9600 bits per second, 96 data bits would be smashed with this one click. Errors usually come in bursts, caused by low noise over long durations, unless the communications link is of poor quality.

Error detection must be defined for line control protocols if the integrity of the data is to be preserved. Defining a mechanism for detecting errors is one part of error control. Error recovery must also be defined. Most protocols use a negative acknowledgement-retransmit technique — that is, the receiving station which detects the error sends a message (**NAK** = **N**egative **AcK**nowledgement) indicating to the system which transmitted the message that an error has been detected. The transmitting system then retransmits the message which was received incorrectly.

There are other techniques for error recovery. Algorithms and techniques exist to provide error correction, for example, but they are not generally used in the transmission of large blocks of data because of the complexity, cost, and overhead of implementing them.

Parity

The use of parity bits is commonplace throughout computer systems. A **parity bit** is a bit appended to a character in the most significant bit and is determined by an odd-parity or an even-parity calculation. **Odd parity** is the counting of the one bits in a character and, if the count is odd, the parity bit is 0. If the count is even, the parity bit is 1, thus guaranteeing that the sum of the 1 bits including the parity bit is always odd. **Even parity** uses the same scheme, except that the sum of the 1 bits must be an even number.

In data communications, the use of a parity bit within each character transmitted can aid in the detection of errors. Such a parity bit calculation within each character is called **Vertical Redundancy Check (VRC)**. However, the effect of two-bit errors using VRC will not be seen. In fact, this simple parity scheme will only catch one-, three-, five-, and seven-bit errors in a seven-bit character. Certainly this is not satisfactory if the integrity of the data is to be preserved.

Another scheme using parity incorporates parity across characters in a message. It is called **Longitudinal Redundancy Check (LRC)**. In this case, all the ones in a particular position of a message are used to determine the parity. For example, if the four characters "ABCD" were being transmitted, the LRC would be computed as shown in Table 4–4.

The LRC in Table 4–4 was computed using odd parity for the calculation of the parity bit in each position. It also used VRC parity bits within each character. In such a case, the parity bit of the LRC can either be set to the appropriate parity or ignored. This depends on the type of protocol which is used.

TABLE 4–4   Determining Odd Parity VRC and LRC

Character	Octal	Binary
A	301	11000001
B	302	11000010
C	103	01000011
D	304	11000100
LRC	173	01111011

It is still possible to have undetected errors using LRC. For example, if characters 1 and 3 (A and C) had been received with errors in the second- and third-bit positions, the VRC and LRC would be correct, but obviously the message would be incorrect — that is, the error would go undetected.

Cyclic Redundancy Check

Today, the most common method of error detection for most data communications is **Cyclic Redundancy Check (CRC)**. CRC check characters are sent with a block of data (i.e, a message) and are appended to the end of the message. The algorithm to compute the CRC is applied at the receiving station; the computed CRC will be the same as the received CRC if no errors occurred in the message while it was being transmitted.

With the CRC technique, each bit in a message is considered to be the binary coefficient of a term x^j in a polynomial. That is, a k-bit message can be represented as a polynomial in a variable x with k terms (of order $k - 1$):

$$M(x) = a_{k-1}x^{k-1} + a_{k-2}x^{k-2} + \ldots + a_2x^2 + a_1x + a_0$$

For example, the message 101101101 is represented by the polynomial

$$x^8 + x^6 + x^5 + x^3 + x^2 + 1$$

The high-order term of the polynomial above is transmitted first. Once we have expressed the message in this convenient mathematical form, we can begin to understand what CRC error-check characters are. It should be noted that these polynomials are manipulated with binary addition, i.e., modulo 2 with no carries (addition and subtraction are identical). While algorithms implementing CRC use exclusive ORs (XOR) and shifts to compute CRC, CRC is able to detect most errors because of the theory on which it is based. The next section describes the theory of the CRC character generation and demonstrates the probability of detecting errors.

Calculation of a CRC error-check character requires a **generating polynomial** which is designated as G(x). If a transmitted message represented by the polynomial M(x) has degree m, G(x) must be of degree g where $0 < g < m$. Note that G(x) will have a unity coefficient. [Martin 1970, pp. 83–89]

Method for Computing CRC

The theory for calculation of the cyclic redundancy check character is as follows:

1. IF M(x) is the message to be transmitted, multiply M(x) by x^g, where g is the degree of the generating polynomial G(x), giving g 0s in the low-order positions (i.e., x^g * M(x) has zero in g low-order coefficients).
2. Divide x^g * M(x) by G(x). This yields a unique quotient Q(x) and a remainder R(x):

$$\frac{x^g * M(x)}{G(x)} = Q(x) \oplus \frac{R(x)}{G(x)}$$

where $\oplus$ represents modulo 2 addition.

3. Add the remainder to x^g * M(x) (the message), placing up to g terms with unity coefficients in the low-order positions. The transmitted message is

$$T(x) = x^g * M(x) \oplus R(x)$$

Note: We have that

$$\frac{x^g * M(x)}{G(x)} = Q(x) \oplus \frac{R(x)}{G(x)}$$

So multiplying both sides by G(x) yields

$$x^g * M(x) = Q(x) * G(x) \oplus R(x)$$

Therefore, adding R(x) to both sides produces

$$x^g * M(x) \oplus R(x) = Q(x) * G(x)$$

(since $\oplus$ and $\ominus$ are the same). Hence, the transmitted message is

$$T(x) = x^g * M(x) \oplus R(x) = Q(x) * G(x)$$

and the transmitted message is exactly divisible by G(x). On the receiving side, the software (possibly the hardware) can divide this T(x) by G(x) and check to be sure the remainder is zero. [Martin 1970]

Figure 4–2 illustrates the CRC computation for **CRC–16** with the polynomial G(X) = $x^{16} + x^{15} + x^2 + 1$. The 16-bit remainder is also called the **Block Check Character** (**BCC**).

FIGURE 4–2   Illustration of Shift/Exclusive OR Technique for Computing
CRC–16 with $G(x) = x^{16} + x^{15} + x^2 + 1$

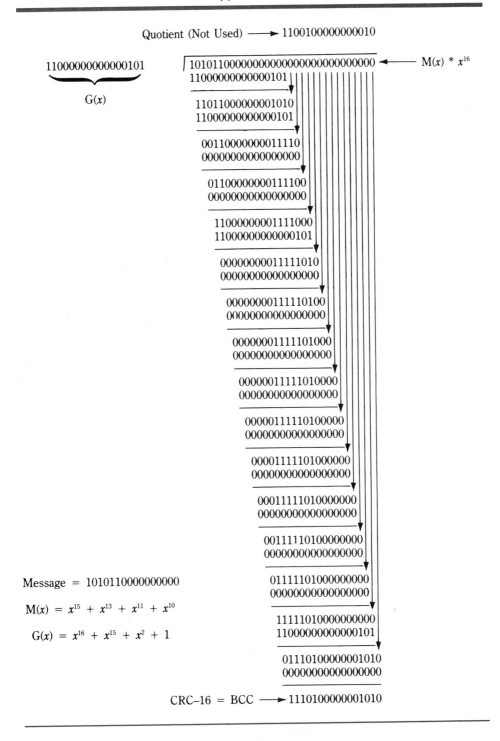

Quotient (Not Used) ⟶ 1100100000000010

$\overbrace{1100000000000101}$

$G(x)$

1010110000000000000000000000000 ⟵ $M(x) * x^{16}$
11000000000000101

11011000000001010
11000000000000101

00110000000011110
00000000000000000

01100000000111100
00000000000000000

11000000001111000
11000000000000101

00000000011111010
00000000000000000

00000000111110100
00000000000000000

00000001111101000
00000000000000000

00000011111010000
00000000000000000

00000111110100000
00000000000000000

00001111101000000
00000000000000000

00011111010000000
00000000000000000

00111110100000000
00000000000000000

01111101000000000
00000000000000000

11111010000000000
11000000000000101

01110100000001010
00000000000000000

Message = 1010110000000000

$M(x) = x^{15} + x^{13} + x^{11} + x^{10}$

$G(x) = x^{16} + x^{15} + x^2 + 1$

CRC–16 = BCC ⟶ 1110100000001010

Summary of Error Detection of CRC–16

The use of parity bits results in many undetected errors. Thus, it is important to know what errors go undetected when using a particular error detection mechanism. Remember that an error is nothing more than 1 bits changed to 0s and vice versa.

It is shown in Appendix A that if $G(x)$ has $(x + 1)$ as a factor and one factor with at least three terms, the probability of detecting errors is as follows:

Type of Error	Probability of Detection
single-bit errors	
two bits in error	
an odd number of bits in error	100%
error bursts of length $< g + 1$	
error bursts of length $= g + 1$	$1-(1/2)^{g-1}$
error bursts of length $> g + 1$	$1-(1/2)^{g}$

where the length of an error burst is the number of bits starting from the first error bit until the last error bit in the message, inclusive. Thus, for CRC–16, the probability of an undetected error burst of length 17 going undetected is $(1/2)^{15}$, which yields a probability of .0000305. Again for CRC–16, the probability of an error burst of length $>$ 17 going undetected is $(1/2)^{16}$, which is .0000152. It should be noted that some error patterns are likely to be more prevalent than others, so that in reality, the probability of error is not *exactly* as shown above. The probability of detecting error bursts greater that 16 bits in length is greater than 99% using CRC–16 error check characters [McNamara 1982, p. 118].

Computation of CRC–16

The necessary division in the CRC algorithm can be accomplished by a series of one-bit shift registers and modulo 2 (exclusive OR circuits). The number of shift registers is exactly the same as the degree of the generating polynomial $G(x)$, e.g., 16 for the CRC–16 polynomial given previously. The number of exclusive OR circuits is equal to one less than the number of one bits in the divisor, e.g., 3 for the CRC–16 polynomial. Figure 4–3 illustrates this shifting/exclusive ORing process which takes place. Note that the BCC computed in Figure 4–3 is indeed the same as the BCC computed in Figure 4–2 using polynomial division.

The generating polynomial $G(x)$ is not the same for all environments. For example, the SDLC and HDLC, the CCITT standard (see Chapter 12) uses $G(x) = x^{16} + x^{12} + x^{5} + 1$. A **CRC–12** generating polynomial often used for six-bit characters is $G(x) = x^{12} + x^{11} + x^{3} + x^{2} + x + 1$. [McNamara 1982, p. 117]

CRC algorithms are often implemented in hardware. Such hardware may compute the CRC while the message is being transmitted and automatically append it to the end of the message. Another possibility is the computation of the CRC using hardware before transmission and then using software to "read" it from the CRC register and append it to the message to be transmitted. [DEC] The last possibility for computing CRC is that of software algorithms.

FIGURE 4–3   Division by Generating Polynomial in Computing CRC–16

	A	B	C	D	E	F	G	H	I	J	K	L	M	N	O	P	Message Bits
Initial	0	0	0	0	0	0	0	0	0	0	0	0	0	0	0	0	V
	0	0	0	0	0	0	0	0	0	0	0	0	0	0	0	1	1
	0	0	0	0	0	0	0	0	0	0	0	0	0	0	1	0	0
	0	0	0	0	0	0	0	0	0	0	0	0	0	1	0	1	1
	0	0	0	0	0	0	0	0	0	0	0	0	1	0	1	0	0
	0	0	0	0	0	x	0	0	0	0	0	1	0	1	0	1	1
	0	0	0	0	0	0	0	0	0	0	1	0	1	0	1	1	1
	0	0	0	0	0	0	0	0	0	1	0	1	0	1	1	0	0
	0	0	0	0	0	0	0	0	1	0	1	0	1	1	0	0	0
	0	0	0	0	0	0	0	1	0	1	0	1	1	0	0	0	0
	0	0	0	0	0	0	1	0	1	0	1	1	0	0	0	0	0
	0	0	0	0	0	1	0	1	0	1	1	0	0	0	0	0	0
	0	0	0	0	1	0	1	0	1	1	0	0	0	0	0	0	0
	0	0	0	1	0	1	0	1	1	0	0	0	0	0	0	0	0
	0	0	1	0	1	0	1	1	0	0	0	0	0	0	0	0	0
	0	1	0	1	0	1	1	0	0	0	0	0	0	0	0	0	0
	1	0	1	0	1	1	0	0	0	0	0	0	0	0	0	0	0
	1	1	0	1	1	0	0	0	0	0	0	0	0	1	0	1	0
	0	0	1	1	0	0	0	0	0	0	0	0	1	1	1	1	0
	0	1	1	0	0	0	0	0	0	0	0	1	1	1	1	0	0
	1	1	0	0	0	0	0	0	0	0	1	1	1	1	0	0	0
	0	0	0	0	0	0	0	0	0	1	1	1	1	1	0	1	0
	0	0	0	0	0	0	0	0	1	1	1	1	1	0	1	0	0
	0	0	0	0	0	0	0	1	1	1	1	1	0	1	0	0	0
	0	0	0	0	0	0	1	1	1	1	1	0	1	0	0	0	0
	0	0	0	0	0	1	1	1	1	1	0	1	0	0	0	0	0
	0	0	0	0	1	1	1	1	1	0	1	0	0	0	0	0	0
	0	0	0	1	1	1	1	1	0	1	0	0	0	0	0	0	0
	0	0	1	1	1	1	1	0	1	0	0	0	0	0	0	0	0
	0	1	1	1	1	1	0	1	0	0	0	0	0	0	0	0	0
	1	1	1	1	1	0	1	0	0	0	0	0	0	0	0	0	0
	0	1	1	1	0	1	0	0	0	0	0	0	0	1	0	1	0
	1	1	1	0	1	0	0	0	0	0	0	0	1	0	1	0	0

XOR

Message Bits

BCC
(CRC–16)

$$M(x) = 1010110000000000$$

Each Input Bit Results in a 1 Bit Shift to Left, except that Previous Value in Column A is Exclusive ORed with Bit to Right of ▮ (Columns B, O, Input Bit, respectively) to Determine Bit to Left of ▮ (Columns A, N, P, respectively).

Terminology

ASCII	EBCDIC
Baudot code	error detection
BCC	even parity
block check character	generating polynomial
CCITT International Alphabet	Hollerith code
Number 2	longitudinal redundancy check
CRC	LRC
CRC-12	NAK
CRC-16	odd parity
cyclic redundancy check	parity bit
data code conversion	vertical redundancy check
data codes	VRC

Review Questions

1. Match a name of the code which has the code whose length is given below:
   a. ASCII   8-bit
   b. BAUDOT   7-bit
   c. EBCDIC   5-bit
2. VRC parity is most often used with _____ code.
3. True or False:
   a. CRC error detection provides better error detection than LRC error detection.
   b. All CRC algorithms produce the same error check character.
   c. A table lookup technique can be used for code conversion between data codes.
   d. IBM introduced ASCII as an extension of the BCD code.
   e. It is difficult to give an example of errors which are not detected by LRC parity checking.
   f. CRC error checking detects 100% of all transmission errors.
4. The two types of parity check characters are _____ and _____ .

Assignments

1. Given the following string of characters:

   THE IDENTIFICATION NUMBER IS 1287A$T69

   Represent this string in Baudot code using

    a. decimal
    b. binary
    c. octal
    d. hexadecimal

2. Given the following string of characters:

*** JOB 498$#123 is Executing for J. DOE ***

Represent this string of characters in ASCII and in EBCDIC
    a. decimal
    b. binary
    c. octal
    d. hexadecimal

3. Using octal or hexadecimal form, represent the message given in Assignment 2 in ASCII with
    a. even parity
    b. odd parity

4. Compute the odd parity LRC for the string in Assignment 3b in octal or hexadecimal.

5. For the message

1100111001010100

compute the CRC-16 check character using the generating polynomial

$$G(x) = x^{16} + x^{15} + x^2 + 1$$

References

DEC. *KG11 Reference Manual.* Maynard, Massachusetts: Digital Equipment Corporation.

Housley, Trevor. 1979. *Data Communications and Teleprocessing Systems.* Englewood Cliffs, New Jersey: Prentice-Hall.

IBM. *System/370 Reference Summary. GX20-1850-4.* White Plains, New York: IBM Corporation.

Lane, Malcolm G., and James D. Mooney. 1983. "A Text Processing System for IBM OS6-Produced Documents on the VAX 11/780 under VMS." United States Department of Energy (for Morgantown [West Virginia] Energy Technology Center).

McNamara, John E. 1982. *Technical Aspects of Data Communication.* Second Edition. Bedford, Massachusetts: Digital Press.

Martin, James. 1970. *Teleprocessing Network Organization.* Englewood Cliffs, New Jersey: Prentice-Hall.

5

Asynchronous Communications

Introduction

Currently, the most common type of data transmission capability is asynchronous data transmission. The smallest microcomputer provides asynchronous interfaces which can control devices like printers and terminals as well as communicate to other computer systems (via terminal emulators — see Chapter 19). This chapter concentrates on the theory of **asynchronous transmission**. "Asynchronous" implies something which is not synchronized. In fact, data characters can be transmitted and received with intervals of random lengths between each character. The mechanism used to allow this is described below.

Since asynchronous transmission allows data to arrive at an arbitrary rate with no predetermined time between characters, there must be a method of recognizing the beginning of a character. This is accomplished by **framing** the beginning of each character received with a **START condition** and the ending of each character with a **STOP condition**. While there is a rate at which bits arrive over an asynchronous line (e.g., 300, 1200, 2400, etc. bits per second), the time between the STOP condition and the next START condition is arbitrarily long. This will be explained in more detail later. Asynchronous transmission is also called **START/STOP transmission**.

Theory

Data in asynchronous transmission is transmitted in a serial manner: that is to say, the binary bits in a character are transmitted one after another. The 1s and 0s are represented by minus (-15 to -5) and plus (+5 to +15) dc voltages, respectively. The **RS–232** interface control signals use +5 to +15 volts as "on" (1) and -15 to -5 volts as "off" (0).

A line on which no transmission of data is taking place is an idle line and has a constant "1" (**mark**) state. It is necessary to recognize when data transmission has begun on a previously idle line and then to identify the beginning and end of the character being received. The transition of the line to a "0" (**space**) state constitutes what is called the START condition. The duration of the START condition is the same as that of a data bit (and thus is dependent upon the speed of transmission, e.g. 1/1200th second for a 1200 bit per second transmission rate).

The information on the line is sampled using a clock which usually operates at 16 times the data bit rate in order to detect the middle of the START condition. Finding the middle will guarantee that the 0s and 1s in the character received are correctly received even if the receive and transmit clock speeds (which are in two different systems) are not exactly the same, which is always the case. The clock then operates for as many bits as the number of bits in the code selected.

Every character must be terminated with a STOP (mark) condition. The duration of the stop condition is hardware-dependent and can be 1, 1.5, or 2.0 times the bit timing. If the STOP condition does not occur at the expected place in the arrival of data bits, i.e., a 0 is detected instead of a 1 at the time when the STOP was expected, a framing error has occurred. This **framing error** can sometimes be interpreted by software as an "interrupt/attention" signal from a terminal user or another computer system.

The **break condition** (generated by a break key on a keyboard or by a hardware transmit interface) forces the line to go to a zero state for longer than the time duration of the START, data bits, and the STOP combined. This forces a framing error which is interpreted by many **timesharing systems** (i.e., one which uses shared interactive terminals attached to a single computer) as an attention condition to stop a program or enter a command.

Note that in asynchronous transmission, the transmitter of one system and the receiver of another are "synchronized" (in phase) between the START and STOP conditions, i.e., while receiving a character. Since there can be an arbitrary amount of time between the STOP and the next START condition, there is no synchronization between characters — hence the name "asynchronous" transmission.

Example

A figure illustrating how the asynchronous transmission works will better illustrate the theory being discussed. Suppose an ASCII character *1* (061 octal) is to be transmitted. Using a square-edged diagram to indicate the digital (discrete) form of the voltages representing 0s and 1s, Figure 5–1 shows a representation of the line. The transmission line begins with the line in an idle state (all 1s are being received). The clock

FIGURE 5–1   Framing of a Character with Start and Stop in Asynchronous Communication

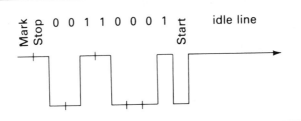

sampling at sixteen times the bit rate detects the START condition and the bit clocking begins and continues for the duration of the 8-bit data character. (Note that the low-order bit of the data character is always transmitted first.) The hardware then detects the STOP condition or state in which all 1s are transmitted, and the character has been received. The character is placed into a hardware buffer accessible by some technique of the software, like a read or move instruction.

If we have a series of characters being received, then there must be an interval after the last data bit of a character of at least the duration of the STOP condition before the START condition for the next character can begin. If the characters "123" are received one after another, the square-edged format of the data is as shown in Figure 5–2.

It should be noted that the software controlling such an interface in asynchronous mode never "sees" the idle (1) bits between characters. This is because the hardware interface only notifies the CPU when a character is assembled in its temporary buffer, that is after the START, the data bits, and the STOP have all been serially recognized and the data bits assembled in this buffer. Just how the interface notifies the CPU depends on the specific interface and computer architecture being used. Usually, either a status bit which can be periodically read (**polled**) by software is sent to the CPU, or an interrupt signal is sent to the CPU, or both (see Chapter 15).

Asynchronous Interfaces

The hardware interfaces used for asynchronous data transmission are similar in the way they are programmed. Often called a **UART (Universal Asynchronous Receiver/Transmitter)**, the transmitter side of the hardware interface takes each character passed to it by means of a character buffer and serializes it between the START and STOP bits.

In simple terms, the software places characters to be transmitted one at a time in a buffer. The interface then becomes "busy" processing each character. As soon as a character is shifted to an internal work buffer of the interface, the interface becomes

FIGURE 5–2   Square-Edged Diagram for "123"

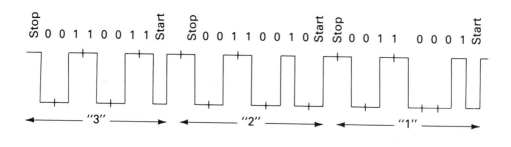

"ready" for another transmit character and notifies the software via a status condition or interrupt that another character may be placed in the transmit buffer. This process continues as long as there is data to be transmitted.

On the receiver side, the data bits in a character which are sent across the line are "assembled" in a work buffer in the interface. When a character is "assembled," it is transferred to a receiver buffer accessible by the receiver software. The interface then signals the CPU and hence the software via a status condition and/or interrupt that a character is available for input. If the character is not taken from the receiver buffer before the next character being received is "assembled" and ready to transfer to this buffer, the result is an **overrun condition** in which data is lost. Such an overrun condition is detected by the receiver hardware logic and is passed on to the software by a status condition (bit) in the interface.

The software continues to set the condition that signals that data is available and to "read" the character from the interface while the data is being received, with the data characters arriving at irregular intervals. The interpretation of the data characters being received is the responsibility of the software. The simple asynchronous interface has no provision for recognizing blocks of data other than the character itself. This function is that of a protocol, which will be presented in Chapter 9.

Multiline Asynchronous Interfaces

Computer systems which support more than one terminal, i.e., timesharing systems, do so by:

1. multiple single-line asynchronous interfaces
2. multiline asynchronous interfaces
3. a combination of single-line and multiline interfaces

Essentially, a **multiline asynchronous interface** supports multiple asynchronous serial lines on a single device.[1] This is accomplished by having the multiple lines supported share the same interrupt facility, clock, and bus interface. Each line has its own transmitter and receiver. The sharing of certain portions of the interface ultimately reduces the cost per line for multiple lines.

When multiple lines in a single interface are supported, characters arrive at different rates on the receiver side of each line. In order to prevent data loss, there must be some additional receiver hardware in the interface. These components are the receiver scanner and the receiver **FIFO (First-In/First-Out)** buffer.

The receiver scanner's job is to detect when a character from a particular line has arrived. Hence, the receiver scanner checks each line in a **round-robin** manner to see if a character is available for that line. If there is, the scanner must read the character, record the line number (scanner position), and set any error flags associated with this

---

[1]Multiline asynchronous interfaces are also called "multiplexers" by some vendors. However, in this book, the term "multiplexer" will be used for devices which provide frequency division multiplexing or time division multiplexing, as described in Chapter 3.

character into an empty position in the FIFO buffer. The pointer to the next position in the FIFO must be adjusted. Obviously, if the FIFO is full, then an error condition called a **FIFO overrun** results.

The presence of characters in the FIFO buffer is made known to the CPU by means of the interrupt facility and/or the device status registers for the multiline interface. Software processing characters from the interface will read a FIFO entry, which will indicate the line number, data character, and error conditions (if any) associated with the character being processed. The receiver software is thus similar to the receiver software for a single line asynchronous interface, except that for each line it must keep track of what user (program) is in control, the address of the input buffer, the current data count, and a pointer to the next position in the input buffer. This is covered in detail in Chapter 18.

Transmit Scanner

On the transmitter side of the multiline interface is another scanner, the **transmit scanner**, which must check the transmit side of each line to determine if its "character-holding" buffer is empty. If it is, the line can handle another output character. Only lines which are enabled for transmit are checked by the scanner. If a line which is enabled for transmission has an empty holding buffer, the scanner reports the condition and the line number to the CPU via the interrupt facility (see Chapter 15) and/or device status registers. The transmit scanner stops until this line is serviced by software.

FIFO Buffer

The **FIFO buffer** allows multiple lines to operate at different speeds and software to react to one line while the scanner places a character from another line into the FIFO. FIFOs are often compared to farm silos because of the way characters arrive and are processed. A typical 16-line interface might have 64 entries in the FIFO, each entry containing the line number, the character, and error flags associated with the character. The hardware can detect when the FIFO buffer is full, which results in a FIFO overrun and loss of at least one character from a line. Note that both the computer and the receiver software must keep up with the arrival rate of characters into the FIFO, or eventually the FIFO will fill up, causing the FIFO overrun condition.

Figure 5–3 illustrates the arrival of characters in the FIFO and the processing of characters by the CPU from the FIFO. Characters arrive from the lines on the input side and are sent to be processed by the CPU on the output side. The hardware, therfore must be able to detect if there is a character "waiting" at the output side of the FIFO. The presence of a character to process on the output side of the FIFO (the receiver side of the multiline interface) is detected by the interrupt facility and/or the device status register.

It is not possible to use a FIFO on the transmit side because the difference in line speeds does not yield a FIFO ordering. Also, there is no real need for such buffering on the transmit side, due to the nature of asynchronous communication, characters can be delayed indefinitely with no loss of data.

Economic Considerations in Number of Lines

Multiline interfaces vary in the number of lines which they support. Most support a number which is a power of 2, i.e. 4, 8, 16, 32, 64, etc. One of the primary motivations for the use of multiline interfaces is to reduce the cost per line. Also, special features are often included in these interfaces, including programmable line speeds, character lengths, and parity.

Taking a simple example, say a 16-port interface for a minicomputer costs $3,600 and a single-line asynchronous interface costs $550. Then 16 lines would cost $8,800. It is therefore $5,200 cheaper to purchase the multiline interface than to purchase 16 single-line serial interfaces, not to mention the fact that it would probably be impossible to plug 16 interfaces into the minicomputer without expanding it. The break-even point is 6 ports: it would cost $3,300 for six single-line interfaces, $3,850 for seven. Thus, if at least six ports are required, it would be better to purchase the multiline interface, in which case the per line cost would be $225.

Often, if only an n-line multiline interface is available and $n + 1$ lines are needed, two such interfaces must be purchased, which might increase the effective per-line cost for lines which are utilized. Using the same set of figures, then, 17 lines require two multiline interfaces at a cost of $7,200. Seventeen single-line interfaces would cost $9,350, which is still $2,150 more than the two multiline interfaces. However, the per-line cost of lines which will actually be used is $7,200/17, or approximately $424, substantially more than the figure ($225 per line) based on all lines being used. It is some-

FIGURE 5–3   Operation of a FIFO Buffer on an Asynchronous Multiline Interface

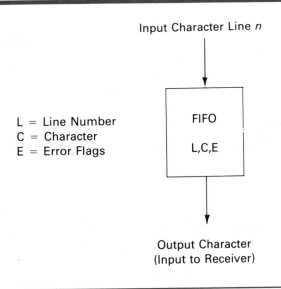

Input Character Line n

L = Line Number
C = Character
E = Error Flags

FIFO

L,C,E

Output Character
(Input to Receiver)

times possible to use a multiline interface and one or more single-line interfaces, because all currently available software supports both concurrently. In this case, seventeen lines could be provided by one multiline interface and one single-line interface at a cost of $4,150, or approximately $245 per line. This is obviously the ideal configuration if cost is the primary criterion, assuming that no expansion in the number of lines was planned in the near future.

One important consideration is whether or not the software to be used on a particular computer supports the multiline interface hardware, because the costs per line increases dramatically if software must be written to support the interface. In general, it is more difficult to program an asynchronous multiline interface than a single-line serial interface. However, if re-entrant coding techniques are used to allow one interrupt handler routine to support multiple single-line interfaces, as discussed in Chapter 18, then the programming techniques are similar.

One disadvantage of a multiline interface is that a failure in the interface results in n lines failing rather than 1. However, the reliability of today's computer systems and interfaces minimizes this concern.

Multiline Interface Control Registers

Figure 5–4 represents the device **control registers** that must be programmed to control a multiline interface. Whether these registers exist as memory locations (as with the DEC PDP–11 and LSI–11 architecture) or as values retrieved or set using some I/O instruction does not change the concepts of how a multiline interface is controlled. Chapter 18 deals with programming techniques for multiline asynchronous interfaces.

═══ Terminology ═══

asynchronous transmission	poll
break condition	round robin
control registers	RS-232
FIFO	space
FIFO buffer	START condition
FIFO overrun	START/STOP transmission
First-In/First-Out	STOP condition
framing	timesharing systems
framing error	transmit scanner
mark	UART
multiline asynchronous interface	Universal Asynchronous
overrun condition	Receiver/Transmitter

FIGURE 5–4   Device Control and Status Registers of a Multiline Interface

```
┌─────────────────────────────────┐   Controls Transmitter and Transmitter
│     Transmit Control Register    │   Interrupts
└─────────────────────────────────┘
  TCR
```

```
┌─────────────────────────────────┐   Controls Receiver and Receiver Interrupts
│    Receiver Control Register     │
└─────────────────────────────────┘
  RCR
```

```
┌─────────────────────────────────┐   Sets Individual Line Characteristics
│     Line Parameter Register      │   (Speed, Character Length, etc.)
└─────────────────────────────────┘
  LPR
```

```
┌─────────────────────────────────┐   Character to Be Transmitted for a
│   Transmitter Buffer Register    │   Particular Line is Placed Here by
└─────────────────────────────────┘   Software
  TBR
```

```
┌─────────────────────────────────┐   Enables/Disables Transmitter for a
│  Transmit Line Control Register  │   Particular Line
└─────────────────────────────────┘
  TLCR
```

```
┌─────────────────────────────────┐   Character Received for a Particular Line
│    Receiver Buffer Register      │   is Placed Here by Hardware and
└─────────────────────────────────┘   "Fetched" by the Software
  RBR
```

```
┌─────────────────────────────────┐   Error Conditions
│     Error Status Register        │
└─────────────────────────────────┘
  ESR
```

Review Questions

1. Characters transmitted in asynchronous transmission are framed by _____ and _____ .

2. A _____ forces a framing error.

3. _____ can be 2, 1.5, or 1 times the length of a data bit in asynchronous communications.

4. Shared   components   in   a   multiline   interface   include _____ and _____ .

5. Another name for asynchronous communications is _____ .

6. True or False:

    a. Asynchronous communications is only used to transmit between computers and interactive terminals.

    b. It is possible to use software to select the bit length of a character received or transmitted in some asynchronous interfaces.

6

Synchronous Communications

Introduction • Synchronization • Clocking • Strip SYN • Controlling
Synchronous Hardware

Introduction

Asynchronous communications provides for the arrival of data characters at an arbitrary rate. This is accomplished by the use of a START condition to begin clocking mechanisms which are synchronized for the duration of the transmission of a single character.

Synchronous communications uses a synchronizing bit pattern to synchronize the transmission and receiving of a block of data. The synchronized timing of bits continues for the duration of the entire data block being transmitted by one system and being received by another. Hence, the synchronizing bit pattern operates in a manner analogous to the START bit in asynchronous transmission, except that the transmit hardware and the receiver hardware must be synchronized for a data block rather than for just one character. Figure 6–1 illustrates the identification of the beginning of the data field within a transmit buffer using this synchronizing bit pattern. Also illustrated is the presence of a trailer of some type, which is analogous to the STOP bits. While this trailer is not present in all synchronous communications environments, some mechanism must exist for identifying the end of the transmission buffer.

As will be discussed in Chapter 12, different protocols define different synchronizing bit patterns. No matter what bit pattern is used to identify the beginning of a message buffer, the principle of detecting this pattern and receiving synchronized data is the same.

Synchronization

Recall that an idle communications line is in a state which is equivalent to the continuous transmission of 1 bits over the line. Just as it was necessary to recognize the beginning of a character in asynchronous transmission, it is necessary to recognize the first character of a data block in synchronous transmission.

In order to do this, the receiver hardware logic incorporates a framing/shift mechanism for searching for the synchronizing bit pattern. Some hardware for synchronous communications uses two consecutive occurrences of an eight-bit **synchronizing character (SYN)** to identify the beginning of a message. For the sake of illustration, assume that the synchronizing bit pattern is 00110010 (EBCDIC synchronizing charac-

FIGURE 6–1   Format of a Transmission Using Synchronous
Communications

sync. pattern	Data Buffer	Trlr

ter — SYN). This mechanism would then **frame** eight bits at a time, shifting the framed pattern one bit to the right when the next bit arrives. When the required bit pattern is recognized, the interface must frame a second SYN character before it is able to recognize the beginning of the message being received. Once this second SYN character has been framed, the receiver has been synchronized with the transmitter and the next eight bits received are the first character of the data block (assuming we are using eight-bit characters). Figure 6–2 illustrates this. [Lane 1984]

Obviously, if the synchronizing bit pattern is the indicator for the beginning of a data block in synchronous data communications, the transmitting station must prefix the data being sent with the appropriate pattern. As shown in Figure 6–2, many synchronization mechanisms require that two identical synchronizing characters precede the data message, i.e., it takes a sixteen-bit synchronizing pattern to recognize the beginning of a message, usually of eight-bit characters. More recent synchronous communication environments use a **FLAG** character for synchronization to identify the beginning as well as the end of the message; the data between the FLAGs must be modified so that no bit pattern identical to the FLAG occurs in the data stream. The modified data is converted back to its original form by the receiving hardware. This is described in more detail in Chapter 12.

The exact format of any given data block transmitted in synchronous data communications is determined by the syntax of the protocol used to send and receive the data. This is discussed fully in Chapter 13.

Clocking

Most synchronous communications modems provide for clocking within the modem. Hence, the interface itself does not clock the bits over the communications line. These modems **clock** bits onto the communications medium at the appropriate rate, which is determined by the speed of transmission. At a speed of 2400 bits per second, 300 eight-bit characters per second are transmitted. A block of 400 characters will take $(400 + n)/300$ seconds to be transmitted and received, where n is the total number of characters in the synchronizing header and the trailer of the data block. If $n = 3$, then it takes $403/300 = 1.34$ seconds to transmit this data.

There is an overhead of a START bit and a STOP bit for every character in asynchronous transmission. In this case, then, for eight bits of data, there are at least ten bits transmitted. The time to transmit 400 characters at 2400 bits per second is (400 *

FIGURE 6–2   Framing of SYN Character to Establish Synchronization

---

```
                Next Bit ───────────┐
                                     \     Hardware
            Data Being Recieved       \
    ─────────────────────────────▶     |  Framing
⟨—char—⟩⟨—char—⟩⟨—SYN—⟩⟨–SYN—⟩        ▼  Register
0010110100000000100110010001100101111    11111111
0001011010000000100110010001100101111    11111111

00010110100000000100110010001100101111   11111111
00001011010000000100110010001100101011   11111111
00000101101000000010011001000110010111   11111111
10000010110100000001001100100011001011   11111111
11000001011010000000100110010001100101   11111111
01100000101101000000010011001000110010   01111111
00110000010110100000000100110010001100   10111111
10011000001011010000000010011001000110   01011111
01001100000101101000000001001100100011   00101111
00100110000010110100000000100110010001   10010111
00010011000001011010000000010011001000   11001011
10001001100000101101000000010011001000   01100101
                                          01100101
10001001100000101101000000010011001000   00110010 ◄──1st SYN Framed
                                             ·
                                             ·
                                             ·
11000001100010011000001011010000000001   00110010 ◄──8 Bits Later
                      ‿‿‿‿‿‿‿‿
                   Data Block
                   Starts Here
                (First Character
                  of Message)
```

1.25)/300 or 500/300 = 1.67 seconds. Hence, the overhead of transmission is higher in asynchronous transmission, even if there are a substantial number of overhead characters in the synchronous protocol **headers** and **trailers**.

Strip SYN

It is possible that one of the synchronizing characters in a two-character synchronization environment might be garbled. Often three or more SYN characters begin a message, so that if the early SYN characters are garbled, synchronization will still occur. In this instance, any extra SYN characters received should be ignored. Synchronous communications hardware usually has a mechanism to **strip** these extra **SYN** characters found at the beginning of a message before signalling the processor that the first character of the message has been received, i.e., the indication of synchronization is delayed until a non-SYN character is received. Figure 6–3 illustrates this process.

Controlling Synchronous Hardware

Programming synchronous hardware is generally more complex than programming a single-line asynchronous interface. The SYN character must be defined to the interface. Then, the STRIP SYN feature must be turned on and off (because SYN characters are generally not removed from the middle of a message). Also, in implementing software for a synchronous interface, since characters are only received after synchronization occurs, determining what characters are actually being received can be quite difficult during debugging. This is discussed further in Chapters 20 and 25.

FIGURE 6-3   Effect of Garbled SYN Character(s) and Stripping Extra SYN Characters from Beginning of Message

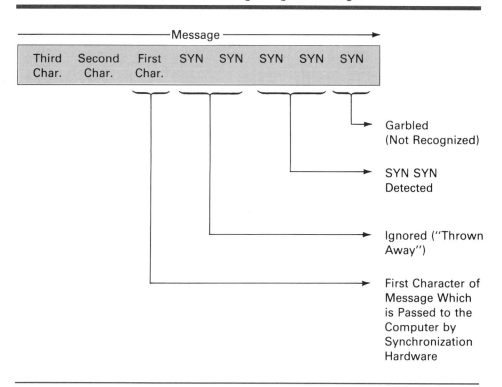

≡ Terminology ≡

Clock	SYN
FLAG	synchronizing character
frame	synchronous communications
headers	trailers
strip SYN	

≡ Review Questions ≡

1. Synchronous transmission involves the framing of a ⎯⎯⎯⎯⎯ of data by ⎯⎯⎯⎯⎯ and ⎯⎯⎯⎯⎯ .

2. A ⎯⎯⎯⎯⎯ character or ⎯⎯⎯⎯⎯ is used to identify the first bit of a message in synchronous transmission.

3. Synchronization of the sending and receiving stations lasts for the length of a ⎯⎯⎯⎯⎯ in asynchronous transmission and a ⎯⎯⎯⎯⎯ for synchronous transmission.

Reference

Lane, Malcolm G. 1984. "Data Communications Protocols." In *Advances in Data Communications Management.* Edited by Jacob Slonim, E. A. Unger, and P. S. Fisher. Volume 2. Chichester, Great Britain: John Wiley & Sons.

7

Modulation/ Demodulation and the RS-232 Interface

Analog/Digital Signals • Manipulating the Signal • Modulation • Phase Modulation • Describing the Speed of a Line • Acoustical Coupling • Programmers' Concerns About Modems • The RS-232 Conventions • Other Signals (Pins) Used with Modems • Cable Wirings

Analog/Digital Signals

Data moving over a communications medium such as a telephone line must conform to the characteristics of the communications link. Generally speaking, information is transferred using an electronically generated analog signal like the one shown in Figure 2–1. Information stored in a computer system is in digital form, consisting of on/off, 1/0, **digital** information. Such digital information is represented with − and + voltages (in the ranges −15 to −5 and +5 to +15, respectively), which are represented by a **square wave**, illustrated in Figure 2–2 [McNamara 1982, p. 37]. Such square waves cannot be transmitted over long distance because of attenuation (see Figure 2–3). That is, the square wave rapidly distorts so that it no longer appears as a square wave on an oscilloscope.

Manipulating the Signal

The problem, then, is to be able to send binary 0s and 1s in any order over media which operate with analog signals. The solution is somehow to manipulate square-edged pulses electronically to fit with the analog transmit frequencies available. A great majority of data communications takes place on **voice-grade** (standard) telephone lines. Since the telephone was developed for voice transmission and the human voice bandwidth is 200–3400 hertz (cycles per second), the restrictions that the characteristics of a voice-grade line tend to present on communications lines impact data transmission.

FIGURE 7–1 Amplitude Modulation

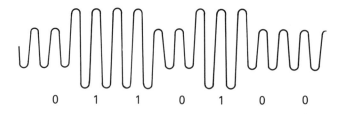

The restriction for the speed of data communications is the bandwidth available, i.e., the frequency range allowed on a particular communications link. In actuality, the bandwidth of communications links is quite large when compared to the bandwidth of the human voice. In order for one communications link to be maximized, the bandwidth is divided into 300–3300 hertz bandwidths, which are electronically shifted throughout the larger bandwidth on the communications medium. This multiplexing of many voice channels over cables or microwave links optimizes the efficiency of these media. Thus, the voice-grade bandwidth of 3000 hertz becomes the bandwidth within which the square-edged pulse can be electronically manipulated.

It was presented in Chapter 2 that the maximum speed of data transmission (measured in bits per second) over a communications line is proportional to the bandwidth [Nyquist 1924; Nyquist 1928; Shannon 1948]. It is easy to see why high-speed data transmission is difficult over voice-grade lines.

Modulation

The process used to "imprint" the binary (square-edged) values on an analog signal is called **modulation**. Essentially, modulation is the modification of some characteristic of an otherwise continuous carrier [McNamara 1982]. This signal is called a **carrier signal** and is the whistle that is often heard on a simple **acoustical modem**.

There are three choices for this modification: the amplitude of the carrier signal, the frequency of the carrier signal, and the phase of the carrier signal. It is even possible to modify a combination of all three. Just how complex the resulting modulated signal is depends on the kind of modulation and the number of discrete states the signal must represent.

Binary 0s and 1s enter a modulator which is generating a carrier sine wave. This carrier signal is modified according to the data and the type of modulation. In the case of **amplitude modulation**, the amplitude is high for 1s and low for 0s, as shown in Figure 7–1. In the case of **frequency modulation**, the frequency is high for 1s and low for 0s, as in Figure 7–2. In either case, the signal received at the other end of a transmission medium is demodulated back to binary 0s and 1s.

FIGURE 7–2   Frequency Modulation

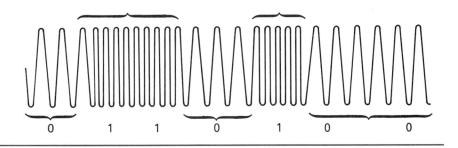

Phase Modulation

Phase modulation represents 0s and 1s by using a sine wave carrier which is shifted electronically so that the peaks do not appear where expected. By using four phase shifts (0, 90, 180, and 270 degrees), we can represent **dibits,** or two bits per signal state. For a Bell 201–compatible modem, the following shifts are used:

0 degrees	00
90 degrees	01
180 degrees	10
270 degrees	11

Figure 7–3 illustrates the phase shifting which takes place to represent these dibits. Each phase change begins with the previous state as a base point for the next phase shift. [Sherman 1981, p. 51]

Describing the Speed of a Line

Often the term baud is used to describe the speed of a modem. However, **baud** is actually the number of times the line condition changes state per second. If each state represents a 1 or 0, then baud is the same as bits/second. On the other hand, if there are four possible states, as in phase modulation, then one line condition change of state represents a dibit, in which case n baud is equal to $2 * n$ bits/second. It is best to use the term **bits per second** rather than "baud" to guarantee an accurate description of data transmission speed.

Acoustical Coupling

Acoustical coupling uses audible tones on the phone line. While many manufacturers have begun to provide direct connect modems, many acoustical couplers still exist. A user makes a connection by placing the telephone handset in cups to pick up signals from the handset's receiver and to send signals using the handset's transmitter. Whether the modem is acoustical or **direct connect** to the phone line, the frequencies used are the same.

There are two types of modems: originate and answer. The **answer modem** provides the carrier signal. The **originate modem** transmits with one set of frequencies which is recognized by the receiver side of the answer modem, while the answer modem uses a different set of frequencies which is recognized by the receiver side of the originate modem.

This is best illustrated by the Bell-103F–compatible modem, which uses the following frequencies for transmitting 0s and 1s when in originate mode:

1070 hertz	binary 0 (space)
1270 hertz	binary 1 (mark)

These are the frequencies recognized by the receiver side of the answer modem. The answer modem transmits using the following frequencies:

FIGURE 7–3   Phase Shift Modulation

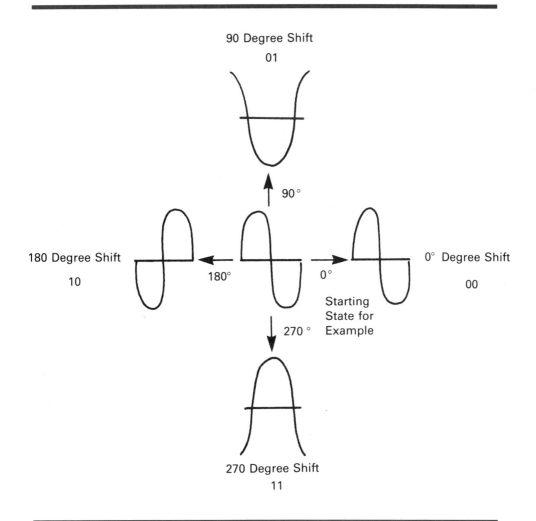

2025 hertz   binary 0 (space)
2225 hertz   binary 1 (mark)

Figure 7–4 depicts the frequency ranges for these answer and originate modems. [McNamara 1982, p. 91]

Full duplex can be accommodated on two-wire facilities, because one channel uses 300–1700 hertz, the other uses 1700–3000 hertz, and appropriate electronic filtering on each end allows the frequencies to be detected correctly. Speeds to 1200 bps can effectively be transmitted with this technique.

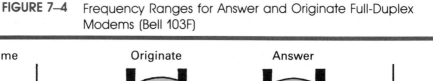

FIGURE 7–4   Frequency Ranges for Answer and Originate Full-Duplex
Modems (Bell 103F)

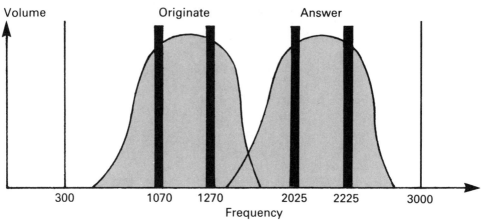

Programmers' Concerns About Modems

It is important to understand how a modem operates, but, from a programmer's point
of view, such knowledge is perhaps less important than an understanding of the signals
generated and required by a modem and a communications interface which is to be
programmed. Only modem setup actually demands an understanding of the principles
of modulation and demodulation principles. Clearly, the failure in communications
between the software of one system and the software of another system or terminal
caused when both acoustical modems are set to answer or both are set to originate is
not a fault in the programming; the solution to the problem is simplified greatly, however, if the principles of frequency modulation are understood.

The RS-232 Conventions

An interface standard called **RS-232** has been developed and approved by the Electrical Industry Association (**EIA**). This standard associates specific signals (by name)
with specific connector pins in a 25-pin RS-232 connector, like the one illustrated in
Figure 7–5. The association between signal and pin has been standardized, but there is
no such thing as a standard cabling, because the use of these defined signals varies
according to the device attached to an RS-232 interface. Figure 7–5 illustrates the
layout of the 25-pin RS-232 connector. One convention that is uniform for all interfaces, devices and modems using RS-232 is that pin 7 is the signal ground and pin 1 is
the protective ground.

While the receive and transmit signals (the IN and OUT signals, respectively) are
on pins 2 and 3, some interfaces (some printers and computers) reverse these. In fact,

FIGURE 7–5   RS-232 Connector Pin Layout

1	2	3	4	5	6	7	8	9	10	11	12	13
o	o	o	o	o	o	o	o	o	o	o	o	o

14	15	16	17	18	19	20	21	22	23	24	25
o	o	o	o	o	o	o	o	o	o	o	o

some devices may be set with switches or jumpers so that pins 2 and 3 may be either IN or OUT. The simplest connection for an RS-232 device is shown in Figure 7–6. The term **null modem** describes a cable connection (shown in Figure 7–6) used for relatively short distance. The null modem connects receive (pin 2) to transmit (pin 3), transmit (pin 3) to receive (pin 2), and ground (pin 7) to ground (pin 7). Via a null modem connection, it is possible to use the square-edged (binary) signal for short distances — say up to 1000–2000 feet, depending on line speed and nearby sources of noise. It must be known which pin of pins 2 and 3 is IN (receive) and which pin is OUT (transmit) in order to correctly wire cables between computers, between computers and modems, and between computers and terminals.

Other Signals (Pins) Used with Modems

The following are used when programming communications interfaces are attached to a modem:

Carrier Detect (CD) — The carrier indicator specifies that the modem detects a carrier signal on the line. This indicator is usually checked by the software. It is critically important, since without a carrier, no modulation takes place, which means that no data communication is possible.

FIGURE 7–6   Null Modem Wiring for Asynchronous Communications

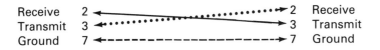

Request To Send (RTS) / Clear To Send (CTS) — In some modems, and in some environments — like a half-duplex environment — it is necessary to wait a certain period of time before the modem can move from receive to transmit. This is called **modem turnaround** and the turnaround time can vary from 50ms (milliseconds) to 200ms.
The Request to Send and Clear to Send signals are used to control this turnaround mechanism. Software that controls transmission and reception via a modem sets Request to Send using the appropriate instructions, which are interface- and computer-dependent. The software must then "wait" (either by polling or interrupts) until the modem sets Clear to Send.
It should be noted that the Clear to Send signal is also utilized when such interfaces are attached to serial printers. In this case, the Clear to Send signal indicates that the printer is on-line and ready to accept another data character.

Data Set Ready (DSR) — The Data Set Ready signal indicates that the modem is powered up and ready. (The term "data set ready" evolved from the use of **data sets** to refer to modems.) This signal is used in programming serial printers to indicate that the printer is on-line; in some cases, Clear to Send and Data Set Ready are combined in one signal and signify that the printer is able to accept data.

Data Terminal Ready (DTR) — This signal gets its name from situations in which modems are attached to terminals. A powered-up and ready terminal sets Data Terminal Ready to indicate to the modem that it is ready. Computer software must set this signal to answer a ringing telephone when a modem is equipped for auto-answer.

Ring — Ring is a signal which indicates that the modem has detected a ringing telephone connected to it. As mentioned above, a computer sets Data Terminal Ready to answer the ringing telephone. When the telephone is answered, the Carrier and the Data Set Ready signals should both be on.

This arrangement of pins and signals within the RS-232 standard is generally available and relatively common. They are not always utilized nor are they always interpreted the same. The programming considerations in an environment requiring modem control will be more fully discussed in Chapter 20.

Cable Wirings

Interfacing different devices seems to require as many cable wiring combinations as there are combinations of the pairings of the pins on each end. This is because of the way various computers, modems, printers, and other devices use and interpret signals. Three "typical" wirings often utilized are shown in Figures 7–7, 7–8, and 7–9.

FIGURE 7-7 Typical Modem-to-Communications-Interface Cable Wiring

Pin	Modem		Interface
2	XMT	– – – – – – – – – ➤	RCV
3	RCV	◄ – – – – – – – – –	XMT
4	RTS	◄────────────	RTS
5	CTS	───────────➤	CTS
6	DSR	───────────➤	DSR
7	GND	◄──────────➤	GND
8	CD	───────────➤	CD
15	TT	───────────➤	TT (Synchronous only)
17	RT	───────────➤	RT (Synchronous only)
20	DTR	◄────────────	DTR
22	RING	───────────➤	RING

Legend

 Set by Interface

─────────➤ Set by Modem

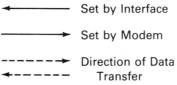

- – – – ➤ Direction of Data
◄ – – – –   Transfer

XMT = Transmit	DSR = Data Set Ready	RT = Receive Timing
RCV = Receive	GND = Signal Ground	DTR = Data Terminal
RTS = Request to Send	CD = Carrier Detect	Ready
CTS = Clear to Send	TT = Transmit Timing	RING = Ring Indicator

FIGURE 7–8   Printer Cable Wiring with DTR = Printer Ready and On-line

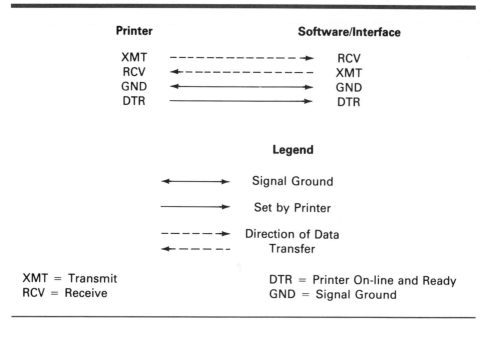

Printer		Software/Interface
XMT	┄┄┄┄┄┄►	RCV
RCV	◄┄┄┄┄┄	XMT
GND	◄────────►	GND
DTR	────────►	DTR

Legend

◄────────►   Signal Ground

────────►   Set by Printer

┄┄┄┄►
◄┄┄┄┄   Direction of Data
Transfer

XMT = Transmit   DTR = Printer On-line and Ready
RCV = Receive   GND = Signal Ground

FIGURE 7–9   Printer Cable Wiring with DTR = Printer On-Line and CTS = Printer Ready (Not Busy)

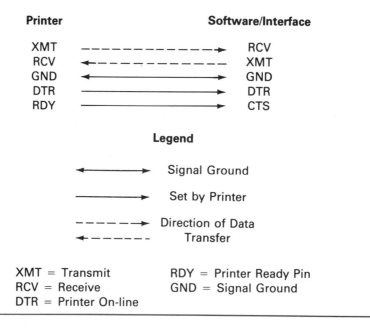

Printer		Software/Interface
XMT	┄┄┄┄┄┄►	RCV
RCV	◄┄┄┄┄┄	XMT
GND	◄────────►	GND
DTR	────────►	DTR
RDY	────────►	CTS

Legend

◄────────►   Signal Ground

────────►   Set by Printer

┄┄┄┄►
◄┄┄┄┄   Direction of Data
Transfer

XMT = Transmit   RDY = Printer Ready Pin
RCV = Receive   GND = Signal Ground
DTR = Printer On-line

≡ Terminology ≡

acoustical coupling	direct connect
acoustical modem	DSR
amplitude modulation	DTR
answer modem	EIA
baud	frequency modulation
bits per second	modem turnaround
carrier detect	modulation
carrier signal	null modem
CD	originate modem
Clear To Send	phase modulation
CTS	Request To Send
Data Set Ready	Ring
data sets	RS-232
Data Terminal Ready	RTS
dibits	square wave
digital	voice-grade

≡ Review Questions ≡

1. Three types of modulation used in modems are _____ , _____ and
_____ .

2. Two bits represented by one state change are called _____ .

3. A common standard for communications interfaces is _____ .

4. A null modem connects _____ on one end to _____ on the other
and vice versa.

5. Modulation in data communications is used to _____ .

References

McNamara, John E. 1982. *Technical Aspects of Data Communication*. Second Edition.
Bedford, Massachusetts: Digital Press.

Nyquist, H. 1924. "Certain Factors Affecting Telegraph Speed." *Transactions
A.I.E.E.*

———. 1928. "Certain Topics in Telegraph Transmission Theory." *Transactions
A.E.E.E.*

Shannon, Claude E. 1948. "Mathematical Theory of Communication." *Bell System
Technical Journal* (July and October).

Sherman, Kenneth. 1981. *Data Communications: A Users Guide*. Reston, Virginia:
Reston.

8

Network Architectures

Requirements for Communications

Early computer communications consisted primarily of information transfers from station to station in a point-to-point environment. Modern network architectures require that information be passed from application (end user) to application running in the same or different computer systems. Such information transfers must be transparent to the application program or end user.

Just as program structure is extremely important in the design of computer software, so is the network structure essential in modern computer networks. The isolation of the many functions required in the management of information transfer results in a design that has clearly delineated functional layers. Conversation between people is analogous to communications between computers and illustrates the necessary functions involved in such information transfer. Human communication can be divided into three levels: cognitive, language, and transmission [Meijer and Peeters 1982, p. 5; Cypser 1978].

The **cognitive level** involves basic understanding and knowledge. For example, conversations and articles involving technical aspects of computer science will have little meaning to someone who is not a computer scientist. Comparable levels of understanding are required in communication between experts in all specialized fields.

The level involving **language** is not concerned with the subject being presented or discussed but, rather, how the information is formulated into words. Two computer scientists attending an international conference, one who speaks only English and one who speaks only German, may well understand common concepts in computer science. However, the lack of a common language for conveying such concepts from one person to the other will prevent a conversation from taking place.

The third and final level of **transmission** is concerned with the physical mechanism used to transfer information. For example, the spoken word is not meaningful to a deaf person, but sign language probably would be. On the other hand, the use of sign language to a person who does not understand this type of communication would not allow information to be transferred. [Meijer and Peters 1982, p. 5]

Each level isolates a specific function required for meaningful conversation to take place. Unless each of the three levels of one party level is compatible with the corresponding level of the other party, meaningful conversation is impossible.

It should be noted that the levels themselves are independent of each other for an individual but dependent in the corresponding level for any other individual if communication is to take place. For example, computer scientists have the basic understanding to discuss many topics in the field. At the language level, there may be several forms: English, German, etc. The transmission level might be telephone, voice conversation, written papers, and so on. The cognitive level might even change, in that a discussion could be held about any topic outside the field of expertise — politics or the stock market, for example — and various combinations of the cognitive, language and transmission levels would result in meaningful conversation.

Implied in all these examples are some rules (etiquette or protocol) which are used in human conversation. Such **protocols** are a major part of the structure of computer networks. While human conversation provides some liberty in the communication process (e.g., a person speaking in "broken" English can still be understood), protocols defined in the layers of a computer network must be very specific and must be adhered to.

Computer Network Architectures

Having laid the groundwork for understanding the need for levels or layers in human conversation, it is appropriate to consider the layering necessary in defining network architectures. The importance of standards in the data processing industry has long been emphasized, but defining and adhering to such standards are not always easy. Fortunately, there is a Reference Model of **Open Systems Interconnection**, defined by the **International Standards Organization (ISO)**, which can be used as a basis for defining the conceptual layers necessary within a network architecture [ISO]. While not every layer is present in every network architecture, it is easier to understand any network structure by comparing it to the open systems model. The purpose of this chapter is to provide a basic understanding of the layers which can be defined in a given network structure and to clearly identify the functions of the **data link control layer**, the layer which provides the protocol for information transfer from one computer system to another via communication lines. The data link control layer will become the major focus of this book, because it involves data transmission *between* computer systems rather than information transfer *within* a computer system. In this layer, one must be concerned with communications links, controlling interfaces and modems, timing, error recovery and other concepts which have been associated with data communications since its very beginning. While the data link control protocol can be implemented in hardware, a software algorithm is the basis of the correct operation of the protocol. Of utmost importance will be the software design techniques for implementing data link control protocols. Such software will control hardware interfaces, the majority of which are synchronous.

The Layers

Applications running in a stand-alone computer system use information local to that computer system (e.g., disk, tape, etc.). Such applications running in a network environment may, if authorized, access information stored in another computer system in the network as well as information stored locally, in the computer system in which it is running. These applications can be programs or terminal operators and might best be described as "end users" [Meijer and Peeters 1982, p. 6]. The purpose of a network is to allow error-free information to be transferred from end user to end user. The actual methods of transfer used should be transparent to the end users. The important thing is to preserve the integrity of the data being transferred within the network from end user to end user.

There are seven layers defined in the ISO Standard Reference Model for Open Systems Interconnection (**OSI**). The purpose of this model is "to provide a common basis for the coordination of standards development for the purpose of systems interconnection, while allowing existing standards to be placed into perspective within the overall Reference Model" [ISO]. The layers in the OSI Model are illustrated in Figure 8–1. The applications or end users reside in the highest layer (7) of the model.

The term Open Systems Interconnection (OSI) "qualifies standards for the exchange of information among systems that are 'open' to one another for this purpose by virtue of their mutual use of the application standards. . . . The fact that a system is open does not imply any particular systems implementation, technology, or means of interconnection, but refers to the mutual recognition and support of the application software" [ISO, p. 2].

By using this reference model as a guide, it is easier to understand the various differences between network architectures, because the model facilitates the development of new architectures. An overview of the OSI model is presented in this chapter. Cypser, Tanenbaum, and Meijer provide detailed descriptions of the OSI model and use it to compare the structures of various networks [Cypser 1978; Meijer and Peeters 1982].

FIGURE 8–1   Layering in the ISO Model

7	Application Layer
6	Presentation Layer
5	Session Layer
4	Transport Layer
3	Network Layer
2	Data Link Layer
1	Physical Layer

The principles of software design presented in Part II of this book rely heavily on modular structures which isolate functions from one module to another. The **layered structure** of the OSI model is an exact parallel to the structuring recommended for the implementation of data link control protocols; therefore, the principles applied at the data link control level can be applied at each subsequent layer in the OSI model when software for a particular network structure is implemented.

Overview

All layers shown in Figure 8–1 do not exist in every network architecture. In many cases, two or more layers are collapsed into a single layer which provides most or all of the functions provided by the two or more original layers.

It should be noted that no data is directly transferred from layers two through seven. Only layer 1, the physical layer, involves a physical transfer of information between computers. [Tanenbaum 1981] Layers three and above involve information transfers between layers within the same computer system. Layer 2, the data link control, controls the transfer of information on the physical medium.

Layers 4 through 7 involve a peer-to-peer [Falk 1983, p. 38] or an end-to-end [Tanenbaum 1981, p. 18] conversation or protocol, in which there is conversation between similar programs on source and destination computer systems. In layers 3 and below, protocols involve conversation with immediate neighbor machines, which may be the source or ultimate destination machine. [Tanenbaum 1981, p. 16] Figure 8–2 illustrates these peer-to-peer protocol conversations.

Figure 8–2 illustrates a path of data flow from an end user which is sending information to another end user. The data to be transferred originates at the application layer. The block of data from the application is passed down through each layer to the physical layer, where it is transferred "out of" the source computer system. Each layer usually adds a header and perhaps a trailer to "frame" the data passed to it by a higher layer. Essentially, the data passed to a particular lower layer is placed into an **envelope** which the layer controls. On the receiving end, the envelope — i.e., the **header** and **trailer** — is removed so that the original data sent will arrive correctly at the next higher layer. After all envelopes are removed by the layers on the receiving end, the data ultimately reaches the application, or end user.

Figure 8–3 illustrates the addition of the headers and trailers to the data at each level. Early communications protocols dealt with envelopes in which only one or two headers and trailers were used to transmit data. The principles applicable to the building of envelopes for messages or data blocks at one level are generally applicable at each level, except that different protocols are used to interpret the headers and trailers at each level.

Application Layer

The highest layer defined in the OSI reference model, the **application layer,** is more or less user-dependent. It is different from all other layers in that it does not interface to a higher layer. However, there must be a way to access the services in the OSI

FIGURE 8–2   Information Flow in OSI Reference Model [Falk 1983, p. 39]

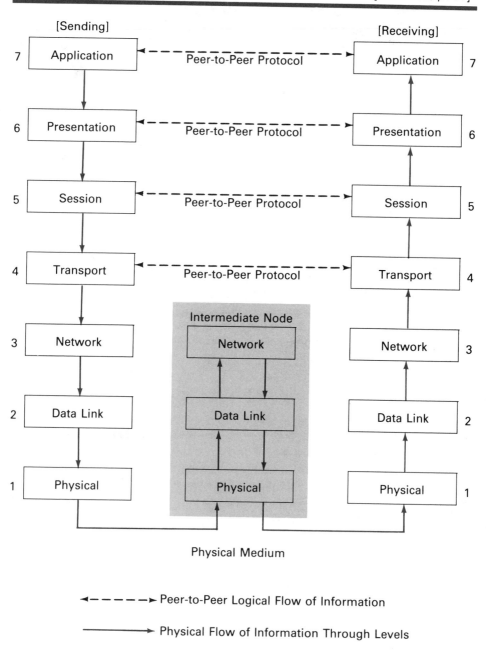

Physical Medium

◄ – – – – – ► Peer-to-Peer Logical Flow of Information

───────► Physical Flow of Information Through Levels

FIGURE 8–3   Illustration of "Envelopes" of Headers and Trailers at Each Layer

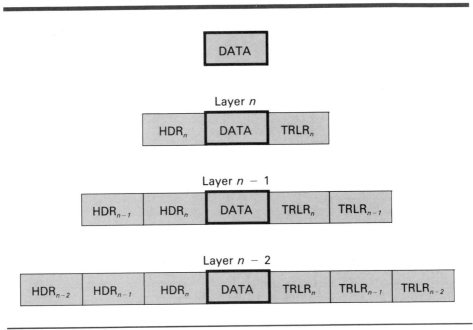

environment. This layer basically serves as a window between corresponding end users using an OSI network for transferring information. [Meijer and Peeters 1982]

All services which can be directly used by application processes must be provided in this level. Such services are outlined in the ISO standard and are listed in Table 8–1.

TABLE 8–1   Possible Application Layer Services Listed in OSI Reference Model [ISO, p. 42]

Identification of intended communications partners — various ways include name, address, definite description, generic description.

Determination of the availability of designated communication partner.

Establishment of authority to communicate.

Agreement on privacy mechanisms.

Authentication of intended communication partners.

Determination of cost allocation methodology.

Determination of adequacy of resources.

TABLE 8–1   Possible Application Layer Services Listed in OSI Reference Model [ISO, p. 42] Continued

Determination of acceptable quality of service (response time, tolerable error rate, etc.)

Synchronization of cooperating applications.

Selection of dialog discipline including initiation and release procedures.

Agreement on responsibility for error recovery.

Agreement on procedures for control of data integrity.

Identification of constraints on data syntax (character sets, data structure).

Presentation Layer

The purpose of the **presentation layer** is to provide "for representation of information that application-entities either communicate or refer to in their dialog" [ISO, p. 44]. (What this text calls "end users" the ISO model calls "application entities.") The presentation layer deals with the representation (syntax) of data being transferred from one end user to another. There are three syntaxes involved at the presentation level: that of the sender, that of the receiver, and that used for the transfer. The mapping of these syntaxes must be determined when the presentation connection is established. [Meijer and Peeters 1982]

Code conversion, as discussed in Chapter 4, is an important function provided in the presentation layer. The presentation layer also provides **data compression** and **decompression**, in which duplicate characters or common "words" are represented by algorithms to improve throughput of information transfers. Chapter 11 discusses various aspects of data compression and decompression. Other important functions at the presentation layer include remote file access (either at the record or at the total file transfer level) and virtual to physical terminal mapping. The terminal mapping is necessary because of the wide variety of terminal control procedures in existence (as discussed in Chapter 3).

The presentation layer must provide for "transparent transfer from application entities" [ISO]. In other words, data appears to be transferred *directly* from an application in one system to an application in another without change, when in fact it has been changed in many ways in passing through the network. Applications invoke the network services for information transfer. It is the job of the presentation layer to provide the first step in this transparent transfer, particularly dealing with syntactic concerns of the data being sent and received by end user applications.

The ISO model provides that application entities can use any syntax. The presentation layer will provide the transformations between syntaxes so that the information can be transferred between applications in a transparent manner.

Session Layer

In the **session layer**, the user negotiates for connections. This layer is essentially the user's interface to the network. As the session layer exchanges data between two users in the network, it must preserve the integrity of the data. Connecting two such users is often called a **session**. [Tanenbaum 1981]

The session layer involves setting up a session between two users and providing services for the dialog which will take place. It is important that the rules for data transfer be established when the session is established. Three types of data exchange are defined in the session layer [ISO]:

1. Two-way simultaneous (TWS)
2. Two-way alternate (TWA)
3. One-way interaction

The session level is concerned with who the communication partner is [Meijer and Peeters 1982]. In order to be able to identify users defined at the session level, it is important to have naming conventions and addressing schemes. Otherwise, conversation between specific users would not be possible.

Setting up a session can be quite complex. Users at each end must be authenticated, the type of transfer must be determined and such things as billing must be taken into account at this level. There also may be some sequence checking done in case messages do not arrive from the next lower layer. [Tanenbaum 1981]

The dialog of data transfer at the session level is managed according to the protocol rules. Typical session services include such things as providing for logging into a timesharing system, transferring files between two computer systems, accessing records in a file on another system, and so on. Hence, the addressing conventions must be provided by the requesting end user (or programs running for such an end user) if such services are to be possible. [Tanenbaum 1981] In addition to these addresses, it is also necessary to know transport addresses, which are used by transport stations. This requires that the session layer be able to map session addresses to transport addresses so that the appropriate transport connection can be established [Tanenbaum 1981].

The session layer must preserve the integrity of the data being transferred. It must prevent aborts in the middle of data base update, for example, or the integrity of the data base will be sacrificed. In the process of doing this management, the session layer really adds application-oriented functions to what otherwise is bit-by-bit transfer at lower levels. [Tanenbaum 1981]

Transport Layer

The **transport layer** is also known as **host-to-host layer** and has as its function the creation of a transport pipe, although the path which is determined by the network layer, is not known. [Meijer and Peeters 1982; Tanenbaum 1981] Data is passed to the transport layer by the session layer. The transport layer passes messages to the network layer. The limitations on the lengths of messages must be taken into account, so the transport layer may map messages onto one or more smaller units, which are called **packets**. The receiving transport layer will reassemble the data in the form required by the receiving session layer. Units or packets must therefore be sequenced in order so that they can be reassembled in the correct order for the session level. As a rule, the transport layer provides data transfer on an error-free point-to-point channel. Messages provided by the session level at the transmitting station are received in the same order in which they are sent, but the transport level might not preserve the ordering, in which case the session level would have to order them. [Tanenbaum 1981]

The transport protocol must provide flow control for the stream of units flowing on the transport connection. That is, at the transport level, there must be a means of suspending and resuming unit traffic.

In most instances, one distinct network connection is established for each transport connection. However, throughput considerations might dictate multiple network connections for a transport connection. One other possibility would be the multiplexing of several transport connections onto the same network connection as a cost-saving measure. [Tanenbaum 1981]

The transport layer is the lowest layer at which there is a **peer-to-peer** [Falk 1983] or **end-to-end** [Tanenbaum 1981] conversation — it is the lowest level at which there is conversation between similar programs on source and destination machines. Levels lower than the transport level converse with immediate neighbor machines, which may be intermediate nodes in the path to the destination system. Figure 8–2 illustrates an intermediate node in which information does not get passed to the transport layer.

Network Layer

The **network layer's** primary function is to provide the routing necessary to move information through the "pipe" defined by the transport layer. An analogy to automobile travel helps to understand the functions of transport and network layers. A decision to drive from Washington, D.C., to Orlando, Florida, is analogous to setting up a transport pipe. The transport layer does not determine the route. Often a travel service will recommend a route to follow in driving from one city to another, and the answers to such questions as "Do you want the shortest route or the most scenic route?" determine the ultimate route to be taken. Also, alternate routes could also be recommended if traffic congestion is heavy (such as taking a bypass around Jacksonville, Florida, instead of driving through the city). These decisions on routing are analogous to the functions provided by the network layer.

In moving data in a network, however, the network layer must be very concerned with finding the best route. There are factors which determine how a best route is determined:

1. fixed route
2. alternate route should the normal route fail
3. dynamic or adaptive routing, in which the route to follow is determined at each moment along the way. Here, an analysis of the state of traffic flow is

needed to determine the best route, i.e., the one with the minimum delay. This is far more complex to implement than 1 or 2. [Meijer and Peeters 1982]

In any case, the network layer must provide the path which will move data through the network from the source system to the destination system by providing an appropriate sequence of transmission links and network nodes. In the process of providing these links and nodes, the network layer should try to avoid local congestion, if possible. [Meijer and Peeters 1982] Figure 8–2 illustrates data moving from a source system to the network layer of an intermediate node and then on to the network layer of the destination system.

Data Link Layer

The **data link layer** controls the message traffic on the physical medium (physical layer). It provides the rules for moving data between nodes. The data link layer's rules are similar to driving rules encountered on a trip. Such signs as stop, yield, one way, slow, and resume speed communication rules which control how one drives along a given road, one link in the trip from one city to another.

In a similar manner, the data link layer must control message traffic on the physical medium. One important function is the **framing** of the data to be transmitted over the physical medium with appropriate delimiters which will be recognized by the receiving station's hardware and data link control layer. Determining when to transmit or receive such frames, acknowledging the correct receipt of a frame, informing a sending node that a frame was not correctly received, and retransmitting erroneous frames are all part of the rules which must be provided at the data link layer.

The data link layer also must provide control for stations connected in a multidrop environment. Here, the data link layer must provide polling procedures for selecting stations to which data is transmitted and from which it is received.

Data link control protocols will be studied thoroughly throughout the remainder of this book. Chapters 9 and 12 concentrate on data link control protocols.

Physical Layer

The **physical layer** involves the transmission of "raw" **bits** over a communications channel. It must convert the bits to be transmitted into the appropriate form so that 0s are recognized as 0s and 1s are recognized as 1s by the receiving physical layer. Hence, the concern at this layer is with electrical and procedural interfacing. [Tanenbaum 1981] Note that it is only at the physical layer that actual data transfer between nodes occurs.

Summary

Figure 8–4 illustrates the basic functions of each layer in the OSI Reference Model. Figure 8–5 provides an overview of the services provided by layers 1 through 6.

FIGURE 8–4   Basic Functions and Information Transfer in the OSI
Reference Model [Falk 1983, p. 39; Martin 1981]

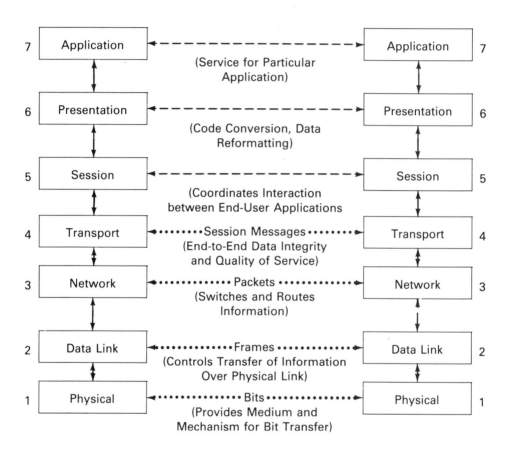

FIGURE 8–5   Overview of Services of Layers 1 Through 6 in the OSI
Reference Model

Layer	Questions Answered (Services Provided) in Layer
PRESENTATION	What are the characteristics of the communications partner? How is data prepared so that it is in the appropriate form?
SESSION	Who is the communications partner? How is the partner identified?
TRANSPORT	Where is the communications partner located? What "pipe" must be set up to get information transferred?
NETWORK	How does information get there? What are the routes to travel from source to destination?
LINK	How is information controlled as it travels along each link?
PHYSICAL	What is the physical mechanism to get the data from node to node?

The layered structure defined by this model is consistent with recommended modular software design techniques. Of course, one of the most important advantages of the layered structure is that any given layer can be modified without causing other layers to be affected. In fact, the layering itself defines a modular structure, in which each layer performs distinct, isolated, and well-defined functions. Two of the principles used by the ISO in defining the layered structure were:

1. The layer boundaries should be chosen so that information flow across the interfaces is minimized.
2. The number of layers should be large enough that distinct functions do not have to be combined in the same layer, yet small enough that the architecture does not become unwieldy. [Tanenbaum 1981]

The ISO Reference Model has indeed adhered to these principles and provides a standard to make order out of what otherwise is a difficult task: comparing and understanding different network architectures.

It is true that the layered structure requires more total overhead than does a single-level implementation of data communications procedures. However, the advantages of modular structure far outweigh the disadvantage of additional overhead.

As was stated earlier, much of this book is devoted to the modular design of software for implementing data link control protocols. The various aspects of link control protocol definition and the techniques for implementing these protocols are generally applicable at each level of a network architecture. Because of the many difficult problems which must be solved at the data link level, higher level protocols will not be studied. Meijer and Peeters, Tanenbaum, and Cypser all provide detailed analyses of network architectures and these higher level protocols [Meijer and Peeters 1982; Tanenbaum 1981; Cypser 1978].

Distributed Processing

Generally, **distributed processing** refers to a processing environment that makes use of more than one processor. Although some might think of multiprocessing environments, the term generally implies a geographic distribution of processors. [Martin 1981] Early computer networks used a **star configuration** with **dumb**, i.e., not programmable, **terminals** accessing the host's computing power (see Figure 2–10). This centralized approach to providing computer access was cost-effective during the 1970s. However, as minicomputers and microcomputers evolved and became less expensive, it became economically beneficial to locate computers at the sites where "dumb" terminals had been located. The less expensive microcomputers and minicomputers soon became extremely attractive to users who often had no control over the centralized host system and in general were dissatisfied with the performance of such centralized systems.

Minicomputers and microcomputers can now be **nodes** in a network and can serve as **hosts** in that network. Data can be stored in a variety of ways in most networks and can easily be transferred from computer to computer. New design questions arise in such networking environments. One of the most important is how to distribute information in a network and still preserve the integrity of the data being stored. Other decisions, such as whether to split the data in the network (one copy of each record stored in a particular computer system and shared by multiple computers) or to replicate the data in the network (multiple copies of the same records for use by multiple computers), are difficult and create difficult management problems. For example, if a data base is distributed or split in the network and system failure occurs at one node in the network, data cannot merely be restored from a backup: the state of the other parts of the data base stored in other computer systems must be considered first. On the other hand, if data is replicated, how can it be guaranteed that an obsolete copy of a record is not being used for processing on a computer in the network? Clearly, setting up and managing a distributed environment is not trivial.

Distributed processing allows users to use local hosts, minicomputers, and microcomputers, as well as remote systems, depending on the needs of a particular user. However, the management of data, error recovery procedures, and so on become quite difficult, and management of such networks must be carefully planned. Martin provides a careful study of distributed processing environments [Martin 1981, pp. 22–56].

Security

The enhanced capabilities provided by computer networks and distributed processing also introduce one additional problem, that of **security**. Access to information is no longer a local problem or a problem of managing a few users. The geographic distribution of users who can access various computers in a network and the desire of **hackers** to access information that does not belong to them create a difficult problem in securing information stored in a computer network.

James Martin points out that network users must be identifiable and their actions authorized and monitored. The network architecture must provide such capabilities. In addition, he states that data, hardware and software must be both protected and locked. Yet all of this is of no value if the transmission itself is not both private and fail-safe. The session level must provide the mechanisms to preserve the integrity of data bases should a system failure occur. The problem of privacy of transmission must entail some type of **cryptography** to guarantee that data which is transmitted has not been "read, copied, or tampered with" [Martin 1981, p. 529].

Providing network security is not easy, and can be quite expensive in dollars and may require a great deal of CPU power to implement sophisticated encryption techniques. The management and security of keys required in such encryption techniques requires careful planning and can become quite complex.

Existing Networks

The **ARPANET** was created by the **Advanced Research Projects Agency** of the U.S. Department of Defense, which first used an experimental four-node network in late 1969. Operating and growing since that time, it provides most of the basic research for theory of networking known today. [Tanenbaum 1981]

The ARPANET used **IMPs (Interface Message Processors)**, which are the switching elements in the network. The IMPs originally were Honeywell DDP-516 minicomputers that had 12K 16-bit words of memory; later IMPs were DDP-316 minicomputers with 16K words of memory. The IMP-IMP protocol is an illustration of the collapsing of two or more layers into one — in this case, mainly layers 2 and 3 of the OSI model. The ARPANET structure has been compared to the OSI model by Tanenbaum and further study of the ARPANET can be done by referring to this book.

Commercial networks like the **Systems Network Architecture (SNA)** of IBM and **DECNET** (also called **DNA — Digital Network Architecture**) of Digital Equipment Corporation provide most of the services described in the OSI reference model for different layers. Once again, the layers of each do not directly correspond on a one-to-one basis to the reference model, but the comparison aids in the understanding of these network structures. Meijer and Peeters and Tanenbaum present details on the network structures of both SNA and DECNET [Meijer and Peeters 1982; Tanenbaum 1981]. The data link control protocols of SNA **(SDLC)** and of DECNET **(DDCMP)** are presented in Chapter 13 of this book.

Protocol Standards

CCITT has defined several protocol standards and they are currently being used in many network implementations. One such commonly used standard is the **CCITT Recommendation X.25**. **X.25** has three levels of protocol definition:

Level 1   for the physical layer, which uses further interface standards **CCITT Recommendation X.21**

Level 2   for the data link layer, which defines the **High-level Data Link Control (HDLC)** protocol (which is similar to the SDLC protocol described in Chapter 12)

Level 3   for the network layer protocol using packet switching

X.25's data link control protocol (level 2) is similar to the SDLC protocol covered in detail in Chapter 12. The network layer (level 3) for packet switching in X.25 provides for logical connections (the establishment of virtual circuits) between terminals and/or computers and other aspects of the network layer. Consult Meijer and Peeters, Cypser, or Tanenbaum for further information on X.25 [Meijer and Peeters 1982, pp. 52ff; Cypser 1978, pp. 593ff; Tanenbaum 1981, pp. 167ff].

≡ Terminology ≡

Advanced Research Projects
  Agency
application layer
ARPANET
bit
CCITT Recommendation X.21
CCITT Recommendation X.25
cognitive level
cryptography
data compression
data link control layer
data link control protocol
data link layer
DDCMP
DECNET
decompression
Digital Network Architecture
distributed processing
DNA
dumb terminal
end-to-end

envelope
framing
hacker
header
host-to-host layer
host
IMP
Interface Message Processors
International Standards
  Organization
ISO
language
layered structure
network layer
node
Open Systems Interconnection
OSI
packet
peer-to-peer
physical layer
presentation layer

protocol	Systems Network Architecture
SDLC	terminal
security	trailer
session	transmission
session layer	transport layer
SNA	X.21
star configuration	X.25

Review Questions

1. The _____ model, developed by _____ , has the following layers:

_____

_____

_____

_____

_____

_____

_____

2. The purpose of the model is _____

_____ .

3. A peer-to-peer protocol is one which _____ .

4. The _____ layer controls data transmission over the physical medium of transmission.

5. _____ was responsible for most of the basic principles used in networking today.

6. IBM's network architecture is called _____ .

7. DEC's network architecture is called _____ .

8. The _____ layer is a responsible for code conversion.

9. The _____ layer breaks data into entities called packets.

10. How is conversation between people similar to communications between computers?

11. Explain what is meant by the term "intermediate node." What layers are used by an intermediate node?

12. What is the significance of ARPANET in the development of network technology?

Assignment

Using Meijer and Peeters 1982, Tanenbaum 1981, or any other appropriate reference, compare the structures of IBM's SNA and DEC's DNA using the ISO/OSI

Reference Model. A chart showing the layers which exist for each along with the seven OSI layers will aid in comparing these network architectures.

References

Cypser, R. J. 1978. *Communications Architecture for Distributed Systems.* Reading, Massachusetts: Addison-Wesley.

Falk, Gilbert. 1983. "The Structure and Function of Network Protocols." In *Computer Communications.* Edited by Wushow Chou. Volume I: Principles. Englewood Cliffs, New Jersey: Prentice-Hall.

ISO International Standards Organization. 1982. *Draft International Standard ISO/DIS 7498: Information Processing Systems — Open Systems Interconnection — Basic Reference Model.* Reprinted in Meijer & Peeters 1982.

Martin, James. 1981. *Computer Networks and Distributed Processing: Software, Techniques, and Architecture.* Englewood Cliffs, New Jersey: Prentice-Hall.

Meijer, Anton, and Paul Peeters. 1982. *Computer Network Architecture.* Rockville, Maryland: Computer Science Press.

Tanenbaum, Andrew S. 1981. *Computer Networks.* Englewood Cliffs, New Jersey: Prentice-Hall.

9

Data Link Control Protocols — Overview

Areas of Protocol Definition • Startup Control • Framing • Line Control •
Timeout Control • Error Control • Sequence Control • Transparency •
Special Cases • Message Types • Data Link Control Protocols and
Synchronous Communications • Basic Data Link Control Protocol Types
• Summary

Areas of Protocol Definition

People communicate with each other using the same language and etiquette. In spite of implications in various motion pictures, computers do not communicate with each other unless they are already programmed to "speak the same language." In fact, unlike humans, computers do not communicate by *knowing* part of the language: that is to say, computers must communicate using specific rules. Any variation from the defined rules results in a failure in the communication between computers.

The set of rules for operating a data communications system is a **protocol**. The **syntax** of information in a protocol is analogous to the language people use to communicate with each other. The **semantics** of a protocol are analogous to the rules that determine when and how people say certain things. For an illustration of semantics, consider the "protocol procedures" used in telephone conversations. The expected response of a party answering a telephone is usually "Hello," with the calling party responding "This is . . . ." Clearly, people use implicit procedures when communicating on a telephone. If those rules are violated, confusion occurs. For example, answering a telephone with "Goodbye" would certainly confuse the calling party and could conceivably result in the calling party hanging up.

It should be noted that there is considerable latitude in the allowable procedures people use on a telephone. For example, "Hi," "Good morning," and so on are acceptable alternatives for "Hello" in answering a telephone. "Bye" is often used to end a telephone conversation.

The rules for operating communications (i.e., the protocol) between computer systems are similar to telephone etiquette in that they must be followed in order for data to be transferred successfully between such computer systems. While people might be able to understand strange responses which do not follow the implicit protocol of telephone conversation, data communications via computer systems requires strict adherence to the rules. [Lane 1984, p. 25]

Communications between computers in the mid 1960s usually provided for one protocol definition for each communication technique: the entire communications system was defined in one layer. While layering was not specifically defined at the time, data was sometimes moved from one computer to another or from a computer to a terminal according to one protocol and the data received was "interpreted" according to a **higher level protocol** [IBM 1971]. The low-level protocol, i.e., the one that allows data to be moved over a communications medium, is essentially the data link control protocol of layer 2 in the ISO Reference Model. Most data link control protocols of the sixties were vendor-defined and vendor-implemented.

One of the most common data link control protocols of this period was IBM's **Binary Synchronous Communications (BSC)** protocol. The IBM HASP multileaving protocol, an example of a higher level protocol, provided for the definitions of record formats for different devices in a remote job entry environment in which multiple records were transmitted by the BSC data link control protocol (see Chapter 11).

The layers of protocols in the ISO OSI Reference Model were shown in Figure 8–1 and the purpose of each layer was discussed in Chapter 8. This text concentrates on the data link control protocol (layer 2) for several reasons. First, much of the difficulty in implementing data communications software results from problems in intersystem communication. Examples of such intersystem problems are timing and noise on transmission media, which changes the data. Hence, it is most important to understand the complexity of implementing this layer. Higher layers are implemented within a specific system and do not involve the problems of the data link control protocol. Second, more readers will be likely to implement simple communications software to "talk" from one computer to another at the data link layer than will implement network architecture software. Third, gaining a thorough understanding of a data link control protocol by implementing a project like the one described in Appendix F is by far the best method of fully understanding the design, implementation, and debugging problems as well as the complexity of data communications software. The remainder of this chapter will concentrate on the rules for data link control protocols.

A **data link control protocol** must provide rules in a variety of areas. The aspects which must be addressed in the definition of a data link control protocol are error control, framing, line control, sequence control, startup control, timeout control, transparency, and special cases [McNamara 1982]. Each of these areas is outlined in Figure 9–1.

FIGURE 9–1   Aspects of Data Link Control Definition

General Characteristics

startup control	=	initiating communication on an idle line
framing	=	method of "packaging" the message
line control	=	which station controls line and when
timeout control	=	action taken if message flow ceases
error control	=	error detection by LRC, VRC, CRC
sequence control	=	message identification
transparency	=	ability to communicate any bit pattern
special cases	=	protocol-dependent

Message Types

Maintenance

Control

Data

Each of these areas will now be described. In the discussion below, a data communications message is a collection of data that is to be sent from one computer system to another as an entity.

Startup Control

Startup control specifies the sequence for beginning communications between computers. Its function is similar to the "Hello," "This is — " sequence of voice conversation on the telephone, illustrated in Figure 9–2. Generally, one computer system must be "listening" (i.e., in receive mode) for a startup message being sent by another computer system. This startup message is in fixed format and usually contains an identification code, which is validated by the receiving system. Startup control specifies the message format of the response to be sent back to the originator of the startup message in order to complete the initialization of a communications session.

Framing

Framing defines how a message is "packaged," i.e., it determines where the message begins and where it ends. In voice communication, a message starts when we begin to speak and ends when we stop. Others can usually "read" our voices to

FIGURE 9–2   Illustration of Startup Sequence in Telephone Conversations

RING!!

DIAL

Dial/Ring

"Hello"

Answer

"Hello,

This is --"

Respond with
Identification

FIGURE 9–3 Illustration of Framing

know when we have finished and expect a response from the other party (see Figure 9–3).

Unlike the human mind, computer systems do not read the "voice" of another computer system. They merely receive bit patterns which will be stored into memory. In synchronous transmission, a computer receives continuous one (1) bits when lines are idle, which is analogous to silence in voice conversation. A protocol must define how a receiving computer system identifies the first bit of the first character of a message. The message is framed when specific bit patterns which begin a message are recognized. Some protocols use the same bit pattern to end a message. The length of these bit patterns is usually a multiple of the character length (in bits). Framing is essentially using headers and trailers to place an envelope around the message at the data link control level, as was discussed in Chapter 8.

Framing, therefore, identifies what portion of the binary bits being received is to be interpreted as data by the receiving computer system as well as where that

FIGURE 9–4 Framing Data to Be Transmitted in Data Link Layer

DATA

Frame Header	DATA	Frame Trailer

data ends. Figure 9–4 illustrates the header and trailer information in the data link layer.

Line Control

Line control in the rules of a protocol specifies when a computer system should be receiving data and when it should be sending data. Half-duplex communications only permits a system either to transmit or to receive data at a given instant in time. Full-duplex communications allows a system to be in both send and receive mode simultaneously.

Obviously, it is essential that the sending and receiving systems be in the appropriate mode required by the protocol, particularly in half-duplex operation, in which receive and transmit are mutually exclusive states. If a system goes into receive mode too late, data will be lost. In particular, the framing character or characters which begin the message will not be recognized, and hence the entire message itself will not be recognized.

In a voice conversation, a message is understood only when it is heard. Figure 9–5 illustrates that normal conversation protocol (etiquette) does not allow people to speak at the same instant in time. (This is, of course, half-duplex mode.) While people can sometimes adapt and understand something that is said to them on the telephone while

FIGURE 9–5   Line Control

"How are you?" (Pause)

(Later) "Fine."

they themselves are talking, a computer system cannot recognize the beginning of the message if it is not in receive mode at the appropriate time. Radio transmission of voice communications illustrates exactly the problems of half-duplex transmission which will be avoided by line control procedures in a protocol. Two voice transmissions sent simultaneously over a radio at the same frequency are heard by neither communicating party (CB operators refer to this as being "walked on").

Timeout Control

Timeout control provides the rules for determining if message flow has ceased, e.g., if the communications connection is broken, one computer system is "down," etc. If a connection is broken or a person leaves the telephone unexpectedly in voice communication, people will respond with such phrases as "Hello," "Are you still there?" "Operator," etc. (see Figure 9–6). We mentally note that the duration of an interval of silence exceeded our expectation of the length of pauses between phrases.

A computer system must recognize a similar condition by the use of a timer within the computer system itself. Timer intervals from one to three seconds for a response while in receive mode are common. Timeout control specifies three things: the timer interval, the response (timeout message) to be sent back by the receiving system after the interval expires with no response (i.e., the system detecting the timeout condition must enter transmit mode), and the action to be taken by a computer system which receives such a timeout message. Of course, if the communications line connection has been broken or if the other computer system is "down," the timeout message will not be recognized by the other system. In fact, if the line connection has been broken, both systems will enter the timeout sequence and send timeout messages, since neither system will be able to receive data from the other.

Timeout control can also specify how many timeouts can occur with no response by the other system before some other action occurs (operator message, re-initializing

FIGURE 9–6   Illustration of Timeout Control

"Hello???"
"Are you there?"

Lost Connection

the system, etc.). Essentially, the computer system experiencing timeouts assumes that the connection between computer systems has indeed been lost and that "drastic" action is required in order to recover.

Error Control

Anyone who uses a telephone recognizes that noise and bad connections often interfere with normal voice communications. If a noisy line prevents one party from understanding something said by the other, the response normally is "What?" or "Say that again" or "The connection is bad, repeat what you said," as shown in Figure 9–7. The speaker is both acknowledging an error in understanding (receiving) a message and requesting the other party to repeat what was said (retransmit the message). This process of recognizing an error and requesting retransmission is usually the technique of **error control** and is defined by today's data link control protocols.

Since the accuracy of data being transmitted and received is critical in a computer system, a protocol must provide a means for error control. This includes error detection and the procedure to be followed after the detection of an error. Such procedures could request retransmission of the message in error (as we just observed in voice communications). Another error detection technique provides for the correction of the received message without retransmission, but this is still rare in common data link control protocols.

Error detection is normally done by such techniques discussed in Chapter 4 as vertical redundancy check (VRC), longitudinal redundancy check (LRC), and cyclic redundancy check (CRC — characters or bits being calculated and appended to or inserted in the message). In all cases (i.e., VRC, LRC, and CRC), calculations are repeated on the received message and compared to the appropriate check character (or bits) sent with the message. If the calculations generated by the receiver do not agree with the error check character sent with the message, then the message is

FIGURE 9–7   Illustration of Error Control

"What?"
"Say that again,
there is a lot of
noise on the line."

rejected (negatively acknowledged to the sender, i.e., "NAKed") and must be retransmitted by the sender.

Each technique for calculating an error check character produces a resulting character whose value depends on the specific message being sent. Different techniques produce different probabilities of an error going undetected, and CRC provides the best probabilities of error detection among CRC, VRC, and LRC.

Sequence Control

During a telephone conversation, it is possible for a line to "cut out" while people are speaking. The result of this is often a lost sentence (or words) or a repeated sentence (or words). The human mind can usually realize that something doesn't makes sense and can respond with "I missed that" or "You already said that," as depicted in Figures 9–8 and 9–9.

Similarly, it is possible for a message to be sent twice by the transmitting system or completely missed by a receiving system because of timing of responses and noise. The mechanism for detecting either is sequence control. **Sequence control** provides for the assignment of a number (modulo some other number, e.g., 8 or 256) to a message so that such situations can be detected when they occur. If a message with the same sequence number as the last is received, a duplicate message condition is detected. If a message is received with a number greater than the previous message number plus one, the missing message condition is detected.

This sequence number also allows the correct receipt of more than one message to be acknowledged with only one acknowledgement (ACK) message. This is particularly useful in full-duplex communications.

FIGURE 9–8   Sequence Control: A Lost Message

"I missed something. Repeat what you just said."

FIGURE 9–9   Sequence Control: A Duplicate Message

"You already said that."

Transparency

It is often necessary to be able to transmit and receive any binary bit pattern as a character of a data message. Since certain bit patterns will specify the beginning and ending of a message, procedures must be provided within the protocol definition to allow the transmission of data bit patterns which may duplicate control character bit patterns. This is called **transparency**. Different protocol types provide distinct methods for transparency.

Special Cases

As with most rules in computer science, there must be some allowance for special cases, which are usually protocol-specific. One example of such a special case is the capability of **downline loading** data, which is software to be run on the computer receiving this data. Each special case is specific to the environment of a given protocol, and there must be rules clearly specified for each such case.

Message Types

Although each protocol provides its own syntax, messages which are handled by data link control protocols can be categorized into one of three types — **maintenance messages**, **control messages** and **data messages**. Understanding these **message types** and the differences in the way various data link control protocols handle them (i.e., in framing and assuring transparency) is essential to a thorough understanding of such protocols and to good design of data communications software, as discussed in Chapter 22.

FIGURE 9–10   Typical Message Traffic Controlled by Data Link Control
Protocol

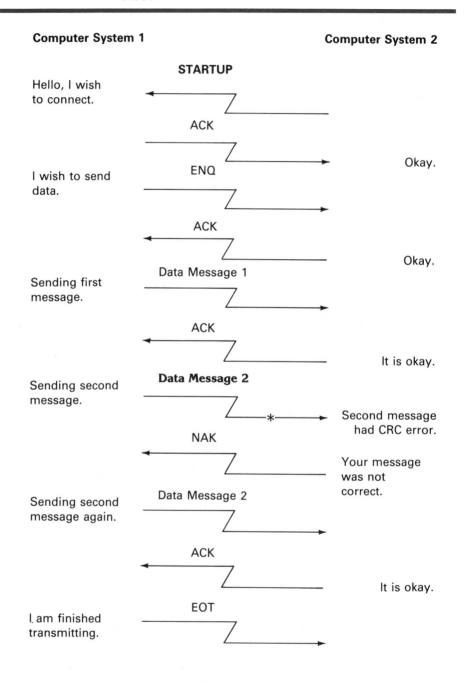

Computer System 1   Computer System 2

STARTUP

Hello, I wish
to connect.

ACK

Okay.

I wish to send   ENQ
data.

ACK

Okay.

Sending first   Data Message 1
message.

ACK

It is okay.

Sending second   **Data Message 2**
message.
                                        —*—   Second message
                        NAK   had CRC error.

Your message
was not
correct.

Sending second   Data Message 2
message again.

ACK

It is okay.

EOT
I am finished
transmitting.

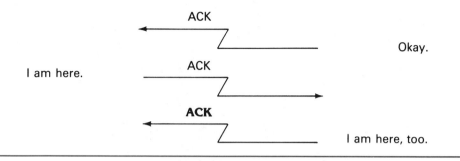

Data Link Control Protocols and Synchronous Communications

Although protocols can be utilized in an asynchronous (START/STOP transmission) environment, most protocols operate using synchronous transmission. In synchronous transmission, once the beginning of a message is recognized, the remaining characters in a message must be received at a specified (synchronous) rate. It is important that the synchronization process which is part of the framing of a message provided by a protocol be thoroughly understood. While protocols differ on what is used to recognize the beginning of a message, the synchronization process is similar for all types of protocols, as was presented in Chapter 6.

Basic Data Link Control Protocol Types

Data link control protocols generally can be classified into one of three categories, based on the technique the protocol uses to frame a message: character-oriented, bit-oriented, and byte-count–oriented. Chapter 12 is devoted to examination of the differences of these types and provides an example of each type of data link control protocol.

Summary

The various aspects of data link control protocols must be considered in defining a protocol. Accurate definition of a protocol is mandatory if communications between computer systems is to be successful. There are two considerations in the definition of a protocol: the format and general use of a message, and the procedures to be followed in transmitting and receiving these messages. The former is referred to as the logical definition, while the latter is the procedural definition (i.e., the syntax and the semantics, respectively). [Davies et al. 1979] Chapter 10 focuses on the considerations for protocol definition.

Figure 9–10 shows sample message traffic with a startup control sequence, data traffic, and error recovery. The procedural rules must define how every aspect of the protocol — i.e., startup control, line control, timeout control, error control, sequence control, transparency, and special cases — is handled.

≡ Terminology ≡

Binary Synchronous	line control
Communications	maintenance message
BSC	message types
control message	protocol
data link control protocol	semantics
data message	sequence control
downline loading	startup control
error control	syntax
error detection	timeout control
framing	transparency
higher level protocol	

≡ Review Questions ≡

1. Two aspects of data link control protocol definition which help preserve the integrity of the data received are _____ and _____ .

2. Two types of messages found in any data link control protocol are _____ and _____ .

3. The purpose of timeout control is _____ .

4. The aspect of a protocol which provides for the transmission of any bit pattern as a data character is called _____ .

5. The three types of data link control protocols are _____ , _____ , and _____ .

References

Davies, D. W., and D. L. A. Barber, W. L. Price, and C. M. Solomonides. 1979. *Computer Networks and Their Protocols*. Chichester, Great Britain: John Wiley & Sons.

IBM Corporation. 1971. *The HASP System*. Hawthorne, New York: IBM.

Lane, Malcolm G. 1984. "Data Communications Protocols." In *Advances in Data Communications Management*. Edited by Jacob Slonim, E. A. Unger, and P. S. Fisher. Volume 2. Chichester, Great Britain: John Wiley & Sons.

McNamara, John E. 1982. *Technical Aspects of Data Communication*. Second Edition. Bedford, Massachusetts: Digital Press.

10

Protocol Definition

Introduction • A Sample Protocol • Procedural Rules and Finite State
Machines

Introduction

Protocols provide the rules for operating a data communications system. It is necessary to define protocols at each layer precisely by specifying both the syntax and the procedural rules (semantics) for the protocol.

Specifying the syntax of the protocol is not particularly difficult. In fact, early protocols provided good definitions of syntax but left the semantics with deep ambiguity. Often, implementors of protocols in communications software resorted to trial and error techniques to determine the procedural rules of a given protocol. Rarely were formal protocol definitions available, to help them design the software, and when the definitions were available, they were often written after the protocol had been implemented.

Just as language syntaxes are defined using a **formal grammar** in **BNF (Backus Naur Form)**, BNF can be used to define message formats for protocol. Hence, an excellent *mechanism* exists for explicitly defining the syntax of protocols.

A Sample Protocol

A hypothetical simple half-duplex data link control protocol ("SHDP") will be used to illustrate the techniques used for defining protocols. The syntax of SHDP is quite simple, consisting of a data message and seven control messages: a start message **(SOH)**, an enquiry message **(ENQ)**, a positive acknowledgement message **(ACK)**, a positive acknowledgement wait message **(WACK)**, a negative acknowledgement message **(NAK)**, an abort data transfer message **(ESC)**, and an end of transmission message **(EOT)**. The control messages are single-character ASCII messages. The data message consists of a single-character **STX header**, a variable data field, a **trailer** which contains an **ETX** character followed by a 16-bit **CRC-16** error check-character. This CRC-16 is computed using all characters in the data message, including the STX and the ETX character. The protocol does not provide for transparent data transmission because the data field may contain ASCII characters, which are limited to the values from 040 (octal) to 177 (octal). The syntax is defined by the grammar in Figure 10–1. Appendix B contains the formal definition of a more complicated protocol (DDCMP — Digital Data Communications Message Protocol. See Chapter 12). Typical techniques

FIGURE 10–1   Sample Grammar for SHDP Messages

⟨msg⟩:= ⟨ctlmsg⟩|⟨datamsg⟩

⟨ctlmsg⟩:= ⟨startmsg⟩|⟨ackmsg⟩|⟨nakmsg⟩|⟨wackmsg⟩|⟨enquirymsg⟩|
        ⟨abortmsg⟩|⟨endmsg⟩

⟨datamsg⟩:= ⟨stx⟩⟨data⟩⟨etx⟩⟨bcc⟩

⟨startmsg⟩:= ⟨soh⟩

⟨ackmsg⟩:= ⟨ack⟩

⟨nakmsg⟩:= ⟨nak⟩

⟨wackmsg⟩:= ⟨wack⟩

⟨enquirymsg⟩:= ⟨enq⟩

⟨abortmsg⟩:= ⟨esc⟩

⟨endmsg⟩:= ⟨eot⟩

⟨soh⟩:= 00000001

⟨ack⟩:= 00000110

⟨nak⟩:= 00010101

⟨wack⟩:= 00010000

⟨enq⟩:= 00000101

⟨esc⟩:= 00011011

⟨eot⟩:= 00000100

⟨stx⟩:= 00000010

⟨etx⟩:= 00000011

⟨data⟩:= ⟨char⟩|⟨data⟩⟨char⟩

⟨bcc⟩:= ⟨byte⟩⟨byte⟩

⟨byte⟩:= 00000000 | ... | 11111111

⟨char⟩:= 00000111 | ... | 00001111 | 00100000 | ... | 01111111

:= means "is produced by"
⟨a⟩⟨b⟩ means "a followed by b"
⟨ ⟩ denotes a metalinguistic variable
⟨a⟩|⟨b⟩ means "a or b"
symbols not enclosed by ⟨ ⟩ are literals or constants
... means "and so on up to"

studied in compiler design can be applied to validation of the syntax of messages. [Gries 1971] The next section provides information on how finite state machine concepts can be used to implement both the syntactic and procedural rules of a protocol in software.

Figure 10–2 gives specific examples of the message types defined by the grammar in Figure 10–1. The data message is the only part of what is transmitted that must be "interpreted" according to the syntax of the protocol: because they are single characters, the control messages are easy to recognize.

Figures 10–3 through 10–8 illustrate the message traffic which takes place using SHDP. As indicated by the various aspects of data link control protocol definition, the

FIGURE 10–2   Message Formats for SHDP

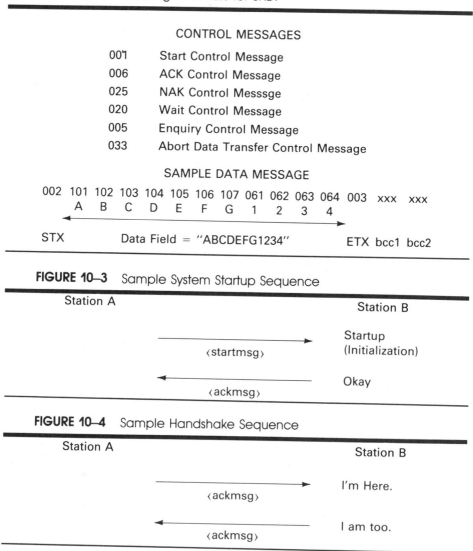

CONTROL MESSAGES

001	Start Control Message
006	ACK Control Message
025	NAK Control Messsge
020	Wait Control Message
005	Enquiry Control Message
033	Abort Data Transfer Control Message

SAMPLE DATA MESSAGE

002 101 102 103 104 105 106 107 061 062 063 064 003 xxx xxx
    A   B   C   D   E   F   G   1   2   3   4

STX   Data Field = "ABCDEFG1234"   ETX bcc1 bcc2

FIGURE 10–3   Sample System Startup Sequence

Station A   Station B

⟨startmsg⟩ →   Startup (Initialization)

← ⟨ackmsg⟩   Okay

FIGURE 10–4   Sample Handshake Sequence

Station A   Station B

⟨ackmsg⟩ →   I'm Here.

← ⟨ackmsg⟩   I am too.

FIGURE 10–5   Sample Data Transfer Sequence

Station A		Station B
─────────────────▶		Request to Send Data
	⟨enquirymsg⟩	
◀─────────────────		Okay
	⟨ackmsg⟩	
─────────────────▶		Data Message 1
	⟨datamsg⟩	
◀─────────────────		Okay
	⟨ackmsg⟩	
─────────────────▶		Data Message 2
	⟨datamsg⟩	
◀─────────────────		Okay, but wait
	⟨wackmsg⟩	
─────────────────▶		Handshake
	⟨ackmsg⟩	
◀─────────────────		Keep waiting
	⟨wackmsg⟩	
─────────────────▶		Handshake
	⟨ackmsg⟩	
◀─────────────────		Okay, continue sending
	⟨ackmsg⟩	
───────────── * ─▶		Data Message 3 with BCC error
	⟨datamsg⟩	
◀─────────────────		Error, retransmit
	⟨nakmsg⟩	
─────────────────▶		Data Message 3 sent again
	⟨datamsg⟩	
◀─────────────────		Okay, continue sending
	⟨ackmsg⟩	
─────────────────▶		End of Data Transmission
	⟨endmsg⟩	
◀─────────────────		Okay (handshake)
	⟨ackmsg⟩	
─────────────────▶		Handshake
	⟨ackmsg⟩	

message sequences represent **startup, handshake, data transfer,** and **error recovery**. The examples help clarify what might be allowed under the procedural rules, but it is difficult to write the software to follow such rules when given only illustrations of message traffic. One particular problem inherent in the protocol is in the area of timeout control. As indicated in Figure 10–8, a timeout during data transfer could occur on station A as a result of either a data message from A being lost or a response from B being lost. The protocol does not provide for acknowledgements being associated with a specific message, and in this instance, the possibility of a duplicate message or a lost message exists. One solution to this problem is to provide an even message ACK (ACK0) and an odd message ACK (ACK1), which then eliminates the problem of duplicate or lost messages by alternating between ACK0 and ACK1 to acknowledge data messages. Chapter 12 illustrates such an ACK0/ACK1 environment using the Binary Synchronous Communications (BSC) protocol. If it allows a duplicate or lost message situation to occur undetected, the protocol is not preserving the integrity of the message traffic. The possibility of such "erroneous" conditions going undetected illustrates the need for careful definition of the protocol's syntax and procedural rules and the validation of such rules whenever possible.

FIGURE 10–6   Receiving Station Aborts Data Transfer

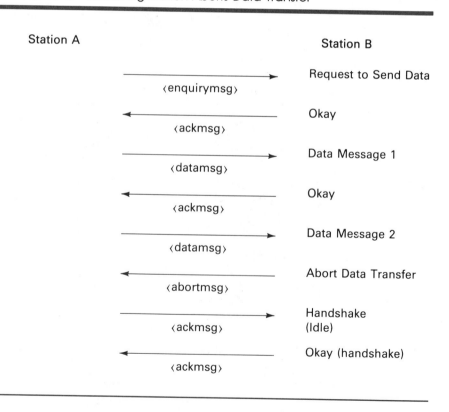

FIGURE 10–7   Sending Station Aborts Data Transfer

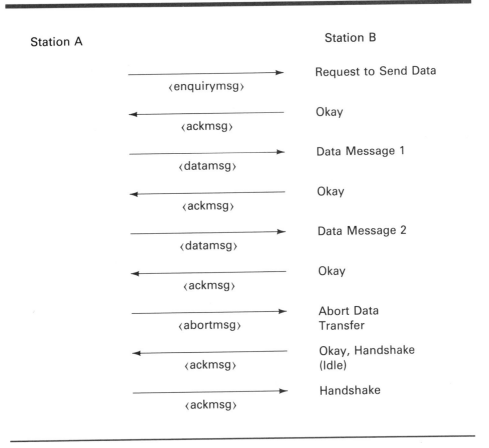

Station A   Station B

⟨enquirymsg⟩   Request to Send Data

⟨ackmsg⟩   Okay

⟨datamsg⟩   Data Message 1

⟨ackmsg⟩   Okay

⟨datamsg⟩   Data Message 2

⟨ackmsg⟩   Okay

⟨abortmsg⟩   Abort Data
                                             Transfer

⟨ackmsg⟩   Okay, Handshake
                                             (Idle)

⟨ackmsg⟩   Handshake

Procedural Rules and Finite State Machines

Procedural rules encompass many aspects of data communications, as implied by the sample message traffic in Figures 10–3 through 10–8. Just how to precisely define exactly what message traffic is "allowed" for a given protocol can be quite difficult. Implementing the procedural rules in software can be even more difficult. As with computer language definitions, any description of these rules in natural language will most definitely lead to ambiguity and confusion on the part of individuals attempting to implement a protocol in software. [Lane 1984]

The procedural rules (as well as the syntatic rules) of a protocol can be defined by the use of **state diagrams** (**finite state machines** or **automata**) or by the use of higher level "computer-type" languages. Such concepts are an integral part of the theory of compiler design. In a finite state machine approach, each procedural action can

FIGURE 10–8   Sample Timeout Sequence

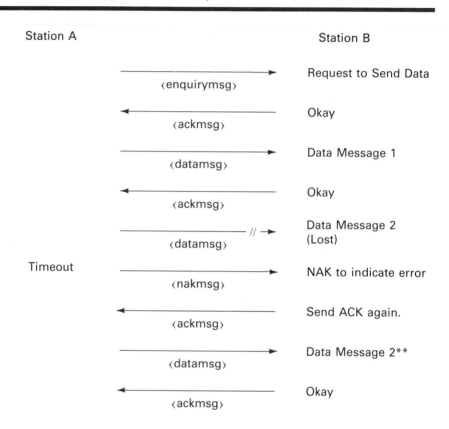

** *Note*: With only a single ACK message, it is not really known if ACK sent after NAK was for Message 1 or 2. It might have been that ACK for Message 2 was sent but lost, in which case Message 2 would be erroneously sent twice.

FIGURE 10–9 Example of State Transitions

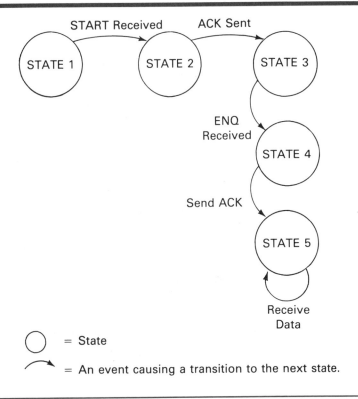

= State

= An event causing a transition to the next state.

be described by a current state, an event which causes transition to a new state (possibly the same as the current state, i.e., no change of state), and the new state. The syntax of a message can also be analyzed by such state machine approaches. Figure 10–9 illustrates a state diagram, which contains states (represented by circles) and events, which cause transitions from state to state (represented by arrows). An event which causes a **transition** to a new state (or the same state) often has an action associated with the event, e.g., place character in buffer or "accumulate" character into CRC-16 calculation. Such action is performed prior to the transition to the next state.

Several distinct states — looking for sign-on, receiving data, and error state, for example — can be recognized in the examples given in Figures 10–3 through 10–8. Each of these major states can have associated with it substates related to the syntax of a message. In SHDP, for example, a data message has a header, text, a trailer and error check characters. The syntax substates for receiving a data message might be as follows:

LOOKING FOR HEADER

RECEIVING HEADER

FIGURE 10–10   Portion of State Diagram for SHDP

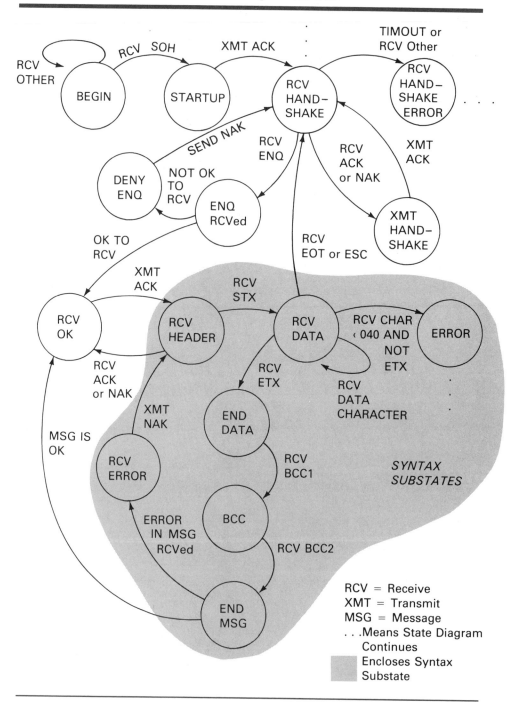

RECEIVING TEXT

RECEIVING TRAILER

RECEIVING ERROR CHECK CHARACTER(S)

Representing the entire finite-state logic of a protocol can be quite difficult, but once completed, the accurate and precise description of the protocol will greatly aid in the implementation of the protocol software. That the diagram can quickly become complex is demonstrated by the portion of a state diagram for SHDP presented in Figure 10–10. This diagram contains only *some* of the state transitions representing procedural rules as well as some of the syntactic rules of the SHDP protocol. Note that in some cases the state remains the same: when the machine is in RCV DATA state, for example, data characters received will be processed and the state machine will remain in the RCV DATA state. Generally, state diagram logic can be implemented by use of data structures representing the states and a finite state machine, which uses such data structures to "interpret" a protocol's procedural rules and the syntax of messages in a protocol. The implementation of such state machine software for data link control protocols is described in detail in Chapter 21.

As mentioned earlier, describing protocol procedural rules using state diagrams can become quite difficult for complex protocols. The alternative to this is the use of higher level languages, which could also serve as a part of the implementation of the protocol itself [Davies et al 1979]. Merely because the state diagrams have been defined does not mean that the protocol is correct. Situations such as infinite loops in a state and erroneous transitions to states caused by lost messages could arise in peculiar data transmission situations. Protocol verification research should eventually provide useful techniques for validating that protocols are correct and that they do not include such pitfalls as infinite loops [Davies et al 1979].

The use of states and transitions from state to state determined by an event (often a data character or complete message received) can simplify programming for implementing a protocol. Protocol definitions which include the finite state machine logic are becoming more and more commonplace and should eliminate the uncertainties in procedural rules which existed in the early days of data communications.

Terminology

ACK	ESC
Backus Naur Form	ETX
BNF	finite state automata
CRC-16	formal grammar
data transfer	handshake
ENQ	NAK
EOT	procedural rules
error recovery	SOH

startup   trailer
state diagram   transition
STX header   WACK

≡ Review Questions ≡

1. How is a formal grammar relevant to defining communications protocols?

2. What are the inputs (events) for a state diagram for representing the syntactic rules of a protocol? For the procedural rules?

3. Give an example of a protocol state in which an input event results in the state remaining the same (i.e., there is no transition to a new state).

≡ Assignments ≡

1. Redefine the SHDP protocol grammar used as an illustration in this chapter so that lost messages and duplicate messages will be detected during data transfer.

2. Complete the state diagram for SHDP shown in Figure 10.10 using the revised definition of SHDP derived in Assignment 1.

References

Davies, D. W., and D. L. A. Barber, W. L. Price, and C. M. Solomonides. 1979. *Computer Networks and Their Protocols*. Chichester, Great Britain: John Wiley & Sons.

Gries, David. 1971. *Compiler Construction for Digital Computers*. New York: John Wiley & Sons.

Lane, Malcolm G. 1984. "Data Communications Protocols." In *Advances in Data Communications Management*. Edited by Jacob Slonim, E. A. Unger, and P. S. Fisher. Volume 2. Chichester, Great Britain: John Wiley & Sons.

11

Line Throughput and Compression

Introduction

No matter how fast a communications line is, the speed of a line is usually the limiting factor in **line throughput** (the amount of data transferred per unit of time). This is particularly true of line speeds less than 19,200 bits per second. Also, as the distances over which the data must be transmitted increases, the probability of errors increases.

In order to improve line throughput and shorten the length of transmitted messages, a technique of data **compression** and **decompression** is employed. Compression techniques are also used by file access methods to reduce the amount of disk storage space required to store data. Compression/decompression eliminates bits in a message to be transmitted without causing the content of information which is received to be changed. [Sherman 1981]

One common technique represents duplicate characters in a data stream by a count of the number of duplicate characters and an indicator as to what character is duplicated. Using this technique, up to n consecutive duplicate characters can be represented by m control characters (m is usually 1 or 2) and hence $n - m$ fewer characters are transmitted for each duplicate character string encountered. It is not unusual for such compression techniques to improve line throughput by 20% to 30%, although this is obviously dependent on the type of data being transmitted.

The most common character compressed in ASCII or EBCDIC data streams is the blank character, because blanks occur so often in consecutive strings. Some protocols compress only trailing blanks. Others compress both embedded and trailing blanks. The most general algorithm would compress any duplicate characters encountered. Only three or more consecutive duplicate characters are usually compressed because there is nothing gained by compressing fewer than three characters.

Protocols generally break data into entities which we will call **character strings**. While character strings are often called by different names, the concept is the same: the representation of a string of nonduplicate characters or a string of duplicate characters in a data message is similar in all protocols.

A Simple Blank Compression Algorithm

The complexity of the compression algorithm in protocols varies. One of the simplest algorithms which will prove useful as an illustration of compression was used by Univac Corporation in a protocol called **NTR (Nine Thousand Remote)**. Every record transmitted in NTR was made up of character strings called "image segments." An image segment consisted of a blank count byte, a character count byte, and data bytes (the number of data bytes is equal to the value of the character count byte). A value of 077 in the blank count byte indicated the end of a record. The protocol only allowed for compression of three or more successive blanks. The collection of image segments and the end-of-a-record image segment makes up a compressed image, or a record, as shown in Figure 11–1.

FIGURE 11–1   Format of an NTR Message Buffer

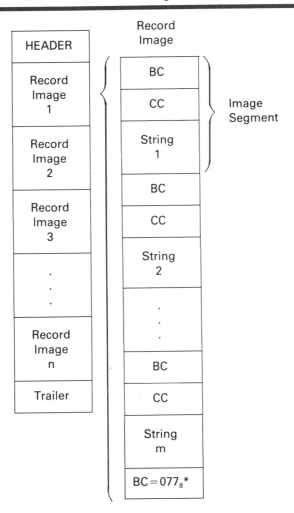

*BC = 077_8 indicates end-of-record

FIGURE 11–2   Compressing a Record Using NTR Method

Record to be transmitted:

JOB014	John Smith	TEST-RUN	12-DEC-83

```
0000000001111111111122222222222333333333334444444444555
1234567890123456789012345678901234567890123456789012
```

Compressed Record:

Image Segment	Image Segment	Image Segment	Image Segment	End-of-Record
0 6 JOB014	6 10 John Smith	5 8 TEST-RUN	8 9 12-DEC-83	077_8
BC CC string	BC CC string	BC CC string	BC CC string	BC*

Length of Compressed Record = 42 bytes
* BC = 077_8 indicates end of record

Let us suppose the record shown in Figure 11–2 is to be transmitted using the NTR protocol. The length of this record is 52 characters. It would be represented in the image segments shown in Figure 11–2.

The compressed image is 42 characters long. Without compression, it would have taken 52 + 1 (count) + 1 (end-of-record) or 54 bytes to represent the record. With compression it takes only 42 bytes. This is a 22.2% improvement in the throughput for this record. This assumes the record was variable length and trailing blanks were not transmitted.

The software preparing a record for transmission builds the image segment according to the specification. The receiving software must expand (decompress) the record by reinserting the blanks. The overhead of the software compression/decompression is negligible compared to the improvement in line throughput which results.

Compressing Duplicate Characters

The NTR protocol merely compressed **duplicate blanks**. It was simple in that only two counts were involved, that of the number of blanks and that of the number of characters in a string. When strings of duplicate nonblank characters are compressed, it is necessary to insert the character being duplicated into the data stream in addition to the count of duplicate characters. In this case, we have the following format:

N   C

COUNT   Character to be duplicated

For example, 013 "A" would indicate that 13 *A*s are in the data stream.

Since strings of duplicate blanks usually occur more often than strings of duplicate nonblank characters, some protocols use the high order bit(s) of the count to indicate if the duplicate string is a blank or some nonblank character. If the count control byte indicates a nonblank duplicate character, the character will follow the count byte as before.

Note that with all of these compression schemes, a count is necessary. The location of the next count control byte is dependent upon the data which precedes it. Hence, the decompression software must "interpret" the data stream to determine where the count control characters are located. This can be done using finite state machine logic to represent the compression technique. [Jones 1981]

A protocol which supports blank and nonblank compression is the IBM **Multileaving Protocol**. First known as the **HASP Multileaving Protocol**, this protocol will be referred to as the multileaving protocol and is covered in more detail in the Chapter 12 [IBM 1971]. Note that compression and decompression do not normally occur at the data link control layer. Higher level protocols normally provide this in a given network architecture and it might be that compression/decompression techniques are implemented in multiple layers.

A message buffer in the multileaving protocol (shown in Figure 11–3) contains multiple records for different devices, each record beginning with control bytes designated as **RCB/SRCB** in Figure 11–3. A record consists of one or more strings identified by a **String Control Byte (SCB)**. It is the SCB that provides for data compression within a data record.

There are four types of SCBs, as shown in Table 11–1. The end-of-record SCB is followed by the RCB for the next record or an end-of-message RCB. In the case of

TABLE 11–1   Multileaving Protocol String Control Byte (SCB) Format

SCB Meaning	SCB Value (Binary)	Format of Count
end-of-record	00000000	
duplicate blanks	100JJJJJ	JJJJJ = # of Blanks
duplicate nonblank character (duplicate character follows the SCB)	101JJJJJ	JJJJJ = # of Times Character Is Repeated
nonduplicate character string (character string of length specified in SCB follows SCB)	11nnnnnn	nnnnnn # Characters in String

duplicate blanks, the SCB is followed by another SCB, since no character is necessary to represent the blank (it is already known). With a duplicate nonblank character, the SCB is followed by the character to be duplicated and then by the next SCB. In the last case of a nonduplicate character string, the number of characters specified follows the SCB before the next SCB is encountered.

FIGURE 11–3   Overview of the Format of a Multileaving Message

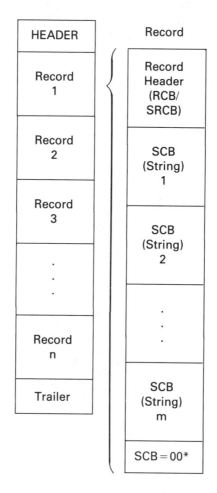

* SCB = 00 indicates end-of-record

Suppose the following were a record in a data stream:

*******TESTҍҍҍҍҍ01/01/84ҍҍҍҍҍҍJOHN DOEҍҍҍҍҍ*******

Then the data record would consist of the following strings represented by SCBs (given in hexadecimal):

A7	*	C4	TEST	85	C8	01/01/84	86	C8	JOHNҍDOE	85	A7	*	00
S	c	S	s	S	S	s	S	S	s	S	S	c	S
C	h	C	t	C	C	t	C	C	t	C	C	h	C
B	a	B	r	B	B	r	B	B	r	B	B	a	B
	r		i			i			i			r	
	a		n			n			n			a	
	c		g			g			g			c	
	t											t	
	e											e	
	r											r	

The 50 characters in the record are transmitted as 31 bytes, including the terminating string control byte. This is a reduction of 38% in the amount of data to be transmitted, so the throughput is improved by 38% for *this* record. This once again illustrates the advantage of using compression in data communications.

Mathematical Algorithms

The previous techniques are known as "brute force" types of data compression [Sherman 1981]. Other rules of data compression are based on **mathematical algorithms**. Working on the probability of a specific sequence occurring in a data stream, such algorithms code sequences with high probability of occurrence with shorter sequences of bits. The bits must be chosen so that the data can be interpreted by the receiving station in such a way as to uniquely identify each bit sequence and its length. Sherman provides more detail on such techniques [Sherman 1981, pp. 191-193].

Summary

Compression/decompression techniques are extremely important to improving communication line throughput. Just where such techniques are applied is dependent on the network architecture and the protocols defined in each layer.

≡ Terminology ≡

character string	multileaving protocol
compression	Nine Thousand Remote protocol
decompression	NTR
duplicate blanks	RCB
HASP multileaving protocol	SCB
line throughput	SRCB
mathematical algorithms	string control byte

≡ Review Questions ≡

1. _____ can improve the effective throughput of a data communications line.

2. A string control byte is used in the _____ protocol.

3. Compression/decompression algorithms which are not "brute force" are based on _____ .

≡ Assignments ≡

1. Using Table 4–3 to look up octal values for EBCDIC and the format for multileaving compression represented by one or more SCBs, decompress the following record extracted from a message log in an operational (HASP) multileaving system:

Beginning SCB
➡

322 310 301 342 327 140 311 311 134 301 134 331 324 362 364 113 327 331 361 244
113 316 342 343 301 331 343 100 321 326 302 100 363 370 365 367 245 113 312 365
113 361 366 113 362 371 100 327 324 202 310 364 100 301 327 331 100 370 361 244
113 311 346 345 325 305 343 100 345 342 361 244 113 305 303 326 307 307 350 203
244 113 316 322 301 331 311 100 322 301 331 311 100 322 301 331 311 246 000 244
113 322 331 324 362 364 113 327 331 361 134 301 134 310 301 342 327 140 311 311
000
⬅

Ending SCB

2. Given the record

******ƀJOB1268900ƀ...ƀƀƀƀƀALƀSMITHƀ...ƀƀƀƀTESTRUNƀƀƀ01/04/95ƀ....ƀ***

where ƀ represents a blank character.

a. Assume the characters are EBCDIC and represent the record in hexadecimal for multileaving format using the correct SCBs (ending the record with a NULL SCB).

b. Assume the characters are in ASCII and represent the record as a series of NTR image segments in octal.

3. In a language that can be run locally, write a subroutine which will take the record given in Assignment 2 and compress the record according to the rules of the multileaving protocol. The subroutine's parameters include the address of the record to be compressed, the address of the data area to store the compressed record in, the length of the input record, and the length of the output record.

4. In a language that can be run locally, write a subroutine which will take the record given in Assignment 2 and compress the record according to the rules of the NTR protocol. The subroutine's parameters include the address of the record to be compressed, the address of the data area to store the compressed record in, the length of the input record, and the length of the output record.

References

IBM Corporation. 1971. *The HASP System*. Hawthorne, New York: IBM.

Jones, James Kenneth, II. 1981. "Implementing HASP Multileaving Data Communications Protocol Using Finite State Logic." Master's Project Report, West Virginia University.

Sherman, Kenneth. 1981. *Data Communications: A Users Guide*. Reston, Virginia: Reston.

12

Data Link Control Protocols

Types • Character-Oriented Protocols • BSC and State Transitions •
Multileaving Protocols • Format of a Multileaving Transmission Block •
Data Transmission Control • Records • SRCBs • Strings • State
Transitions • Byte-Count-Oriented Protocols • DDCMP Message Traffic •
Bit-Oriented Protocols • SDLC Message Traffic • Conclusion

Types

The three types of data link control protocols — character-oriented, byte-count-oriented, and bit-oriented — will be presented in this chapter. The first two types of protocols establish synchronization by using a synchronizing character, while bit-oriented protocols utilize a unique FLAG character to frame a message.

Character-Oriented Protocols

Character-oriented protocols rely heavily on the insertion of control characters around the data as an envelope; they also rely on the insertion of a special control character (DLE) to provide transparency, because without it, data can otherwise be interpreted as ending control characters. On the receiving end, it is necessary to scan messages for control characters in the header, in the data field itself, and in the trailer.

Such functions as **Start of Header** (SOH), **Start of Text** (STX), **End of Text** (ETX), and **End of Transmission Block** (ETB) are indicated by specific control characters. These characters are used to delineate message fields and control protocol functions. Figure 12–1 illustrates the general format of messages in a character-oriented protocol. Synchronization is accomplished by the detection of (at least) two **synchronization characters** (SYN) immediately preceding the message being received (see Figure 6–2). The value used for the SYN character is dependent on the specific protocol. These SYN characters are not part of the message stored by the receiving system. Most hardware interfaces provide synchronization capability for character-oriented protocols by scanning for two consecutive synchronization characters (i.e., the synchronizing bit pattern length is 2 * character length, as illustrated in Figure 6–2). Figure 12–1 shows a **Block Check Character** (BCC), which is used to detect errors. The BCC is usually computed using the **LRC** or **CRC** methods discussed in Chapter 4.

One of the most widely used and oldest examples of a character-oriented protocol is IBM's **Binary Synchronous Communications** (BSC) protocol, which operates

FIGURE 12–1   General Format of Character-Oriented Protocols

General Description: Special characters are used to delineate the data field and control protocol functions.

General Format:

SYN	SYN	SPECIAL CHARACTER	HEADER	SPECIAL CHARACTER	DATA	SPECIAL CHARACTER	BCC

in **nontransparent** or **transparent** mode. There are quite a few different control characters and/or control sequences in BSC. Table 12–1 lists these control characters and a brief description of the use and purpose of each. The values in parentheses are the values of the control characters and sequences in hexadecimal when the EBCDIC data codes are used. [McNamara 1982]

TABLE 12–1   Binary Synchronous Communications Control Characters

SYMBOL	MEANING (HEXADECIMAL VALUES FOR EBCDIC)		USE
SOH	START OF HEADER	(01)	Beginning of BSC Header
STX	START OF TEXT	(02)	Start of Data Field.
ETB	END OF TRANSMISSION BLOCK	(26)	Indicates the end of block of characters which began with an SOH or STX. BCC follows ETB. Requires a response: NAK, ACK0, ACK1, WACK, or RVI.
ITB	END OF INTERMEDIATE TRANSMISSION BLOCK	(1F)	Separates message into sections for error detection purposes without causing reversal of transmission.

TABLE 12–1   Binary Synchronous Communications Control Characters (continued)

SYMBOL	MEANING (HEXADECIMAL VALUES FOR EBCDIC)		USE
ETX	END OF TEXT	(03)	Same as ETB, except it also means there are no more data blocks to be sent.
EOT	END OF TRANSMISSION	(37)	Indicates end of transmission, which may contain a number of blocks including text and headings.
ENQ	ENQUIRY	(2D)	Used to bid for line in point-to-point communications. Also, used to request retransmission of ACK/NAK response when either is garbled.
ACK0 ACK1	POSITIVE ACKNOWLEDGEMENT	(10 70) (10 71)	Means previous block was accepted without error; Another block may be sent. ACK0 used for even "numbered" blocks; ACK1 for odd ones.
WACK	WAIT BEFORE TRANSMIT POSITIVE ACKNOWLEDGEMENT	(10 6B)	Basically same as ACK, but also indicates receiver is not ready to receive another block. Response is usually ENQ with WACK as response until receiver is ready, at which time the appropriate ACK is sent.
NAK	NEGATIVE ACKNOWLEDGEMENT	(3D)	Means previous block was received in error.

TABLE 12–1   Binary Synchronous Communications Control Characters (continued)

SYMBOL	MEANING (HEXADECIMAL VALUES FOR EBCDIC)		USE
DLE	DATA LINK ESCAPE	(10)	Used to create WACK, ACK0, ACK1, and RVI 2 character sequences. Primary use is to control transparent data transfers.
RVI	REVERSE INTERRUPT	(10 7C)	Positive Acknowledgement but also requests transmitting station to terminate transmission because of need to send high priority message.
TTD	TEMPORARY DELAY	(03 2D)	Used by transmitting station not ready to transmit but wishes to retain line

While most control sequences are single characters, some are two character sequences, specifically: **ACK0**, **ACK1**, **WACK**, **RVI**, and **TTD**. BSC can be used with either **ASCII** or **EBCDIC**. The values listed in parentheses in Table 12–1 are for EBCDIC. Table 12–2 lists the values of these control characters and sequences for both EBCDIC and ASCII.

TABLE 12–2   BSC Control Character/Sequence Values for ASCII and EBCDIC [IBM n.d.]

Two-Character BSC
Data Link Controls

Function	EBDIC	ASCII
ACK0	DLE, 70_{16}	DLE, 0
ACK1	DLE, 71_{16}	DLE, 1
WACK	DLE, $6B_{16}$	DLE, ;
RVI	DLE, $7C_{16}$	DLE, ‹

As can be seen in Tables 12–1 and 12–2, the BSC protocol uses the following control messages: a single control character for control messages, **ENQ** for enquiry (bid for the line), ACK0 and ACK1 for positive acknowledgement, NAK for negative acknowledgement, WACK for wait before transmit positive acknowledgement, RVI for reverse interrupt, and TTD for temporary delay. Hence, short, fixed-length messages are used for control messages.

Data messages for BSC operating in nontransparent mode consist of an optional fixed-length header consisting of a control character (**SOH**) followed by **header** fields, a text (data) area consisting of a control character (**STX**) followed by data, and a **trailer** consisting of an ending control character (**ETX** or **ETB**) followed by a block check character (BCC), which is used to preserve the integrity of the transmitted data message. Figure 12–2 illustrates the format of BSC nontransparent data messages.

FIGURE 12–2   Message Format in BSC Nontransparent Protocol

Control Messages: ENQ   WACK
                     ACK0   RVI
                     ACK1   TTD
                     NAK

Data Message:

SYN	SYN	SOH	Header	STX	DATA	ETX	BCC

Figure 12–3 illustrates the type of message traffic which might exist using BSC communications. Since the protocol is a half-duplex protocol, the line must alternate between transmission and receiving of information.

The BSC protocol operating in nontransparent mode is relatively simple, although the implementation of it in software is not trivial, since there are many different types of control characters and sequences. Also, as the name implies, it does not provide the transparency feature previously described: it is not capable of transmitting any bit pattern as a data character without the possibility of it being misinterpreted as a control character. For instance, in the example for data messages shown in Figure 12–2, a bit pattern identical to ETX within the data would be mistaken as an end-of-text indicator and the end of the data would be assumed after the next byte (or bytes) were taken as the BCC.

BSC protocol operating in transparent mode solves this problem by **stuffing** a **DLE** in front of each intended control character in a data message. Control messages

FIGURE 12–3   Sample Point-to-Point Message Traffic in BSC Protocol

SYSTEM A		SYSTEM B	
ENQ	⟶		Wish to Send
	⟵	ACK0	Okay
Data Message	⟶		Received OK
	⟵	ACK1	Acknowledge
Data Message	⟶		Received OK
	⟵	ACK0	Acknowledge
Data Message	⟶		Received OK but not ready for next message
	⟵	WACK	Acknowledge with Wait
ENQ	⟶		Received OK Still Busy
	⟵	WACK	Acknowledge with Wait
ENQ	⟶		Received OK
	⟵	ACK1	Okay to Send
Data Message	⟶		Received OK
	⟵	ACK0	Acknowledge
EOT	⟶		Finished Transmitting

FIGURE 12–4   Data Message Format in BSC Protocol Operating in
Transparent Mode

Data Message:

SYN	SYN	DLE	SOH	Header	DLE	STX	DATA	DLE	ETX	BCC

are the same as in nontransparent mode. Figure 12–4 illustrates the format for data messages for transparent mode; the delimiting control characters in the data message are preceded by a DLE. Including a character which is the same bit pattern as a DLE in the text of the message is an example of a special case which requires a stuffing of a DLE into the text field, i.e., to transmit a DLE as a data character in transparent mode, it must be transmitted as two DLEs. This is similar to a programmer's placing two quotation marks in a literal string delineated by quotation marks in order to include a quotation mark as a character in the literal string. The BSC protocol operating in transparent mode allows for communications in which control characters can be included as a part of the text. The framing techniques employed are identical to those used BSC operating in nontransparent mode, except that in each instance in which a control character is intended, it must be preceded by a DLE, i.e., a control character actually becomes a tandem of control characters, the first of which is always a DLE. [Lane 1984]

BSC and State Transitions

As mentioned earlier, the use of states and transitions from state to state determined by an event (often a data character or complete message received) is an ideal technique for specifying the syntax and semantics of a data link control protocol. Using finite state machine techniques can greatly simplify programming for a protocol, particularly a protocol like BSC that has so many different control messages and the need to scan the data field for control characters. Techniques for implementing data link control protocols using finite state machines are outlined in Chapter 21. Figure 12–5 is a partial **state diagram** for receiving using the BSC protocol. Notice that the analysis of an input character in a message determines the next state. The data state in transparent mode has a loop for every character except the DLE (Data Link Escape), which allows the protocol to "escape" to another state to see if a DLE precedes a control character or another DLE. In the latter case, the second DLE is a data character and forces a return to the data state.

FIGURE 12–5   Partial State Diagram for Receive in BSC Protocol

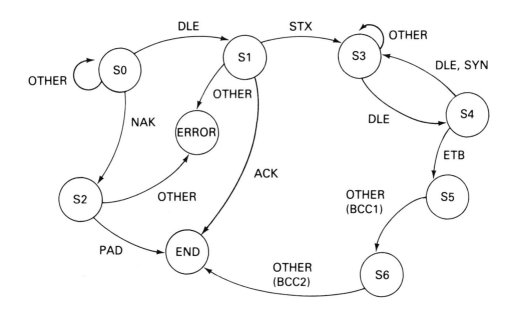

Multileaving Protocols

The early days of synchronous transmission using the Binary Synchronous Protocol resulted in one-way-at-a-time data transfer (e.g., the **IBM 2780** protocol allows for reading of cards and printing of data, but transfer of data in one direction must complete before transfer of data in the other direction can begin). Many delays were encountered. Users wanting to transmit card-image data had to wait until the printer finished before data could be sent in the other direction. Line throughput was also a problem.

Because of the need to eliminate this waiting and to improve line throughput, a concept called multileaving evolved [IBM 1971]. The IBM 2780 point-to-point Binary Synchronous Protocol allowed data transfers in one direction with acknowledgements (ACKs) and negative acknowledgements (NAKs) in the other direction at any given time. Data contained in a received message was destined for one specific device.

The **multileaving protocol** of the HASP (Houston Automatic Spooling) System was one of the first examples of the use of a layering of protocols, and the protocol is still in use today in many installations [IBM 1971]. Multileaving allows data to be transferred in both directions concurrently (based on the protocol being used). That is,

FIGURE 12–6   Format of a Multileaving Transmission Block

BCB	- Block Control Byte
FCS	- Function Control Sequence
FCS	- Function Control Sequence
RCB	- Record Control Byte
SRCB	- Sub-Record Control Byte
SCB	- String Control Byte
DATA	- Character String
SCB	- String Control Byte
DATA	- Character String
SCB	- Terminating SCB for Record 1
RCB	- RCB for Record 2
SRCB	- SRCB for Record 2
SCB	- SCB for Record 2
DATA	- Character String
SCB	- Terminating SCB for Record 2
RCB	- Transmission Block Terminator

multileaving eliminated the need to wait until data was completely transferred in one direction before beginning data transfer in the other direction. Basically, the Binary Synchronous Communications protocol was used as the data link control protocol with a few slight differences (ACK sequences), and although BSC is a half-duplex protocol, it appeared to the operator of a multileaving terminal that data was being transferred simultaneously. IBM called the capability **"pseudosimultaneous, bidirectional transmission,"** because for the first time in a BSC environment, data could be sent alternately in both directions. In addition, data for more than one device is included in a single data transmission buffer. The data records for multiple devices are "multileaved" in one communications buffer. Up to seven "streams" of data for the same type of device (printer, cards, punches, etc.) are supported. [IBM 1971; Jones 1981; Gesalman 1983]

In the next section, an overview of the operation of the HASP multileaving protocol will be presented. Other multileaving protocols now exist. The presentation of the HASP (later known as JES2) multileaving protocol will help clarify the basic concepts involved in a higher level multileaved protocol.

Format of a Multileaving Transmission Block

A Hasp **multileaving transmission block** is shown in Figure 12–6. The format shown here does not include control characters for Binary Synchronous Communication in transparent mode. Recall that BSC does not provide sequencing of data buffers transmitted. The multileaving transmission block provides a sequencing modulo 16 in a **Block Control Byte (BCB)**. This allows for the detection of lost blocks and duplicate transmission blocks and for the resetting of the expected BCB. Figure 12–7 shows the format of the BCB.

FIGURE 12–7   Format of the Block Control Byte

OXXXCCCC

O = 1	Always on
CCCC	Modulo 16 Block Sequence Count
XXX	Control Information
000	Normal Block
001	Bypass Sequence Count Validation
010	Reset Block Sequence Count to CCCC

Data Transmission Control

In BSC, message traffic is controlled by the use of a **wait-a-bit** (busy) control message (WACK). Since multiple data streams are to be supported for multiple buffers in a single transmission block in the multileaving protocol, the use of such a busy technique would violate the goals of improved throughput and "pseudosimultaneous" data transmission. The two **Function Control Sequence (FCS)** bytes shown in Figure 12–8 control the various data streams which can be included in a transmission block. By clearing a particular bit representing a device in a particular stream of data, data transmission for that stream can be suspended without affecting other data streams. Data transmission typically would be suspended when no buffers are available for a particular device or when the device is not ready.

FIGURE 12–8   Function Control Sequence Format [Gesalman 1982, pp. 23, 25; IBM 1971]

Function Control Sequence (FCS) — Two byte sequence giving the status of the various data streams. If a bit corresponding to a stream is turned off, that stream's transmission is suspended until reinstated in another FCS.

```
O S R R A B C D    O T R R W X Y Z
```

O = 1 must always be on
S = 1 suspend all stream
       transmission
   = 0 normal state
T = remote console stream
       identifier
A = reserved
ABCD_WXYZ = function stream identifiers

Records

The remainder of a transmission block consists of records for devices in various data streams. Each record begins with and is identified by a **Record Control Byte (RCB)**. There are three basic types of RCBs — Transmission terminator (RCB = 00000000), a Control Record (1III0000, where III represents control information) and a Record Type Identifier (OIIITTTT, TTTT ≠ 0000) — as shown in Figure 12–9. In the last type, III represents the data stream of the device.

Most devices require that permission to send be requested by the sender and permission be granted by the station to which data is to be transferred before transmission for a device may begin. This is done by setting the control information field III = 001 for Request Permission, placing an image of the device RCB into the **Sub-Record Control Byte (SRCB)** and transmitting it in a buffer. The software in the transmitting station

FIGURE 12–9   RCB Format [Gesalman 1982, pp. 25-26; IBM 1971]

$$\boxed{\text{O I I I T T T}}$$

O = 0 end of transmission block (IIITTT = 0)
   = 1 all other RCB's
TTTT = record type identifier
   = 0000 control record
   = 0001 operator message display request
   = 0010 operator command
   = 0011 normal input record
   = 0100 print record
   = 0101 punch record
   = 0110 data set record
   = 0111 terminal message routing request
III = control information (if control record)
   = 001 request to initiate function trans.
   = 010 permission to init. function trans.
   = 111 general control record

cannot send data for this device until a record containing both the permission-granted RCB (III = 010) and the SRCB equal to the transmitted prototype RCB is received.

Once permission has been granted, data for this device in a multileaving transmission block is identified by the appropriate RCB. The SRCB for such data records provides device-specific control information. [IBM 1971] RCBs and FCS's for various data streams are shown in Table 12–3.

TABLE 12–3   Illustration of RCB and FCS Values for Streams 1–4

| Stream | Device | RCB | | | FCS | |
		Binary	Octal	Hex	Octal	Hex
1	Printer	10010100	224	94	004000	0800
2	Printer	10100100	244	A4	002000	0400
3	Printer	10110100	264	B4	001000	0200
4	Printer	11000100	304	C4	000400	0100
1	Reader	10010011	223	93		
2	Reader	10100011	243	A3		
3	Reader	10110011	263	B3		
4	Reader	11000011	303	C3		

SRCBs

The Sub-Record Control Bytes (SRCB) are used to provide supplemental information about a record. For request permission and grant permission RCBs, the SRCB contains a "prototype" RCB of the device. For printers, carriage control information is given in the SRCB. For "readers" and "punches," the unit value for the string control bytes is provided. The SRCB always follows the RCB unless the RCB is transmission block terminator (RCB = 0000 [hexadecimal]).

Strings

Each record identified by an RCB/SRCB consists of one or more strings identified by a **String Control Byte (SCB)**. Chapter 11 illustrated how the strings are identified using the SCB and how the SCB provides for data compression within a data record.

State Transitions

Figure 12–10 lists the finite state transitions for the request to initiate and permission to initiate a function transmission in a multileaving environment. The higher level multileaving protocol state transitions for interpreting data message syntax are given in Figure 12–11.

The multileaving protocol has been in use for many years and it is still in use today. It is part of the evolution of communications protocols into a layered environment. The software which supports the multileaving protocol must interpret the data at two levels, at the BSC data link control and at the multileaving protocol itself. Such software could most easily be implemented using finite state logic at both levels and a modular structure which isolates the functions of the data link control and the multileaving protocol interpetations.

Byte-Count–Oriented Protocols

Byte-count–oriented protocols use special characters along with a fixed-length header, which contains a byte count for the length of the text to control protocol functions (see Figure 12–12). Synchronization is accomplished by the use of two or more SYN characters preceding the message, as in character-oriented protocols. Digital Equipment Corporation's **Digital Data Communications Message Protocol (DDCMP)** is an example of such a protocol. DDCMP makes use of a single control character in a fixed-length header to determine the type of control message (see Figure 12–12). Framing data messages is simply an extension of framing control messages, the major differences being that a different control character (SOH) begins the fixed-length header, which contains a field with a byte count for the text length, and that the text follows the header. Having the length of the text included in the header of a data message makes these DDCMP data messages similar to variable-length data records. The length of the text following the header is recorded in the header and this text is followed by a two-byte CRC (cyclic redundancy check) character to assure the

FIGURE 12–10 Request to Initiate and Permission to Initiate a Function Transmission in a Multileaving Environment [Gesalman 1982, p. 124]

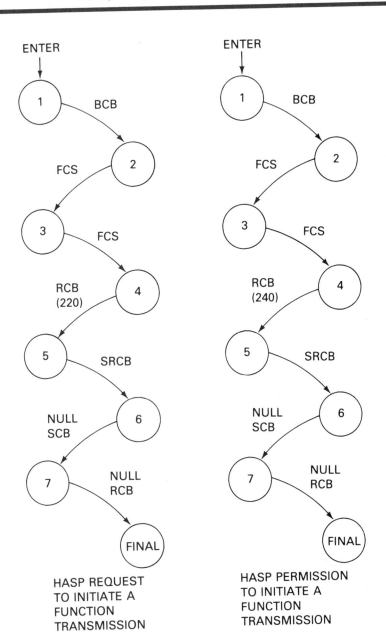

HASP REQUEST TO INITIATE A FUNCTION TRANSMISSION

HASP PERMISSION TO INITIATE A FUNCTION TRANSMISSION

validity of the transmitted data. A two-byte CRC is always included as the last field in the fixed-length header to establish its integrity. [Lane 1984]

Thus, framing is achieved by the byte-count protocols through the use of a synchronization character, a control character (first character of the message), fixed lengths for header and trailer, and a byte count for the text. Transparency is automatically provided, since bit patterns are important only in the case of the message's first character and received text information need only be counted by the receiving protocol software to determine the end of a received message.

FIGURE 12–11   Receive State Transitions for Syntax of Multileaving
Protocol [Gesalman 1982, p. 116]

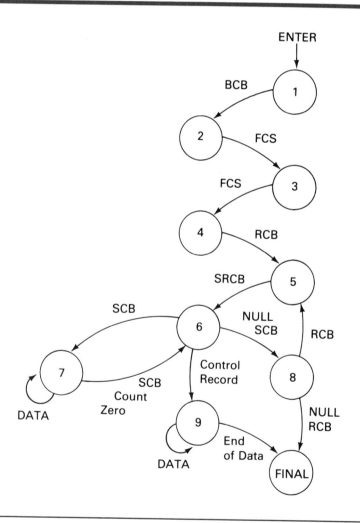

FIGURE 12–12   General Format of Byte-Count–Oriented Protocols

General Description: Special fixed-length control messages are used to control protocol functions. Fixed-length header containing the length of the data field is used for data messages.

General Format:

SYN	SYN	SPECIAL CHARACTER	Fixed Length Header	BCC	DATA	BCC

BSC and similar character-oriented protocols provide for half-duplex transmission. Using fields within the header, DDCMP provides both for the sequencing of data messages (using the NUM field in Figure 12–13) and for the acknowledgement of a message received (using the RESP field), thus allowing full-duplex communication with message acknowledgement "riding" on the data message itself. Hence, DDCMP provides for the correct sequencing of messages and for efficient line utilization by allowing the simultaneous use of lines in both directions.

DDCMP provides relatively few message formats. The categories of message types include the control and data messages shown in Figure 12–13 and maintenance messages, which will not be discussed. Data messages contain SOH as the first character of the header. All control messages start with ENQ. Table 12–4 lists the possible control messages and their uses.

The specification document for DDCMP includes a BNF definition of the protocol as well as state tables. As indicated in Chapter 10, this provides the designer of the software for DDCMP a precise definition of the protocol which can be used to implement the protocol with finite state machine techniques. Appendix B includes the BNF definition of the DDCMP protocol.

TABLE 12–4   DDCMP Control Messages And Their Use

Control Message	TYPE (binary)	SUBTYPE and FL Bits** (binary)	Use
ACK	00000001	000000QS	Acknowledge Messages, Response contains number of Last Good Message
NAK	00000010	xxxxxxQS	Negative Acknowledgement to Message. RESP contains number of last good message. SUBTYPE indicates reason for NAK:
		000001	Header BCC Error
		000010	Data BCC Error
		000011	Rep Response (see REP below)
		001000	Buffer Unavailable (Similar to WACK in BSC except that data is rejected and must be sent again)
		001001	Receiver Overrun (Last character not processed before next arrived)
		010000	Buffer too long. (One system may have been generated with buffers longer than the other or count was wrong, and BCC did not detect it [very unlikely])
		010001	Header Format Error.
REP	00000011	00000011	Reply Requested. Used to ask "Have all messages through the message number in NUM field been received correctly?"
STRT	00000110	00000011	Startup message used for system startup. Expected reply is STRT or STACK.
STACK	00000111	00000011	Reply to STRT on system startup

** Q = 1   "Quick SYNC" indicates to receiving station that message is followed by SYN characters and use of "Strip synch" feature of hardware will prevent filling receiving station with SYN characters.

   S = 1   S is the Select Flag, which is used to indicate that this is the last message which transmitting station is going to send and the addressed station is now permitted to send. Useful in multidrop lines and in half-duplex, where stations are polled or must release the line periodically.

FIGURE 12–13 Message Format in DDCMP Protocol

Control Messages:

SYN	SYN	ENQ	TYPE	SUBTYPE	FL	RESP	FILL	ADDR	CRC

Number of bits	8	8	6	2	8	8	8	16

Data Message:

SYN	SYN	SOH	COUNT	FL	RESP	NUM	ADDR	CRC

Number of bits	8	14	2	8	8	8	16

SYN .... Synchronizing Character (226)
ENQ .... Designates Start of Control Message (005)
TYPE .... Specifies Type of Control Message
SUBTYPE .... Information Related to Particular Control Message
RESP .... Response Number — Message Number (Modulo 256) of Last Good Message Received
FILL .... Filler Not Used for Particular Message
CRC .... CRC-16 Using $x^{16} + x^{15} + x^2 + 1$ as Generating Polynomial
SOH .... Designates Header for Data Message (001)
COUNT .... 14-bit count specifying number of characters in data field
FL .... Two Bits Containing flags used in line control
NUM .... Message Number (Modulo 256) of data message
ADDR .... Address of station in multidrop environment

DDCMP Message Traffic

System startup is done by a station sending a **STRT** message. The receiving station also sends a STRT message, after which the originator of the first STRT sends a **STACK**. The station receiving the STACK responds with an ACK and the startup sequence is completed. Figure 12–14 illustrates this startup sequence.

DDCMP allows data traffic in both directions in both half- and full-duplex environments in either point-to-point or multidrop configurations. In half-duplex, the line control for transmission is retained until the **select bit** of the flag FL is set to 1 in either a control or data message, in which case the line is turned around from one direction to

FIGURE 12–14   Startup Sequence in DDCMP

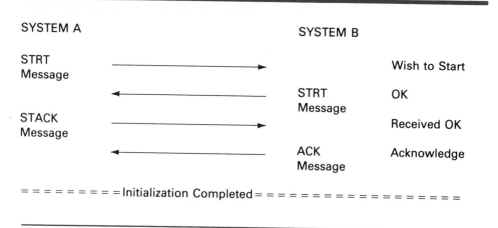

the other. The receiving station can then turn the line around and transmit one or more data messages in the other direction until it sets the select bit in a message. Figure 12–15 illustrates how line control is implemented in half-duplex DDCMP. [Meijer and Peeters 1982]

The select bit is also used to **poll secondary stations** in **multidrop lines**. When the **primary station** turns on the select bit in a data message or a control message, secondary station can send data or a control message back to the primary station until it sets the select bit in a message sent to the primary station. The multidrop use of DDCMP in which polling is used is very similar to the half-duplex message traffic in a point-to-point environment in Figure 12–15: once a station on a multidrop line is polled, traffic from the secondary station to the primary is identical to what is shown in Figure 12–15.

Several messages can be sent in a sequence at any time once a station has control of the line for transmission, as shown in Figure 12–15, but it is possible that the receiver will not be able to process the message. For example, if there is no buffer space, the receiver will respond with a NAK, indicating "buffer not available" in the SUBTYPE (see Table 12–14). Hence, the WACK concept of BSC, in which the station transmitting data is "told" to wait before sending the *next* message, is replaced with a data message rejection after the fact. The WACK tells the transmitting station to wait to send the next message, while this NAK ("buffer not available") of DDCMP indicates that the message already sent could not be handled. Depicted in Figure 12–16 is the message traffic when such a NAK is sent. The sending station will continue to send the data message after each such NAK until it is accepted. NAKs sent for other reasons, shown in Table 12–4, are similar to the "buffer not available" NAK shown in Figure 12–16, except that the reason for NAK in the SUBTYPE changes.

It is not necessary to get an acknowledgement for every message, as illustrated in Figures 12–15 and 12–16. However, there can never be more than 255 outstand-

FIGURE 12–15   DDCMP Line Control in Half-Duplex Point-to-Point Environment

Primary Station*		Secondary Station*
$DATA_{S=1}$	(NUM = 1,RESP = 0) →	Received Message 1 OK
	← (NUM = 1,RESP = 1) $DATA_{S=0}$	Send Message 1
	← (NUM = 2,RESP = 1) $DATA_{S=0}$	Send Message 2
	← (NUM = 3,RESP = 1) $DATA_{S=0}$	Send Message 3
	← (NUM = 4,RESP = 1) $DATA_{S=1}$	Send Message 4 (Last Message)
$ACK_{S=1}$	(RESP = 4) →	Receive ACK
	← (NUM = 5,RESP = 1) $DATA_{S=0}$	Send Message 5
	← (NUM = 6,RESP = 1) $DATA_{S=1}$	Send Message 6 (Last Message)
$DATA_{S=1}$	(NUM = 2,RESP = 6) →	Receive Message 2 OK
	← (RESP = 2) $ACK_{S=1}$	Send ACK

* $DATA_{S=0}$ Select Bit Is Off

$DATA_{S=1}$ Select Bit Is On

FIGURE 12–16   DDCMP Line Control When a Buffer Is Not Available

Primary Station*		Secondary Station*	
$DATA_{S=1}$	→ (NUM = 1,RESP = 0)		Received Message 1 OK
	← (NUM = 1,RESP = 1)	$DATA_{S=0}$	Send Message 1
	← (NUM = 2,RESP = 1)	$DATA_{S=0}$	Send Message 2
Buffer not Available	← (NUM = 3,RESP = 1)	$DATA_{S=0}$	Send Message 3
	← (NUM = 4,RESP = 1)	$DATA_{S=1}$	Send Message 4 (Last Message)
$bNAK_{S=1}$	→ (RESP = 2)		Receive NAK
	← (NUM = 3,RESP = 1)	$DATA_{S=0}$	Send Message 3 Again
	← (NUM = 4,RESP = 1)	$DATA_{S=0}$	Send Message 4 Again
	← (NUM = 5,RESP = 1)	$DATA_{S=1}$	Send Message 5 (Last Message)
$ACK_{S=1}$	→ (RESP = 5)		Receive ACK
	← (NUM = 6,RESP = 1)	$DATA_{S=1}$	Send Message 6 (Last Message)
$DATA_{S=1}$	→ (NUM = 2,RESP = 6)		Receive Message 2 OK
	← (RESP = 2)	$ACK_{S=0}$	Send ACK

* $DATA_{S=0}$ Select Bit Is Off
$DATA_{S=1}$ Select Bit Is On
$ACK_{S=1}$ Select Bit Is On
$bNAK_{S=1}$ "Buffer Not Available" NAK with Select Bit On

ing messages before an acknowledgement must be made, because the message number is eight bits long and cannot wrap to a number equal to the first outstanding message. Also, a transmitting station in a full-duplex environment can force a reply by transmitting a **REP** message, which requests the receiver to reply with information about the last good message received. Figure 12–17 shows a primary station in a full-duplex environment sending four messages and getting no response from the secondary station. A response is forced from the secondary station when the primary station sends a REP message indicating the last message number sent in the NUM field.

Appendix B lists state tables for procedural rules of the protocol as presented in the DDCMP specification. These procedural rules produce the type of traffic shown in the figures presented for DDCMP. The state transitions for data message syntax are very straightforward in DDCMP because of the use of a byte count in the data message header. Figure 12–18 illustrates the simplicity of these state transitions.

FIGURE 12–17   Using REP Message to Force Reply on Outstanding
Messages

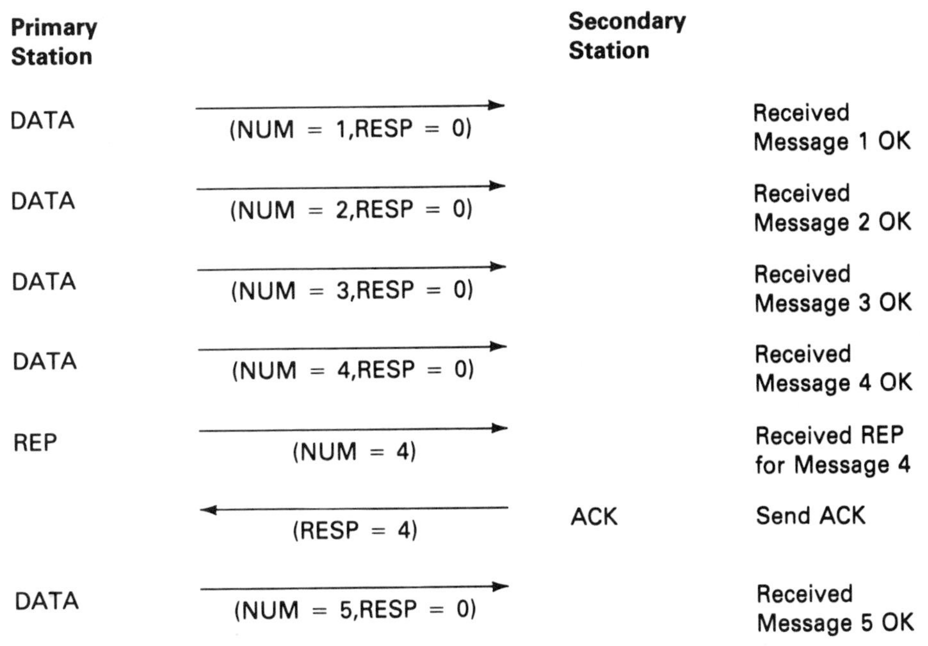

Primary Station		Secondary Station
DATA	(NUM = 1,RESP = 0) ⟶	Received Message 1 OK
DATA	(NUM = 2,RESP = 0) ⟶	Received Message 2 OK
DATA	(NUM = 3,RESP = 0) ⟶	Received Message 3 OK
DATA	(NUM = 4,RESP = 0) ⟶	Received Message 4 OK
REP	(NUM = 4) ⟶	Received REP for Message 4
	⟵ (RESP = 4) ACK	Send ACK
DATA	(NUM = 5,RESP = 0) ⟶	Received Message 5 OK

FIGURE 12–18   Receive State Transitions for DDCMP Data Message
Syntax [Gesalman 1982, p. 115]

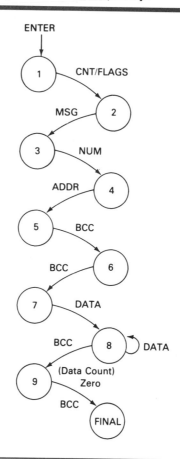

Bit-Oriented Protocols

Bit-oriented protocols rely on a unique bit pattern (special character) to delineate messages by means of a control character (**FLAG**) in a short header to control protocol functions (see Figure 12–19). This unique bit pattern is used for synchronization in place of the synchronization character(s) which precede the messages in the protocols discussed previously. Also, the end of a message is indicated by a FLAG character, i.e., the message is framed by FLAG characters. An example of such a protocol is IBM's **Synchronous Data Link Control (SDLC)** protocol, which is similar to the **High Level Data Link Control (HDLC)** protocol specified by the International Standards Organization. [ISO]

SDLC supports full-duplex transmission with centralized control using a serial bit transmission. A unique bit pattern, called a FLAG, consisting of a 0, six 1s, and a 0

FIGURE 12–19   General Format of Bit-Oriented Protocols

General Description: Special character, i.e., FLAG (01111110) is used to delineate messages with special character in header to control protocol functions.

Note: Because this type of protocol works bit by bit, a 0 bit must be inserted into the transmitted data stream after each series of five continuous 1 bits is detected.

General Format:

FLAG	HEADER	TEXT	FRAME CHECK	FLAG

(01111110) identifies the beginning and end of a message. This uniqueness is guaranteed by the manipulation of the data signal by the hardware: a string of six 1s is allowed only in the characters intended to be FLAGs. The communications hardware inserts a 0 after five consecutive 1s are transmitted at any point within the message between the FLAGs. Naturally, the hardware must eliminate any 0 found after a bit pattern of five 1s on the receive side. Figure 12–20 outlines the bit insertion/deletion technique and presents an example of its operation. [Lane 1984]

The framing technique used by the bit-oriented protocol employs FLAGs which are unique to delineate both control and data messages. Transparency is achieved by including header, text, and frame check trailer within the FLAGs, so that all message bit patterns are subject to the pattern checking and altering, as shown in Figure 12–21.

There is one special case with regard to framing, which should be pointed out here for future reference. Two FLAGs are not always associated with each message. In a full-duplex communications environment, for instance, one message may follow another immediately. If this is the case, the trailing FLAG for the first message represents the leading FLAG for the second message as well.

Figure 12–21 shows the general format of SDLC messages. The information field is present only in certain message types. There are three formats of messages: **information transfer, supervisory**, and **nonsequenced**. The control byte formats for each are given in Figure 12–22. The low-order bit (bit 0) of the control byte is transmitted first.

There are many types of supervisory and nonsequenced messages. Table 12–5 gives the control byte values for each of them, and Table 12–6 describes the use of each supervisory and nonsequenced control message.

FIGURE 12–20   *Zero-Bit Insertion in SDLC*

Rule: Whenever five 1 bits appear consecutively between FLAG characters, the transmitting station must insert a 0 bit in the data stream. The receiving station will remove the inserted zeroes after the detection of five 1 bits and a 0 bit in the data stream. Characters are reassembled into 8-bit bytes by the hardware.

Example: Suppose the following data stream is being transmitted.

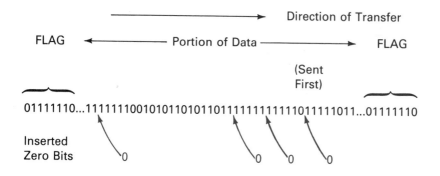

The message transmitted on the line is:

On the receiving side, the inserted zeroes (0 above) are removed upon the detection of the sequence of five 1 bits and a 0 bit.

FLAG is framed by a shifting mechanism similar to that used to frame SYN characters, except only a single 8-bit FLAG is used to establish synchronization.

FIGURE 12–21   Format of SDLC Messages

Only for
Information Message,
Nonsequenced Information Message,
and
Command Reject Message

Address specifies address of secondary station when sent by master and specifies address of station sending to master when sent by secondary station.

FIGURE 12-22 Control Byte Formats in SDLC

Information Transfer Format

7	6	5	4	3	2	1	0
N_R			P/F	N_S			0

Supervisory Format

7	6	5	4	3	2	1	0
N_R			P/F	MODE		0	1

Nonsequenced Format

7	6	5	4	3	2	1	0
C/R			P/F	C/R		1	1

N_S = Sending Sequence Number

N_R = Receiving Sequence Number

P/F = Primary Station **P**oll when set to 1 and sent from Primary Station or Secondary Station **F**inal transmission for current time when set to 1 and sent from secondary station

Note: Bit 0, i.e., low-order bit, is transmitted first.

TABLE 12–5   SDLC Message Control Fields

					Transmitted First	
	INFORMATION					
INFORMATION**		N_R	P/F	N_S	0	
	SUPERVISORY					
Receiver Ready	RR	N_R	P/F	00	01	
Receiver Not Ready	RNR	N_R	P/F	01	01	
Reject	REJ	N_R	P/F	10	01	
	NONSEQUENCED					
Nonsequenced Information**	NSI	000	P/F	00	11	C,R
Request for Initialization	RQI	000	F	01	11	R
Set Initial Mode	SIM	000	P	01	11	C
Set Normal Response Mode	SNRM	100	P	00	11	C
Request On-Line	ROL	000	F	11	11	R
Disconnect	DISC	010	P	00	11	C
Nonsequenced ACK	NSA	011	F	00	11	R
Command Reject**	CMDR	100	F	01	11	R
Optional Response Poll	ORP	001	1	00	11	C

** Information Field I follows Control Field
and is followed by CRC.

TABLE 12–6 Use of Supervisory and Control Messages

MESSAGE TYPE	USE
RR	Acknowledges receipt of I-frames from primary or secondary station.
REJ	Requests retransmission of I-frames from primary or secondary station.
RNR	Inhibits secondary station from sending I-frames when sent by primary station. Indicates secondary station is not able to accept additional I-frames from primary station until certain conditions are cleared.
RQI	Sent by secondary station to request initialization by having primary station send SIM message.
SIM	Initiates specific procedures at receiving station for initialization. N_R and N_S are set to 0 at both stations. Expected response to SIM is an NSA message.
SNRM	Subordinates receiving secondary station to the transmitting primary station. In this mode, secondary station is not to send any transmissions unless requested to do so (via polling) by the primary station. Expected response to SNRM is an NSA message.
ROL	Sent by secondary station, which is disconnected when it is requesting to go on-line.
DISC	Sent by primary station to place secondary station off-line. Secondary station cannot send or receive information frames and remains in this mode until an SNRM or SIM is received. Expected response to DISC is an NSA message.
NSA	Nonsequenced acknowledgement used to acknowledge SNRM, DISC, or SIM messages.
CMDR	Command Reject is sent by secondary station to indicate it has received a nonvalid command. An information field is included, containing the control field of the rejected command, the secondary station's N_R, the N_S, and four bits which indicate one of the four conditions: Invalid or nonimplemented command Information field in message which should not contain one Information field was too long N_R from primary station does not make sense given the N_S which was sent to it

SDLC Message Traffic

Message traffic in SDLC can become quite complex, as can the state diagrams for representing the protocol. Figures 12–23 through 12–27 illustrate various message traffic possibilities for SDLC. SDLC operates on a **master/slave** or **primary/secondary** station basis, with the primary or master station controlling the line. A secondary station cannot send unless polled by the primary station. However, once a secondary station has been polled, it may send up to seven data messages before giving up control of the line for transmission. The poll (P) bit shown in Figure 12–22 is set in the control byte by the primary station when the secondary station is being polled. The address of the secondary station is also set into the message, as indicated in Figure 12–26. When a secondary station sends to the primary station, it places its address in the address field of messages. The final (F) bit is set by a secondary station when it is giving up control of the line for transmission. Note that the bit position is the same for both the poll bit and the final bit. When a primary station transmits, the bit is a poll bit; when a

FIGURE 12–23   Startup Sequence in SDLC

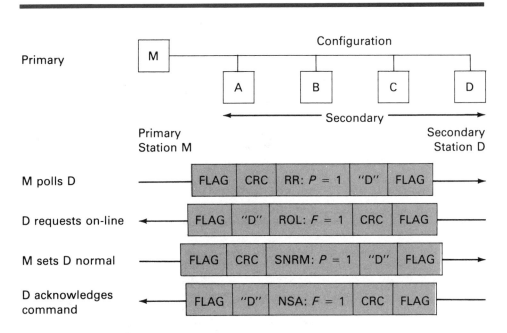

F = Final Bit Value   P = Poll Bit Value
RR = Receiver Ready   ROL = Request On-line
SNRM = Set Normal Response Mode   NSA = Nonsequenced ACK

secondary station transmits, it is a final bit. Table 12–5 illustrates that nonsequenced messages are either commands (sent by the primary station) or responses (sent by the secondary station).

A secondary station is off-line until it is polled by the primary station and then requests on-line via the ROL message. Figure 12–23 illustrates the startup sequence for bringing a secondary station on-line, and Figure 12–24 illustrates the disconnect sequence for placing a secondary station off-line.

Figure 12–25 shows half-duplex message traffic in SDLC and illustrates the use of the polling and final bits, represented by P and F, respectively. In a half-duplex mode, several messages may have to be discarded by the receiving station because of an error in an earlier message and because of the fact that the line cannot be turned around until the poll bit is set by the primary station or the final bit is set by the secondary station (see Figure 12–27).

Full-duplex SDLC message traffic is illustrated in Figure 12–27. Note that the primary station M can send to one station on a multidrop line after it has polled and is receiving data from another station. Two succeeding arrows of the same type in Figure 12–27 indicate when full-duplex (simultaneous) transmission is actually taking place.

Conclusion

Descriptions of character-oriented (BSC and BSC multileaving), byte-count–oriented (DDCMP), and bit-oriented (SDLC) data link control protocols have been presented in this chapter. Each protocol provides the basic aspects of protocol definition required in a data link control protocol and discussed in Chapter 9. Areas such as error control and line control, while similar, have very specific rules for a given protocol. The implementation of the protocol rules for each protocol in software using techniques like finite state machines must accurately represent both the protocol's syntax and procedural rules. Chapters 21 through 25 will concentrate on the software implementation details for data link control protocols.

FIGURE 12–24   SDLC Disconnect Sequence

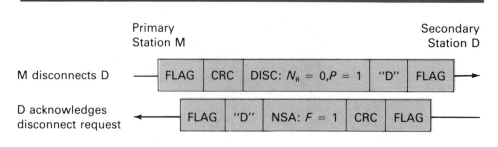

FIGURE 12–25 SDLC Half-Duplex Message Traffic Using Polling in a Multidrop Environment

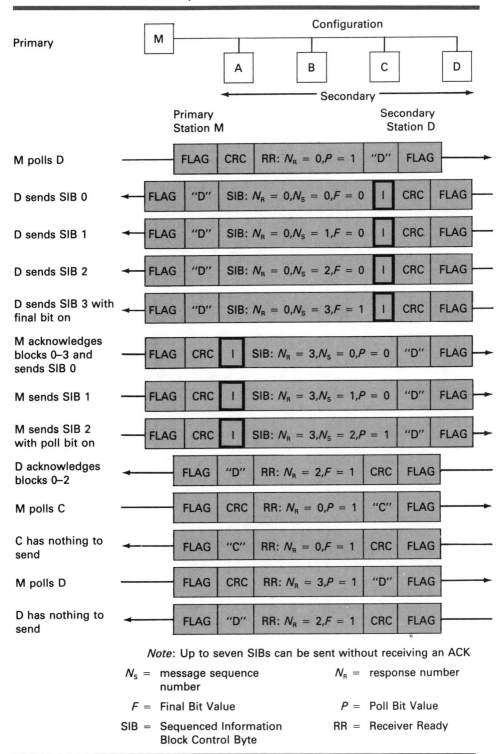

Note: Up to seven SIBs can be sent without receiving an ACK

N_S = message sequence number

N_R = response number

F = Final Bit Value

P = Poll Bit Value

SIB = Sequenced Information Block Control Byte

RR = Receiver Ready

FIGURE 12–26 Error Recovery in SDLC

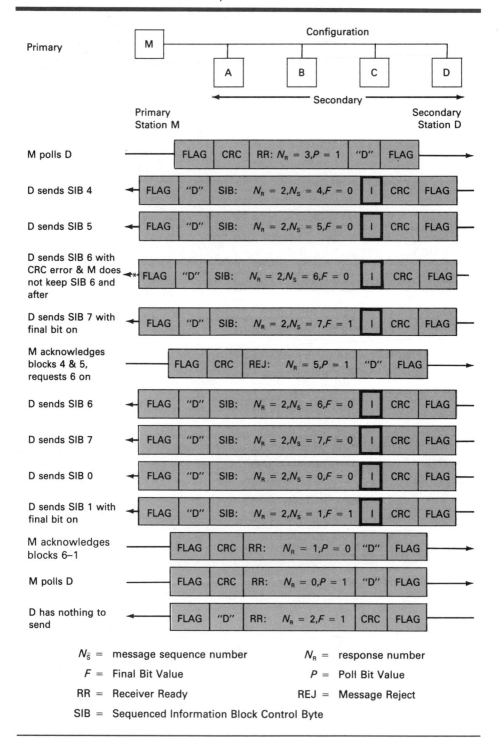

$N_{\bar{s}}$ = message sequence number N_R = response number

F = Final Bit Value P = Poll Bit Value

RR = Receiver Ready   REJ = Message Reject

SIB = Sequenced Information Block Control Byte

FIGURE 12-27 SDLC Full Duplex Message Traffic

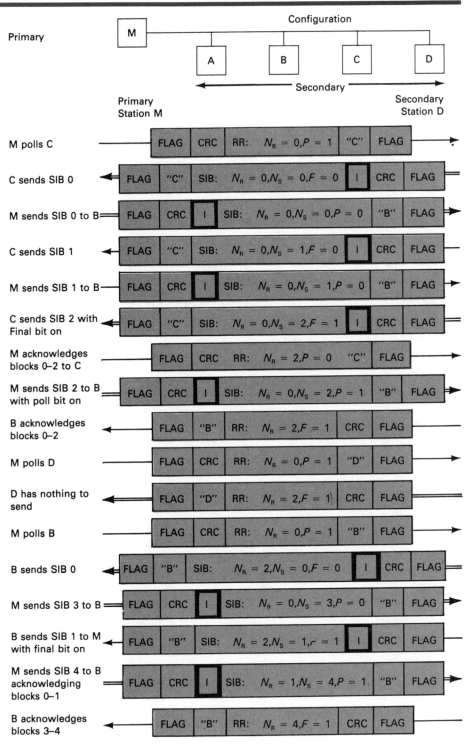

Note: Whenever succeeding two arrows are the same, e.g., a ➡ right before a ⬅ or a ➡ right before a ◄, then simultaneous transmission is taking place. M can always send to a secondary station. The secondary station which is polled may send data at the same time M is transmitting to the same or a different station.

Terminology

ACK0
ACK1
ASCII
BCB
BCC
Binary Synchronous
  Communications
bit-oriented protocol
Block Check Character
block control byte
BSC
byte-count–oriented protocol
character-oriented protocol
CRC
DDCMP
Digital Data Communications
  Message Protocol
DLE
EBCDIC
End of Transmission Block
End of Text
ENQ
ETB
ETX
FCS
FLAG
Function Control Sequence
HDLC
header
High Level Data Link Control
IBM 2780
information transfer message
LRC
master/slave stations
multidrop line
multileaving protocol

multileaving transmission block
nonsequenced
nontransparent
poll
primary station
primary/secondary stations
pseudosimultaneous, bidirectional
  transmission
RCB
Record Control Byte
REP
RVI
SCB
SDLC
secondary station
select bit
SOH
SRCB
STACK
Start of Header
Start of Text
state diagram
String Control Byte
STRT
stuffing
STX
Sub-Record Control Byte
supervisory
SYN
synchronization character
Synchronous Data Link Control
trailer
transparent
TTD
WACK
wait-a-bit

≡ Review Questions ≡

1. What is the purpose of each of the following control characters in Binary Synchronous Communications protocol?
   a. STX
   b. ETX
   c. DLE
   d. ACK0
   e. ACK1
   f. ENQ
2. DDCMP data messages are similar to ——————— ——————— disk or tape records.
3. What is the purpose of FLAG characters in SDLC? How are these FLAG characters guaranteed to be unique?
4. What is the purpose of each of the following fields in a header of DDCMP data message?
   a. RESP
   b. NUM
   c. ADDR
   d. COUNT
   e. SOH
   f. FL
   g. CRC
5. BCC is an abbreviation for ——————————— . Computation of BCC usually uses ————— or ————— ————— .
6. Explain the method used to provide transparency in the BSC protocol.
7. What is the multileaving protocol? How is sequencing provided in the multileaving protocol?
8. Which of the protocols studied in this chapter provide for a reason for NAK when a message is rejected? What are the reasons which can be provided to a station whose message is rejected?

≡ Assignments ≡

1. Compare how SDLC and DDCMP control full-duplex message traffic in a multidrop environment.
2. How does the multileaving protocol differ from SDLC and DDCMP in suspending and resuming data message traffic?
3. Compare the message framing techniques of SDLC, BSC, and DDCMP.

13

Local Area Networks

LANs and WANs

A network class called a **Local Area Network** has become quite popular in recent years. It is not exactly easy to define just what a local area network (**LAN**) is. Thurber and Freeman provide the following definition:

The properties of LANs as a class of network-like systems are:

1. single organization proprietorship
2. distances involved are of the order of a few miles and in the general locality [Thurber 1979]
3. the deployment of some type of switching technology [Cheong and Hirschheim 1983]

One common feature of an LAN is a shared transmission medium which is used to move information from computer to computer. Another standard feature is that LANs tend to be peer-to-peer — any device can directly communicate with any other device. [Graube & Mulder 1984] LANs are high speed, particularly when compared to **Wide Area Networks (WAN)**, which use "standard" communications facilities (e.g., dial-up telephone and leased lines): LANs have data transmission speeds as high as 10 megabits per second. The term "local" is used because LANs communicate between systems which are from 1 to 10 km apart. [Graube and Mulder 1984]

Why LANs?

Advances in microcomputer technology, particularly in the lower cost and greater power of microcomputers, helped to force the development of LANs. Microcomputers are often purchased for certain applications, but as these applications grow or other applications are added, the microcomputers also need to grow. Being able to add other microcomputers which share such things as disks and printers in order to obtain more processing power allows users to start out with small systems that can handle increased workloads in the future by the use of LAN technology. As early as 1977, Datapoint Corporation introduced a concept called **ARC** (Attached Resource Computer, a trademark of Datapoint Corporation), a local area network (even though it was not called it at the time, since the concept of an LAN had not yet been defined). The original press release stated that this new network "will dramatically alter the way the business world thinks and uses computers" [Datapoint 1983]. By 1983, 5000 such local area networks had been installed for customers by Datapoint Corporation. Figure 13–1 depicts the ARC environment with multiple processors.

Today LANs are used to allow small microcomputers to be sold in environments where previously minicomputers and medium-scale computers were sold. By using

FIGURE 13–1   The Datapoint ARC LAN

The ARC® Local Area Network
Datapoint Corporation
San Antonio, Texas

Sample ARC Network Configuration
(Note: Resource Interface Modules are internal to processors.)

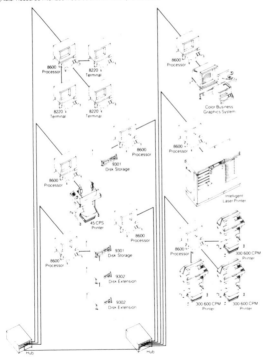

Attached Resource Computer® (ARC) Network:
Datapoint processors, peripherals, software and ARCNET™ components form an ARC local area network

ARCNET Network Components:
Resource Interface Modules (RIMs) implemented with LSI chips, coaxial cable, and hubs (junction boxes)

Topology:
ARCNET Network operates logically as a bus, but any arbitrary physical topology is allowed as long as no loops are formed

Transmission Method:
Baseband

Line Access Method:
Token Passing

Addressing:
8 bits

Transmission speed:
2.5 million bits per second

Transmission Protocol:
Serial asynchronous

Number of Supportable Processors:
255 per segment

Maximum Geographical Span:
4 miles

Maximum Distance between Nodes:
2000 feet

ISO Model Support:
Yes, layers 1 and 2

Remote Communications:
SNA/SDLC, 3270, 3780, DATAPOLL™, and MULTILINK™ (for interface to an X.25 LAPB host, Burroughs, Univac, or Honeywell equipment)

Applications:
Data processing, data communications, word processing, electronic message services (including interface to Telex,* TWX and Teletype*), financial modeling, telex management, color graphics, communications management, intelligent printing

Date Announced:
1977

Date of First Delivery:
1977

Installed Base:
Over 5000

Average Cost per Attachment:
ARCNET interface is $400.00 on the Datapoint 1560 processor, integral attachment on most other Datapoint processors

multiple processors and LAN technology, the power of these larger computers can be obtained, but more processors can be added only as required.

The connection of personal computers for peripheral sharing, particularly disks and printers, is very attractive in office environments and, hence, to vendors which manufacture such computers. This is because 80% of communications in such environments takes place within a local area (1 to 10 km) [DEC 1982, p. 13]. An example of a small business system which relies heavily on this LAN technology is the family of microcomputers (IWS, AWS, and N-GEN) developed and manufactured by Convergent Technologies and marketed by many different companies, like Burroughs Corporation (B-20, B-25, both of which are trademarks of Burroughs), the NCR Corporation (the Worksaver, a trademark of NCR) and Gould, Inc. (PowerStation, a trademark of Gould). Using an architecture called the "distributive intelligence" architecture, workstations (computers) with very few peripherals attached can be added to form a cluster environment so that workstations can share disk drives and printers via LAN technology. ["Convergent Technologies" 1983, pp. 11–12] Again growth can be gradual, and the initial investment nominal. Hence, local area networks permit a large number and a great variety of computer systems to share peripherals and exchange large amounts of information at high speed over limited distances. [DEC 1982, p. 14]

Design Goals

One of the major factors which affects the performance of an LAN-based system is its speed. No matter how many users the LAN is to accomodate, the speed and capacity of the network should approximate the speed of the computer I/O bus itself. This is particularly true since the power of an LAN-based system is obtained by the addition of processors in order to approximate the speed of larger and faster computers. If an LAN is susceptible to bottlenecks, the performance of the system will not approximate these larger systems, and the LAN-based system will not be accepted by today's users, who generally will not tolerate systems with slow response times. [DEC 1982, p. 10]

Assuming the speed of the LAN approaches that of the I/O bus, other design goals include such things as reliability, maintainability, low cost, flexibility, extendability, and compatibility. All of these are design goals for most computer systems. After the high speed requirement, one of the most important features of LANs is the ability to have a large number and variety of devices be able to exchange data on the network. Such equipment includes computers, intelligent copiers, word processors, high speed printers, and other similar equipment. LAN technology which provides such compatibility to a wide variety of equipment will most likely be that selected for offices and industries which have such a large diversification of equipment. In particular, there is a need to be able to attach equipment of different manufacturers for such information exchange on the LAN. [DEC 1982]

Finally, LANs should be simple to configure and install, and connections to the LAN should be easy to make. Users should not be aware of the LAN which provides device sharing and, in most cases, should feel as though the devices being shared "belong" to them. Of course, in such a shared environment, security of information stored in shared disks and files in the LAN is essential.

Design Factors

The performance and power of an LAN are dependent upon several design factors:

1. Control of message traffic and access to the network — Since the most important factor in the use of LANs is the performance and, hence, how fast information moves from one computer (node) to another, the mechanisms for controlling message traffic and access to the network are extremely important. The protocol used to gain access to the network and control the network traffic greatly impacts the speed of data transfer.

2. **Network topology** — The selection of the number of nodes, how they are connected (links), the kinds of systems that can be connected, and the location of the nodes.

3. Network performance — The speed of data exchange is impacted by the protocol that controls network access and message traffic, but it is also impacted by the medium and signalling technology being used for data transmission. The projected response time on a given processor must take into account the factors affecting performance, such as potential bottlenecks and application environments which might cause contention for certain devices as well as the network channel.

4. Requirements for hardware and software — The software for providing the LAN should be an integral part of the operating system supported on the processors. The cost of such software and the required hardware for providing the LAN capability is a major factor in the selection of a particular LAN. The initial cost of a base system and the expansion cost (on a per-node basis) are very important to potential users of an LAN.

5. Applications — Just what applications can be implemented in a particular LAN environment determine the usefulness of the LAN-based system in that environment. Merely being able to "run a program" is not sufficient in such an environment. The sharing and protection of data, and critical section problems requiring **record** and **file lockout** are of utmost importance in the success of applications in an LAN. The ability to lockout records should be provided automatically in **turnkey** applications and also should be relatively simple to use in the implementation of application programs for the system. Access methods should be uniform within the LAN, and they should be standard in some way (most likely implemented as part of the operating system support running on a processor in the LAN) in order to avoid "home grown solutions" to such common problems in shared user environments. Also, the use of equipment of different types should be supported by software which takes into account data code differences and architectural differences wherever possible. [DEC 1982]

The Network Channel

Control, access, and allocation of the network channel are critical aspects of LAN design affecting performance. **Channel control** can be either centralized in a single node in a manner similar to the polling techniques of SDLC and DDCMP in a multidrop environment, or it may be distributed to all nodes. Channel control is determined by the protocol used for data exchange in the LAN. **Channel allocation** deals with the allocation of the capacity of the channel so that it may be used in the most efficient manner possible. [DEC 1982]

   Channel control techniques are used by nodes to gain permission to use the common network channel for data transmission. Again determined by the LAN protocol, channel access techniques provide access to the network channel to nodes which are competing for the use of this resource. Two categories of channel access control are noncontention-oriented and contention-oriented. [DEC 1982] No matter what techniques are used for control, access, and allocation of a network channel in an LAN, nodes must follow the LAN protocol rules in order to access and use the network channel.

LAN Network Topologies

A network topology is made up of the nodes and **links** (communications paths) between nodes. There are three topologies for implementing LANs: stars, rings, and buses. [Graube and Mulder 1984] Figures 13–2, 13–3, and 13–4 illustrate these topolo-

FIGURE 13–2   Star Topology for an LAN

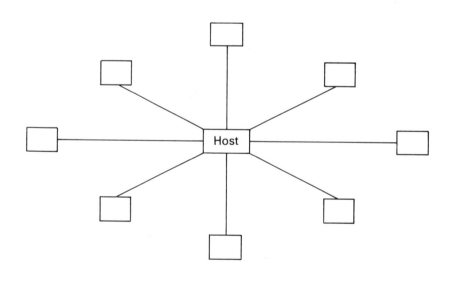

FIGURE 13–3   Ring Topology in an LAN

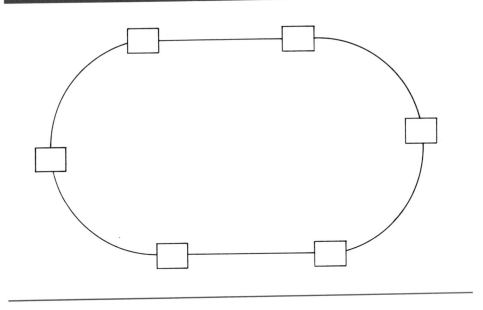

gies. LAN implementations provide for logical data exchange, whether or not there is a direct physical connection between the source node and the destination node for a data transfer. In the cases where there is no direct physical connection, the LAN must provide for switching and routing of the data being sent to the appropriate destination node.

A **star** topology can use either centralized or distributed control. The central node must generally route message traffic to outer nodes. If traffic tends to move between the central node and the outer nodes, the data transfer is fairly efficient. However, if message traffic from one outer node to another tends to be heavy, the switching required at the central node could degrade network performance considerably.

FIGURE 13–4   Bus Topology in an LAN

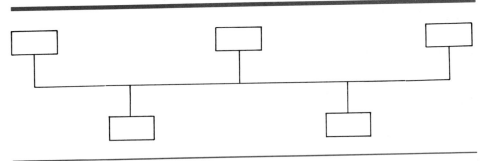

A **ring** topology has nodes which must act as active repeaters. In a star configuration, the central node had to determine how a particular message received is to be routed (switched) to another node. In a ring topology, messages are usually passed on to the next node. A token is often used to give a particular node permission to use the channel. Note that when a node fails in a ring topology, the network itself fails.

A **bus** topology shares a single physical channel. It is similar to a multidrop environment, discussed in Chapter 2, in that messages are broadcast to all nodes and a node must be able to recognize its address in a message received. There is no repeating of a message as there is in a ring topology. An obvious advantage of a bus topology is that failures in one node do not generally cause a failure in the entire LAN. [DEC 1982]

Transmission Media

The transmission medium and signalling technology used for the network channel also impact the speed of data transfer within the LAN. There are two signalling technologies: baseband and broadband. **Baseband** is the more prevalent of the two and either coaxial cable or a twisted wire pair is used for signalling. In this technology, the only signal on the transmission medium is that of the LAN itself. [Graube and Mulder 1984] The signalling bandwidth for baseband transmission is usually no more than 50 MHz.

Broadband transmission uses bandwidths of 300 MHz or greater and often has the channel split into two channels of 150 MHz for two-direction use. Either frequency division multiplexing or time division multiplexing techniques can be applied to the channel. One obvious advantage of broadband signalling is that multiple signals, e.g., video, can coexist on the transmission medium. [Cheong and Hirschheim 1983]

Since Shannon's Law tells us that the maximum data transmission rate is proportional to the bandwidth, it is obvious that broadband signalling will provide a far greater transmission rate than will baseband signalling. In spite of this and the fact that baseband signalling does not provide for other signalling capability on the transmission medium, it is still most attractive for most LAN environments because it is far less expensive than broadband signalling. [Cheong and Hirschheim 1983]

One other medium offers excellent possibilities: fiber optics. However, since this medium is not easily tapped, it is most attractive in a ring topology with point-to-point connections. [Graube and Mulder 1984]

LAN Protocols

Just as protocols are defined at each layer of a wide area network (WAN), a well-defined protocol must be used for data exchange in a particular LAN. There are two common techniques used in defining LAN protocols: a centralized or distributed polling technique, like token passing; a collision detect technique like Carrier Sense, Multiple Access/Collision Detect (CSMA/CD).

Polling Techniques

Polling LAN protocols can be either **centralized** in a manner similar to that illustrated by a multidrop environment using either SDLC or DDCMP, as described in Chapter 12, or **distributed**, using either a token-passing or slotted ring technique. **Token passing** is a mechanism whereby only one device may transmit on the LAN network channel at a given time. Each device or node receives and passes the right to use the channel (by passing the token) in an order determined by the protocol. While token passing is most often associated with ring topologies, it can be used in a bus topology. For example, Datapoint's ARC LAN implementation uses token passing with a bus topology. Figure 13–5 illustrates token passing in a ring topology.

A **token** is simply a special bit pattern which is sent from node to node when there is no message traffic. Once a node has possession of the token, it has exclusive access to the network for transmitting a message. No other node can transmit on the channel without the token. In order to prevent a node from dominating the channel, the LAN token-passing protocol prohibits a node from using the token twice in a row and specifies that it must be passed on. A node which has no data to send simply passes the token on to the next node according to the LAN protocol.

A node which has the token and wishes to transmit will hold the token until the message is sent to the destination node. The message transmitted includes source and destination addresses. As with protocols in WAN environments, some type of acknowledgement must be sent back to the source node to indicate whether or not the message sent was received successfully. The token will not be given up until this response is received, which introduces the potential for long delays in a ring topology using token passing. [DEC 1982].

FIGURE 13–5   Token Passing in an LAN

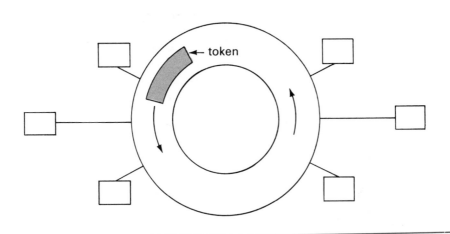

A **slotted ring** is another mechanism for distributed polling in LANs used in a ring topology. Rather than having just one token giving nodes permission to send, there are a number of **slots** or **frames** sent around the ring. Included in each ring are source and destination addresses, control and parity information, and the data being sent from one node to another. In the slotted ring technique, a node must merely wait for an empty slot which it can fill with data, setting the appropriate source and destination addresses and control bits (e.g., a bit indicating that the frame is now full) before it sends the frame on to the next node. As the frames are transmitted around the ring, each node determines if a particular frame belongs to it and if so removes the data from the frame and marks it empty by setting the appropriate control bit(s). [DEC 1982]

Figure 13–6 illustrates the slotted ring. Notice the similarity of the diagram to a freight train traveling on a circular track with box cars. Empty box cars (frames) can be filled at any given station (node) with the destination of the cargo being marked in some manner (address) on the car. Full cars are examined to see if the cargo is destined for the current station, and if so, the car is emptied and it is marked empty. Obviously, the removal of data from a frame is magnitudes of order faster than the unloading of a box car and the speed of the movement of a train is magnitudes of order slower than the speed of data transmission in an LAN.

Contention Techniques

Contention techniques anticipate collisions of data transmission on the network channel. No polling is required if the common channel is shared and the nodes can detect collisions. An example of a contention protocol is the **Carrier Sense Multiple Access with Collision Detection (CSMA/CD)** such as that used in **Ethernet,**

FIGURE 13–6   Slotted Ring in an LAN

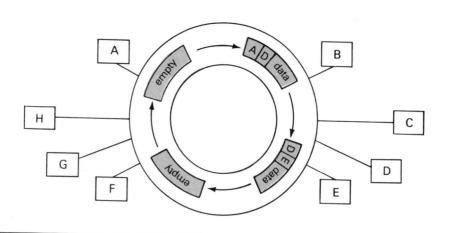

whose LAN standard was developed by and is supported by Digital Equipment Corporation, Xerox Corporation, and Intel Corporation.

The way to understand CSMA/CD is to take apart the name, which is essentially the combination of names of three different abstract capabilities: carrier sense, multiple access, and collision detection. Multiple access capabilities are made possible by carrier sense and collision detection. The term **multiple access** refers to the fact that a CSMA/CD protocol permits any node to send a message immediately upon detecting that the channel is free of message traffic. The obvious advantage of this is that the substantial amount of waiting time resulting from polling techniques is no longer required.

Carrier sense is used to determine if the channel is free: with carrier sense capability, each node can "listen" before sending a message. Because of the propagation delay of messages being sent on the channel, it is indeed possible that two nodes could sense that the channel was free at approximately the same time and begin transmitting. When this occurs, a **collision** results.

The term **collision detect** means that the hardware and protocol rules must provide for detecting collisions when they occur and some type of recovery from such collisions. Collision detection is possible because collisions cause a change, which can be detected by hardware, in the electrical signal level (energy level) on the channel. The hardware interprets such a change in energy level as a collision and recovery of a collision is performed according to the CSMA/CD protocol rules.

Upon detection of a collision, a node must interrupt its transmission and must wait for a specified interval. After this interval, it uses the listen-before-transmitting technique to retransmit. The interval of time for waiting may be a fixed or random interval. It is obvious that subsequent collisions can still occur. When this happens, the wait intervals get longer. To help detect collisions and avoid subsequent collisions. a node can send **jams**, or noise bursts, so that other nodes involved are sure to detect the collision. [DEC 1982]

Figures 13–7 and 13–8 illustrate analogically how CSMA/CD operates. In polite voice conversation, people listen before beginning to speak, as shown in Figure 13–7. On occasion, however, even though they listen, two people sometimes begin speaking at "exactly" the same instant in time. When this happens, one or both say something like "I'm sorry, you go ahead" (see Figure 13–8). Eventually, one party speaks and, after the first has finished, the other speaks. Parents often experience many conversational "collisions," in which two or more children speak, and often must resort to jamming, i.e., a loud reprimand, in order to restore proper conversation among those attempting to speak.

LANs and OSI Model

LANs correspond to physical and data link layers of network architecture, but in order to be truly effective, there must exist higher layer network services. [DEC 1982] LANs are connected to WANs at the network layer [Graube and Mulder 1984]. Connections from one LAN to another are also needed. Such internetwork connection can be accomplished by a **gateway**, which is basically a packet conversion from the source

FIGURE 13–7 Listen-Before-Talking in Carrier Sense Multiple Access

Okay to talk,
no one is talking.

listen
????

protocol to the target protocol. [Cheong and Hirschheim 1983] The implementation of such gateways is not necessarily trivial because of such things as differences of speed between two networks. Even when the same protocol is used in two networks (LANs and/or WANs), different node addresses in the two networks can create difficult problems. [Cheong and Hirschheim 1983]

LAN technology generally uses two of the ISO layers, the physical and data link control layer. Standards exist for LANs at the physical layer: the CSMA/CD technique is equivalent to the IEEE Standard 802.3 or the ISO standard 8802/3. These standards are similar to the Ethernet standard developed by Xerox Corporation, Digital Equipment Corporation, and Intel Corporation. Standard 802.3 is a baseband bus operating in coaxial cable at 10 megabits per second [Graube and Mulder 1984]. CSMA/CD standards at link layer are IEEE standard 802.2 and ISO standard 8802/2. Other standards have been developed for token passing (IEEE Standard 802.4 and ISO standard 8802/ 4). [Graube and Mulder 1984]

Summary

Standards in LAN implementation are particularly important in accomplishing the compatibility required to allow the variety of equipment in office and industrial environments to be attached to and operate in the LAN. Local area networks are an important part of today's communications technology. The techniques for implementing the protocol rules to support data transfer within the LAN are extremely important to the performance of the LAN.

Part II of this book deals with protocol implementation at the data link layer. Since the LAN protocols discussed in this chapter are implemented at the physical and data link layer, the implementation techniques which will be describe in Part II can be applied to the implementation of LAN protocols. In particular, the timing and debugging problems found in the implementation of a data link control protocol in a point-to-point

FIGURE 13–8   Listening While Talking to Detect a "Collision" in CSMA/CD

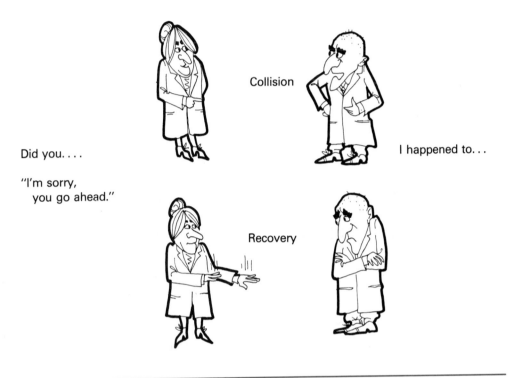

Collision

Did you. . . .

"I'm sorry,
   you go ahead."

I happened to. . .

Recovery

environment are very much a part of the LAN environment, particularly in a star or ring topology. With the high rate of data transfer typical in LAN implementations, software designers will find quite a challenge in the testing and debugging of protocols supporting data transfer within an LAN.

≡ Terminology ≡

ARC
baseband
broadband
bus
Carrier Sense Multiple Access
   with Collision Detection

carrier sense
centralized control
channel allocation
channel control
collision
collision detect

contention techniques	network topology
CSMA/CD	polling LAN protocols
distributed control	record
Ethernet	ring
file lockout	slot
frame	slotted ring
gateway	star
jam	token
LAN	token passing
links	turnkey
Local Area Network	WAN
multiple access	Wide Area Network

Review Questions

1. Why are LANs becoming so popular?
2. Which of the following are distributed polling techniques?
   a. CSMA/CD
   b. token passing
   c. slotted ring
3. Performance and power of an LAN are dependent upon the following design factors:

   _____

   _____

   _____

   _____

   _____

4. List and explain two LAN topologies.
5. Broadband uses bandwidths of _____ while Baseband uses bandwidths of _____ .
6. What is a gateway?
7. _____ anticipate collisions of data transmission on a network channel.
8. Ethernet uses a _____ protocol.

Research Assignment

What are some of the LANs available for microcomputers today? Are there any which easily connect microcomputers of different architectures and manufactured by different vendors? If so, list them.

References

Cheong, V. E., and R. A. Hirschheim. 1983. *Local Area Networks: Issues, Products, and Developments*. Chichester, Great Britain: John Wiley & Sons.

Convergent Technologies. December 1983. "Convergent Technologies: A Major Success, A Well-Kept Secret." *Business Microworld*. Pp. 11–12.

Datapoint. 1983. "The Datapoint ARC Local Area Network Milestones and Fact Sheet." San Antonio, Texas: Datapoint Corporation.

DEC. 1982. *Introduction to Local Area Networks*. Maynard, Massachusetts: Digital Equipment Corporation.

Graube, Maris, and Michael C. Mulder. October 1984. "Local Area Networks." *Computer*. Pp. 242–247.

Thurber, K. J., and Freeman, H. A. October 1979. "Architecture Considerations for Local Area Computer Networks." *Proceedings of the First International Conference on Distributed Computing Systems*. Pp. 131–142.

Part 2

Communications
Software
Design

14

Introduction to Data Communications Software Design

Traditional Approaches ● The Receiver and Transmitter Functions ●
Modular Design

Traditional Approaches

Much information has been published about data communications protocols, interface standards, packet switching, local area networks, and hardware interfaces. Yet, without good software, data communications and computer networks cannot exist. More research is needed in the area of data communications software methodology and implementation experiences. [Lane 1984, p. 1]

Various approaches have been used to implement data communications software. In the past, it appears that many designers of data communications software have ignored various principles in operating system design and have far too often used "brute force" techniques in implementing such software. In these cases, structured programming and modular programming have not been applied, and in many instances, the communications software has proved to be impossible to modify because of its complexity and lack of structure. Software maintainers often find it difficult to understand why some of this communications software works at all, for its logic is impossible to follow.

Literature searches for data communications articles find far too few publications on software methodology for data communications. Data communications is an area in which structured and modular programming are absolutely essential. Complex protocols, error conditions, timing problems, and the many other factors often external to the computer for which the communications software is being developed make it wise to apply the "Keep It Simple, Stupid" (KISS) principle and to use structured and modular programming techniques.

The **software methodology** presented in this book will focus on software for controlling asynchronous and synchronous interfaces and, most important, for implementing data link control protocols. If the techniques for implementing such **low-level protocols** are clear, understanding the various layers of protocols defined by the OSI model, described in Chapter 8, and their protocol implementations in software should follow. After all, data transfer between systems is controlled and most of the timing and error recovery are supported at the data link control layer; these aspects tend to make protocols difficult to implement and debug in software. The software methodology will not focus on software design techniques for higher level protocols for system network architectures.

As will be discussed later, many techniques used in the implementation of operating systems are important in the design of data communications software. Many different events occur in a data communications environment, like receiving of data complete, transmission of data complete, and timeouts. Communications functions can therefore be implemented as concurrent tasks, taking on the characteristics of tasks in a multiprogramming operating system. The use of data structures (usually **linked lists** called **control blocks**) for representing such tasks is standard in operating system design. Also, queue structures which pass information from one communication task to another will prove to be useful as well. Such **queue structures** are also useful in passing information from one layer to another in the OSI model. In such implementations of communications software, the software becomes highly **event-driven**.

Applying the appropriate techniques (operating systems principles, structured programming, modularization, and finite state machines) will result in less time spent debugging and in software which is easier to understand and modify. The net effect is, of course, a lower cost for the implementation and maintenance of such software.

The Receiver and Transmitter Functions

The two major functions in any data communications system are receiving and transmitting data. There is a great need for event synchronization between the receiver and the transmitter. Recall that the protocol is the language of data transmission and reception. The procedural rules of a protocol will specify what information must be passed from the receiver side of the software to the transmitter side of the software. In particular, information relating to the detection of errors (CRC, VRC, or LRC) by the receiver side must be provided to the transmitter side so that negative acknowledgements (NAKs) can be sent by the transmitter to the other computer system. Included in this information is the message identification number of the erroneous message. Hence, the synchronization of events (in the operating system sense — that is, the execution of one task must be synchronized with that of another) is critical to the correct operation of the communications software implementing a particular data link control protocol.

Assume that the receiver and transmitter functions are provided by a **receiver task** and a **transmitter task**, respectively. There must then be some mechanism to give control to the receiver and transmitter tasks at the appropriate times. This can be done by a simple **round-robin driver program**, which gives control to each function in turn, or by a **priority-driven dispatcher** in which each function becomes one or more independent tasks.

In order to present the receiver and transmitter tasks in a simple environment, let us assume that the receiver and transmitter are operating in a point-to-point environment that requires that data be read from and written to various files and/or devices. Data which is read from such files/devices must be packaged for transmission over the communications line by the transmitter task. Data which is received by the receiver task must be unpackaged and written to the files/devices. Figure 14–1 illustrates the structure and the flow of data in such a simple environment. The packaging and unpackaging of data which is passed to and from the transmitter and receiver respectively is called the "higher level protocol" in this figure.

FIGURE 14–1   Overview Structure of Data Communications Software

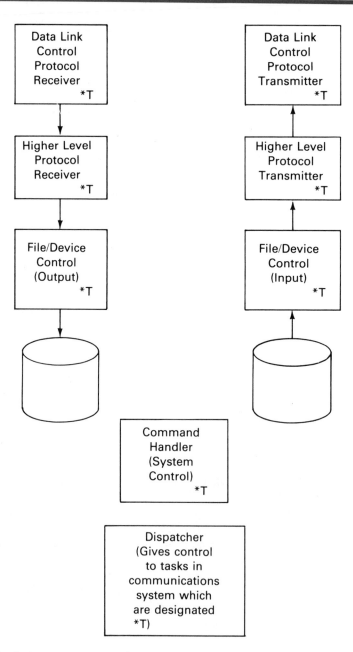

*T Can be independent task in software
↑↓ = Data Paths

Modular Design

Each of the major modules presented in Figure 14–1 can be implemented as an independent task in the data communications software. In fact, the data communications software itself is often a task in a multiprogramming operating system. Data being received from the communications line must be stored in a receiver buffer and validated according to the syntactical rules of the protocol implemented by the software. Part of the validation of the data is the application of the error detection algorithm defined by the protocol to determine if the received data is correct. Information which indicates that a received data message is correct or in error is provided to the transmitter task so that the appropriate procedural rules (send ACK, send NAK, etc.) may be invoked to pass this information on to the computer system which sent the message.

One of the simplest environments that can be used to illustrate the implementation of a data link control protocol is the environment that uses a simple compression or decompression algorithm as the higher level protocol, shown in Figure 14–1. Recall from Chapter 11 that the purpose of compression and decompression is to increase line throughput. No data link control protocol discussed in this book provides for compression and decompression; this is usually left to the "higher level" protocols in the system, which describe how the received and transmitted data is packaged. Compression and decompression can even be provided in more than one layer.

Figure 14–1 can be modified slightly, as depicted in Figure 14–2, to illustrate a simple remote job entry communications software similar to that used for an IBM HASP multileaving workstation. Such RJE software provides compression/decompression and the routing of data within a data buffer to and from the appropriate device or file. [Lane 1975]

Figure 14–2 assumes that a compression technique is being supported before data is transferred to the transmitter and a decompression technique supported before data is transferred to the appropriate device or file. In this case, data messages received by the data link control receiver modules must later be interpreted according to a higher level protocol (layer) in order to determine how the data should be "unpackaged" and to determine the destination file or device for the data. Similarly, the transmitter is passed data which has been packaged according to the same higher level protocol rules.

Figure 14–2 shows the decompression and compression functions being implemented as tasks in the communications software system. It is assumed that compression must process data from various input queues from devices and/or files and place this information in output buffers in a queue which is used as input to the transmitter task. The transmitter task must then use the syntactic rules of the data link control protocol to package data in the correct **envelope** for transmission.

Similarly, the decompression task processes data messages which have been validated (as correct) by the receiver task and places the decompressed data into buffers in the appropriate queues for files and/or devices, according to the higher level protocol decompression rules. The movement of data in both cases is illustrated by the arrows in Figure 14–2.

Perhaps the environment depicted in Figure 14–2 appears quite simple. However, a great deal of complexity — involving timing, message validation, error detection and recovery, acknowledgement of correct and incorrect messages, the interpretation of

FIGURE 14–2   RJE Model

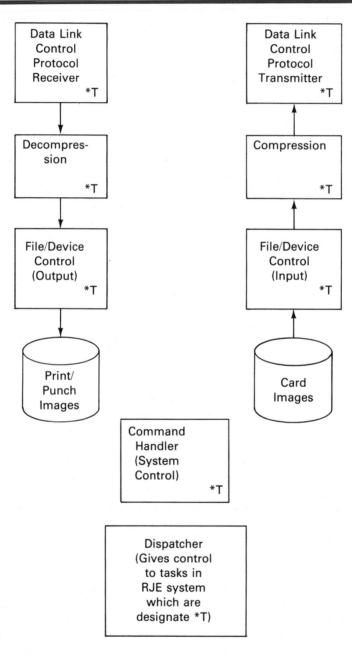

*T Can be independent task in software
↑↓ = Data paths

data received according to protocol rules, and the processing of data to be transmitted — is encountered in the implementation of the software. In combination with the number of concurrent events, this complexity makes implementation and debugging a difficult process. Careful structuring of the communications software is important to simplifying these processes. Chapter 22 presents a modular structure which can be used to isolate functions and make testing and debugging much easier.

Terminology

control block	queue structure
envelope	receiver task
event-driven	round-robin driver program
linked lists	software methodology
low-level protocol	transmitter task
priority-driven dispatcher	

Review Questions

1. How are linked lists used in designing data communications software?
2. Communications software is often highly _____ .
3. Control can be given to the modules in a data communications software by a _____ or _____ dispatcher.
4. The two primary tasks in a data communications software are the _____ task and the _____ task.
5. The syntactic rules of a protocol are used to package data into the correct _____ for transmission.

References

Lane, Malcolm G. 1975. "HASP Remote Workstation Enhancements." *Proceedings of SHARE XLIV*. Los Angeles, California. Pp. 248–260.

Lane, Malcolm G. 1984. "Data Communications Protocols." In *Advances in Data Communications Management*. Edited by Jacob Slonim, E. A. Unger, and P. S. Fisher. Volume 2. Chichester, Great Britain: John Wiley & Sons.

15

Interrupts and Their Use in Data Communications Software

Introduction • Overview of Interrupt Facility

Introduction

It is difficult to understand and write data communications software without understanding how hardware interrupts operate. Those who are already familiar with interrupts and interrupt handlers may choose to skip this chapter.

There are two basic techniques used to drive input/output devices: polling and interrupts. Using a **polling technique**, the software must periodically or continually check (poll) a device to see if it has finished the previous operation, e.g., a character has been received or transmitted. Chapter 17 illustrates the use of a polling technique in receiving and transmitting data from an asynchronous interface. Such a polling technique wastes a great deal of CPU time doing nothing useful. On the other hand, if the program did something else and only occasionally looked to see if the interface was ready, the throughput of the device would be adversely affected. Interrupt facilities allow a device to get service when needed without being continually polled.

Some analogies from everyday activities can illustrate how interrupts work. In cooking a roast, you could place a thermometer in the roast and constantly check it for the correct temperature (polling). Modern ovens provide a probe and an automatic reading of the temperature of the meat, shutting off the oven and perhaps generating an audible alarm when the meat has reached the desired temperature. You can go about other tasks knowing that the oven will inform you of the completed event.

The "interrupts" generated by the oven will likely call you away from another task. When leaving an interrupted task, it is very important to remember precisely where you were in performing that other task.

For example, say you were reading a book and the oven began signalling the completion of the event. If you closed the book without marking the place where you were reading, it might be difficult to find your place quickly (in fact, if you really weren't absorbing what you were reading, you might never find your place).

As human beings, we sometimes find it difficult to remember our place in what we were doing when more than one "interrupt" occurs in a short period of time (if an oven signal, telephone, and doorbell all ring within 15 seconds, for example). A computer which is interrupted must "remember" precisely what was executing (the address of the instruction that would have been executed) and preserve the integrity of its environment (processor status and register contents).

FIGURE 15-1   Human Interrupt Processing

"Ring"

Unlike human beings, computers handle thousands of interrupts per second. For every interrupt that occurs, hardware and software must remember what was interrupted and guarantee that nothing is changed in the expected environment of the program which was interrupted. With the analogy to interrupts which occur in everyday life in mind, let us consider how interrupts work in a computer system.

Overview of Interrupt Facility

Without the presence of interrupts within a computer system, execution proceeds sequentially from one instruction to the next until a branch instruction causes a transfer of control to another memory location. With the introduction of an **interrupt** facility, transfer of control within a CPU can occur automatically when an interrupt condition is

FIGURE 15-2   Multiple Interrupt Handling with the Human Mind

"Ding Dong"
(Door Bell)

signalled (by a device). This automatic transfer mechanism must provide the capability to automatically save (e.g., on a hardware stack) the address which would have been the next instruction executed had the interrupt not occurred. While different computer architectures provide different ways of saving this address (and appropriate status bits or condition codes), the basic concept is the same. The interrupt process is basically as follows: after each instruction is executed, the equivalent of the following algorithm is performed in the hardware:

IF INTERRUPT THEN DO

Save Execution Address (PC)

Save Status Information

Transfer Control to Interrupt Handler

END

Just what address is branched to is dependent on the computer's architecture. Some systems, like the DEC PDP-11, provide the capability of a different interrupt handler address for each device. The algorithm then becomes:

IF INTERRUPT THEN DO

Save Address

Save Status

CASE INTERRUPT — TYPE OF

DEVICE1: . . .

.

.

.

DEVICE2: . . .

.

.

.

END CASE

END

That is, the cause of the interrupt can be determined before the rest of the program executes. Other systems, like the IBM mainframe architecture (3000 and 4000 series), have categories of interrupts. For example, all input/output interrupts cause control to pass to a **first level interrupt handler (FLIH)**, which then interrogates the hard-

FIGURE 15-3 Single Level Interrupt Handler (PDP-11)

FIGURE 15-4 Hierarchical Interrupt Handling (IBM Mainframe Architecture)

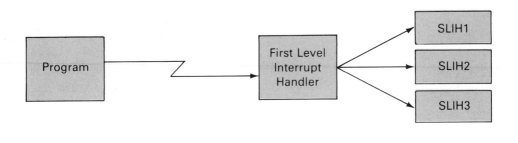

ware facility to determine which channel caused the interrupt. The FLIH then branches to the specific **second level interrupt handler (SLIH)** to process the interrupt.

Just how can the execution address and the status be saved? Two basic techniques are prevalent: one technique automatically pushes information onto a hardware stack upon the occurrence of an interrupt; the other stores this information in fixed (low) memory locations for a particular class of interrupts. A few processors have multiple sets of registers, so that each interrupt level may operate in its own register environment without destroying lower priority environments (e.g., IBM 3705 communications controller).

Let us consider an example from the PDP-11. Each device on the PDP-11 has assigned to it a unique address (by hardware configuration) in low memory, called an **interrupt vector**. Each interrupt vector is used to determine the destination address of the generated branch as well as the new **status word** to be used upon the occurrence of an interrupt caused by that device. Each vector consists of two 16-bit words. The first is the address of the interrupt handler; contents of this word are placed into the **program counter (PC)** after the necessary information about the interrupted program has been saved on the stack. The second word is a new status word to be transferred to the **processor status word (PS)** before control is transferred to the interrupt handler. The previous PC and PSW are saved via a stack. The algorithm for the hardware interrupt facility invoked after each instruction on the PDP-11 is equivalent to:

```
IF INTERRUPT THEN DO
    PUSH PS
    PUSH PC
    IF CAUSE = DEVICE1 THEN DO
        PC = VECTOR(DEVICE1)
        PS = VECTOR + 2(DEVICE1)
    END
    IF ...



                    .

                    .

                    .


    END
```

No matter how the address at which the interrupt occurred is saved and no matter how the appropriate interrupt handler is branched to, a return mechanism from the interrupt handler gives control back to the interrupted program. The return to the interrupted program could be done at the end of the servicing of a device interrupt, or it could be delayed due to the need to execute a higher priority task in a multiprogramming operating system. In any event, when the interrupted program gets control back, the contents of the registers and status information are restored to their values at the time of the interrupt.

The simplest case for communications software is for a device (communications interface) to interrupt when it needs service, then for the interrupt handler to service the device and then return to the interrupted program. Figure 15–5 illustrates this.

FIGURE 15–5   Simple Interrupt Servicing in a Communications Environment

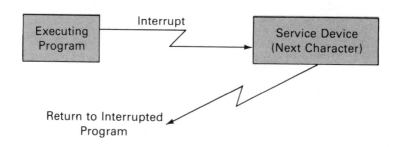

One important concept that is used with interrupt handlers has to do with setting **event flags** or **event control blocks** to indicate to other software modules that some event is complete. For example, if a communications interface transmits one character at a time, interrupting at the end of each character sent, then the interrupt handler could service each interrupt and set this event flag (whose address is known to other modules) when the last character has been sent, thus indicating that the requested transmit operation has finished. The use of such status or event flags is very important in communications software implementations. This software now polls such event flags or can use these flags as indications that an independent task in the communications software can now continue (i.e., the task is blocked from executing until the flag is set).

≡ Terminology ≡

event control block	polling technique
event flag	processor status word
first level interrupt handler	program counter
FLIH	PS
interrupt	second level interrupt handler
interrupt vector	SLIH
PC	status word

≡ Review Questions ≡

1. Compare polling techniques and interrupt-driven techniques for controlling I/O devices.

2. Compare first level interrupt handlers and second level interrupt handlers. Are both always required? Why or why not?

3. What role does each of the following play in interrupt processing in a computer system:

    a. processor status word or processor status

    b. program counter

    c. interrupt vector

    d. event control blocks

    e. I/O device

16

Implementing Error Detection Algorithms

Overview

Chapter 4 introduced the requirements for error detection and error recovery using parity checking techniques. Hardware for computing the error check characters may or may not exist in a given computer system. Hence, the error check characters may be computed solely in software or with a combination of hardware and software.

Hardware Parity Error Detection

Parity bits for **VRC** are often generated by the communications interface. Such interfaces permit the selection of parity as **even, odd, mark** (always 1), and **space** (always 0). Parity generation and checking can also be disabled.

The software driving the interface must set the hardware accordingly if it is to be used for parity generation and checking. The parity is generated for each character as it is sent and checked for each character as it is received. A parity error is reported to the software via an error condition in a status register.

Software Parity Error Detection

The parity bit in a character can be generated in several ways in software. One technique is to use the character with a zero parity bit as an index into a table which has the parity bit on or off (according to whether it is an odd parity or even parity table). With 7-bit characters, there will be 128 positions in the lookup table. Table 16–1 lists the parity table for **odd parity** and **even parity** using 7-bit ASCII characters as the index into the table.

TABLE 16–1 Parity Lookup Table for 7-Bit ASCII Characters

Decimal Index	Hex	Octal	Symbol	Octal Parity Odd	Octal Parity Even	Hex Parity Odd	Hex Parity Even
0	00	000	NUL	200	000	80	00
1	01	001	SOH	001	201	01	81
2	02	002	STX	002	202	02	82
3	03	003	ETX	203	003	83	03
4	04	004	EOT	004	204	04	84
5	05	005	ENQ	205	005	85	05
6	06	006	ACK	206	006	86	06
7	07	007	BEL	007	207	07	87
8	08	010	BS	010	210	08	88
9	09	011	HT	211	011	89	09
10	0A	012	LF	212	012	8A	0A
11	0B	013	VT	013	213	0B	8B
12	0C	014	FF	214	014	8C	0C
13	0D	015	CR	015	215	0D	8D
14	0E	016	SO	016	216	0E	8E
15	0F	017	SI	217	017	8F	0F
16	10	020	DLE	020	220	10	90
17	11	021	DC1	221	021	91	11
18	12	022	DC2	222	022	92	12
19	13	023	DC3	023	223	13	93
20	14	024	DC4	224	024	94	14
21	15	025	NAK	025	225	15	95
22	16	026	SYN	026	226	16	96
23	17	027	ETB	227	027	97	17
24	18	030	CAN	230	030	98	18
25	19	031	EM	031	231	19	99
26	1A	032	SUB	032	232	1A	9A
27	1B	033	ESC	233	033	9B	1B
28	1C	034	FS	034	234	1C	9C
29	1D	035	GS	235	035	9D	1D
30	1E	036	RS	236	036	9E	1E
31	1F	037	US	037	237	1F	9F
32	20	040	SP	040	240	20	A0
33	21	041	!	241	041	A1	21
34	22	042	"	242	042	A2	22
35	23	043	#	043	243	23	A3
36	24	044	$	244	044	A4	24
37	25	045	%	045	245	25	A5
38	26	046	&	046	246	26	A6
39	27	047	'	247	047	A7	27
40	28	050	(	250	050	A8	28
41	29	051	)	051	251	29	A9
42	2A	052	*	052	252	2A	AA
43	2B	053	+	253	053	AB	2B
44	2C	054	,	054	254	2C	AC
45	2D	055	-	255	055	AD	2D
46	2E	056	.	256	056	AE	2E
47	2F	057	/	057	257	2F	AF
48	30	060	0	260	060	B0	30
49	31	061	1	061	261	31	B1
50	32	062	2	062	262	32	B2
51	33	063	3	263	063	B3	33
52	34	064	4	064	264	34	B4
53	35	065	5	265	065	B5	35
54	36	066	6	266	066	B6	36
55	37	067	7	067	267	37	B7
56	38	070	8	070	270	38	B8
57	39	071	9	271	071	B9	39
58	3A	072	:	272	072	BA	3A
59	3B	073	;	073	273	3B	BB
60	3C	074	<	274	074	BC	3C
61	3D	075	=	075	275	3D	BD
62	3E	076	>	076	276	3E	BE
63	3F	077	?	277	077	BF	3F
64	40	100	@	100	300	40	C0

TABLE 16–1 Parity Lookup Table for 7-Bit ASCII Characters Continued

Decimal Index				Octal Parity		Hex Parity	
	Hex	Octal	Symbol	Odd	Even	Odd	Even
65	41	101	A	301	101	C1	41
66	42	102	B	302	102	C2	42
67	43	103	C	203	303	43	C3
68	44	104	D	304	104	C4	44
69	45	105	E	105	305	45	C5
70	46	106	F	106	306	46	C6
71	47	107	G	307	107	C7	47
72	48	110	H	310	110	C8	48
73	49	111	I	111	311	49	C9
74	4A	112	J	112	312	4A	CA
75	4B	113	K	313	113	CB	4B
76	4C	114	L	114	314	4C	CC
77	4D	115	M	315	115	CD	4D
78	4E	116	N	316	116	CE	4E
79	4F	117	O	117	317	4F	CF
80	50	120	P	320	120	D0	50
81	51	121	Q	121	321	51	D1
82	52	122	R	122	322	52	D2
83	53	123	S	323	123	D3	53
84	54	124	T	124	324	54	D4
85	55	125	U	325	125	D5	55
86	56	126	V	326	126	D6	56
87	57	127	W	127	327	57	D7
88	58	130	X	130	330	58	D8
89	59	131	Y	331	131	D9	59
90	5A	132	Z	332	132	DA	5A
91	5B	133	[	133	233	5B	DB
92	5C	134	\	334	134	DC	5C
93	5D	135	]	135	335	5D	DD
94	5E	136	^	136	336	5E	DE
95	5F	137	_	337	037	DF	5F
96	60	140	`	340	140	E0	60
97	61	141	a	141	341	61	E1
98	62	142	b	142	342	62	E2
99	63	143	c	343	143	E3	63
100	64	144	d	144	344	64	E4
101	65	145	e	345	145	E5	65
102	66	146	f	346	146	E6	66
103	67	147	g	147	347	67	E7
104	68	150	h	150	350	68	E8
105	69	151	i	351	151	E9	69
106	6A	152	j	352	152	EA	6A
107	6B	153	k	153	353	6B	EB
108	6C	154	l	354	154	EC	6C
109	6D	155	m	155	355	6D	ED
110	6E	156	n	156	356	6E	EE
111	6F	157	o	357	157	EF	6F
112	70	160	p	160	360	70	F0
113	71	161	q	361	161	F1	71
114	72	162	r	362	162	F2	72
115	73	163	s	163	363	73	F3
116	74	164	t	364	164	F4	74
117	75	165	u	165	365	75	F5
118	76	166	v	166	366	76	F6
119	77	167	w	367	167	F7	77
120	78	170	x	370	170	F8	78
121	79	171	y	171	371	79	F9
122	7A	172	z	172	372	7A	FA
123	7B	173	{	373	173	FB	7B
124	7C	174	|	174	374	7C	FC
125	7D	175	}	375	175	FD	7D
126	7E	176	~	376	176	FE	7E
127	7F	177	DEL	177	377	7F	FF

While setting up the parity table takes time, such a table can save a great deal of time in the long run, because computing the correct parity for transmission is simply the use of the character as an index or offset into the table. This table lookup is quite fast, particularly when implemented in assembler language. When a character is received, it can be saved, the parity bit stripped, and the result used as the index to "fetch" the correct parity. The original character received can be compared to the table entry fetched. If it is the same, the parity was correct; if not, a parity error has occurred.

Both even and odd parity characters can be supported in an environment by having two such tables or by using only one such table and reversing the parity bit via an eXclusive OR (XOR) with 200 (octal) of a character in the table when it is looked up.

Computations using shifts, ANDs, and eXclusive ORs are usually most suitable in assembler language. Beginning with 0 in a work register W, the received character C can be ANDed with a 001 and XORed with and stored in the work register. The character is then shifted one bit to the right, ANDed with 001 and XORed with and stored in the work register. This is done until every bit has been shifted into the low-order bit, ANDed, and XORed. If the result in the work register is 0, parity was even; if 1, parity was odd. Figure 16–1 illustrates this process.

On receive, the result determines the correct parity. On transmit, if the parity is to be odd and the result is 0, set the parity bit to 1 (with an OR operation); if the parity is to be even and the result is 1, set the parity to 1. Otherwise, the parity bit is correct (0).

FIGURE 16–1   Computing Parity with Exclusive ORs and Shifts

Shift	Shifted	AND 00000001 Resulting	XOR Previous W Yields
			W = 00000000 (initial value)
	C = 01011001	00000001	00000001
1 →	00101100	00000000	00000001
2 →	00010110	00000000	00000001
3 →	00001011	00000001	00000000
4 →	00000101	00000001	00000001
5 →	00000010	00000000	00000001
6 →	00000001	00000001	00000000
7 →	00000000	00000000	00000000
			Result → Parity was even.

→   Shift 1 bit to right
C   Received character
W   Work register

LRC

LRC is fairly simple to implement in software. A work location TEMP, which is one character long, is cleared to zero. Then, as each character to be "accumulated" in the LRC is processed, XOR it with TEMP. After all characters have been accumulated, a 0 in a bit position of TEMP indicates that the parity in that position was even, a 1 indicates that it was odd. LRC for even parity is the value in TEMP; LRC for odd parity is the 1's complement of TEMP.

Hardware CRC Error Detection

CRC calculations are usually implemented in hardware for synchronous interfaces. Some interfaces have a fixed CRC calculation, e.g., CRC-16, while others may allow the selection of the **CRC algorithm** to be used. If the interface itself supports the protocol, then the CRC mechanism is implemented according to the rules of the protocol the interface supports.

If the CRC error detection is controlled by software rather than as a part of the protocol running in the interface, then certain procedures should be followed in setting up a message for transmission. Before a message is transmitted, the CRC value must be cleared before the interface accumulates each character into the CRC value as it is transmitted. On closing out the sending of a message, the CRC is normally transmitted as part of the trailer of the message. There are variations among the rules of the protocol and the rules of the hardware interface in accumulating the CRC. Some protocols, like BSC, do not include all characters (e.g., DLEs in a transparent mode) in the CRC calculation. A CRC algorithm in the interface usually accumulates all characters between the beginning and the end of the message.

FIGURE 16–2   LRC Calculation with XORs

ASCII Character	Binary	XOR Previous TEMP TEMP	
		00000000	(Initial Value)
A	01000001	01000001	
B	01000010	00000011	
3	00110011	00110000	
E	01000101	01110101	⟵ even LRC
		10001010	⟵ odd LRC (1's complement)

Some systems provide a CRC hardware algorithm independent of the communications interface. The KG-11 of the DEC PDP-11 is an illustration of such a hardware feature. The CRC can be computed on any string of data before it is sent to a communications interface. When such a feature is used, characters are put into the CRC algorithm one at a time; therefore, characters in a message which are not to be accumulated are not selected by software to be processed by the CRC algorithm in hardware.

Software Algorithm for CRC-16

The CRC algorithm for CRC-16 can be implemented in software by emulating the algorithm shown in Figure 4–3. This algorithm requires the use of XORs and shifts to accomplish the desired result. In assembler language, XOR, SHIFT, and AND instructions can be used. In higher level languages, such operations are often difficult to emulate.

═══ Terminology ═══

CRC algorithm	odd parity
even parity	parity bits
LRC	space parity
mark parity	VRC

═══ Review Questions ═══

1. How can parity be computed using software?
2. If both hardware and software are available for computing CRC-16, which would be best to use? Why?
3. What happens when parity is set to mark? To space?

═══ Assignments ═══

1. Given the following ASCII string to be transmitted,

Now is the time for all good programmers to come to the aid of their computers.
TESTING 13598GHB!

    a. Write the string in octal with even parity.
    b. Write the string in octal with odd parity.
    c. Write the string in octal with mark parity.

d. Write the string in octal with space parity.

e. Write the string in hexadecimal with odd parity.

2. In a language that can be run locally, write a subroutine SETPAR to convert ASCII characters in a data area to odd or even parity depending on the parameter PARITY. Calling sequence of SETPAR is

CALL SETPAR(DATA,LENGTH,PARITY)

where DATA is the area containing the string to be set to even or odd parity, LENGTH is its length, and PARITY is a string variable with a value of "ODD" or "EVEN." The parity bit should be set in each character in the data area DATA (i.e., do not move the character string).

3. In an appropriate language that can be run locally, write a subroutine CRC16 to compute the CRC-16 block check character using the "algorithm" illustrated in Figure 4-3 for the generating polynomial shown in this figure. The calling sequence for CRC16 is

CALL CRC16(DATA,LENGTH,CRC)

where DATA is the string which to be used to compute the CRC-16 block check character, LENGTH is its length, and CRC is to contain the result of the CRC calculation.

17

Programming Asynchronous Interfaces

Introduction

As described in Chapter 5, the asynchronous interface assembles each character which is "framed" by a START and STOP condition into a 1-character buffer. Some interfaces provide for programmable character lengths of 5, 6, 7, or 8 bits, although the characters are usually placed into an 8-bit buffer. Only after the bits, which arrive serially, are assembled into this buffer is the character transferred in parallel to the CPU.

Different computers provide various mechanisms for the transfer of data characters to and from an asynchronous interface. However, techniques for character-by-character transfer are similar (i.e., each character requires transfer by a program executed by the CPU). All such interfaces have facilities on both the receive side to indicate if it is ready to provide a data character or on the transmit side to indicate if it is ready to be given a data character.

Programming Techniques

Two basic programming techniques are used to control an asynchronous interface: **polling** and **interrupt-driven**. Chapter 15 introduced the basic concepts of interrupts and how they are used in communications software. This chapter will cover both polling and interrupt-driven techniques for controlling an asynchronous interface and will illustrate these techniques with pseudocode.

Receive Software

An asynchronous interface normally has the equivalent of a **receiver status register** (RCV-STAT), a **receiver data register** (RCV-DATA), a **transmit status register** (XMT-STAT), and a **transmit data register** (XMT-DATA), accessible by either absolute memory locations (PDP-11) or by the use of I/O instructions.

To be more specific, the Digital Equipment Corporation PDP-11 architecture provides an I/O structure in which all device registers are referenced by memory locations in high memory in an area called the **I/O page**. This **UNIBUS** (a trademark of Digital Equipment Corporation) provides for fairly simple I/O device programming. An **asynchronous serial interface** on the PDP-11 has four device registers, two for receive and two for transmit. The format is illustrated in Figure 17–1. The status registers provide communications between the device and the CPU. For most PDP-11 asynchronous interfaces, the data registers are for data transfer one character at a time.

Assume that the condition RCV-READY means that the interface has an input character available for processing from the communications line (usually indicated by a receiver ready condition signalled by a status in the the status register). Also assume that the names of the four registers are RCV-STAT, RCV-DATA, XMT-STAT, and XMT-DATA, as shown in Figure 17–1, and the contents of these registers are accessible to the program driving the interface by these names. Then the program to receive data using such an asynchronous interface can be written as:

$I = 0$

DO UNTIL $I = N$

    DO WHILE NOT RCV-READY

    END

    DATA(I) = RCV-DATA

    $I = I + 1$

END

This program receives N characters into a data area called DATA (which must be defined elsewhere in the program). The loop on NOT RCV-READY might appear strange, since there seems to be no way out of the loop. However, since receiver hardware will asynchronously set the ready condition upon the receipt of a character, the RCV-READY condition will eventually be true and execution will continue.

Asynchronous interfaces are often used to attach terminals whose users terminate data input early by the use of an "enter" or "carriage return" key. In many cases, therefore, the software will require less than N characters. In this case, the program must provide for the detection of a carriage return (015 octal) and exit from the receive loop early. This is illustrated below:

FIGURE 17–1   Receiver and Transmit Device Registers (PDP-11)

RECEIVER STATUS REGISTER	(RCV-STAT)
RECEIVER DATA REGISTER	(RCV-DATA)
TRANSMITTER STATUS REGISTER	(XMT-STAT)
TRANSMITTER DATA REGISTER	(XMT-DATA)

```
END-RCV = FALSE
I = 0
DO UNTIL (I = N OR END-RCV)
    DO WHILE NOT RCV-READY
    END
    DATA(I) = RCV-DATA
    IF DATA(I) = CR THEN END-RCV = TRUE
    I = I + 1
END
```

The data movement in this receiver algorithm is illustrated in Figure 17–2.

At the machine level of execution, the wait on the receiver's not being ready can be either an instruction sequence using a "TEST STATUS" input/output instruction or a test of a bit or byte in a certain memory location where the device status register is located (e.g., PDP-11). Similarly, the data movement from the receiver buffer RCV-DATA can be a machine language sequence containing a "READ" I/O instruction or a move instruction from the receiver data register in a certain memory location (PDP-11).

These algorithms poll the device to determine when a character is available. Much CPU time can be wasted polling the device, even if the time between characters is short. For example, at 1200 bits per second, the minimum time for an 8-bit character is 8 bits plus START time, plus STOP time. If the STOP bit is assumed to be one data **bit time**, then 10 bit timings are required to receive one character. This means that the maximum rate of character transfer is 120 characters per second. Hence, the loop above will take 1/120th of a second, during which useful work could have been done by the CPU.

FIGURE 17–2   Data Movement in Receiving Data with an Asynchronous Interface

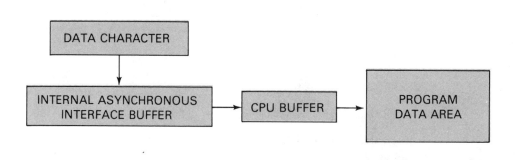

FIGURE 17–3   Sample Interrupt Mechanism for Receiver

```
        CALL RCV(DATA,N,RCV-FLAG)

    .
    .   Other useful tasks performed here
    .
        DO WHILE NOT RCV-FLAG
        END
```

Setup Routine
```
    RCV(DATA,N,RCV-FLAG)
    Save DATA address
    Save Character Count N
    Save address of RCV-FLAG
    I = 0
    Enable Receiver Interrupts
    RETURN
```

Receiver Interrupt Handler
```
    RCV-INT**
        Save all
        DATA(I) = RCV-DATA
        I = I + 1
        IF I = N THEN DO
          RCV-FLAG = 1
          Disable Receiver Interrupts
        END
        Restore All
    RETURN
```

** Variable names used are the same as those in the calling program in order to simplify illustration. Normally parameter addresses would be saved in RCV for later use by RCV-INT.

It is for this reason that interrupts exist. For our purposes in this book, an **interrupt** is a hardware mechanism which is triggered by a signal from a device needing service and which automatically saves the current execution address of the program in control of the CPU and transfers to an **interrupt** (device) **service routine**. When interrupts are used, a **device handler** is normally split up into a setup routine and an interrupt handler, which will be called RCV and RCV-INT, respectively. The address of RCV-INT must be placed into the appropriate hardware mechanism so that it will receive control when a receiver interrupt occurs.

Figure 17–3 illustrates the logic of the program requesting a receive operation from the interface, the setup routine RCV, and the interrupt routine RCV-INT. A call to the RCV routine provides the address of the data buffer (DATA), the number of characters to be read (N), and the address of an event flag (RCV-FLAG) which is used to signal to the caller that N characters have been received by the interrupt handler.

After RCV is called, the receiver operation is started and the calling program can continue with other instructions while the receiver interrupt handler RCV-INT periodically gets control when the next character is ready and returns when it is processed. Eventually the calling program will need the data being received, in which case the RCV-FLAG can be checked (finally polled). Notice that on this polling, the entire N characters will have been received when the RCV-FLAG is set.

The RCV module sets up the interface for using interrupts. If the address of RCV-INT has not been set into the interrupt mechanism (usually, but not always, an interrupt vector), then RCV must provide this function. RCV saves the parameters, mainly the address of the data area, the count of the number of characters to be received, and the address of the event flag RCV-FLAG. It clears the count of received characters and enables receiver interrupts (sets a bit or performs an I/O operation). RCV can then return to the calling program, since the receiver will interrupt on each character which is received, with this interrupt being serviced by RCV-INT.

RCV-INT must save the processor status and registers to preserve the integrity of the environment of the interrupted program. It then moves the received character into the next location in the data area, advances the pointer, and checks to see if all characters have been received. If so, i.e., $I = N$, then RCV-FLAG is set to indicate that all requested data has been received and further receiver interrupts are disabled. In all cases, registers and status are restored and control is returned to the interrupted program.

The time which was previously used to poll for each character is now available for other tasks before checking RCV-FLAG. In a multiprogramming environment, RCV-FLAG could be an event flag in a task control block, which prevents the particular task requesting the receipt of data from using the CPU until the receiver event has completed, thus allowing other "ready" tasks to use the CPU.

Figure 17–3 shows that receiver interrupts are disabled. In many environments, receiver interrupts continue with data being received into an internal (ring) buffer until a program calls for the data, at which time it is transferred to the user's data area in order to prevent a loss of data in a full-duplex environment (see Chapter 18).

Transmit Software

Transmit programming is similar to receive programming. Assume that the asynchronous interface has one internal buffer from which data is serialized as output and that the transmitter becomes ready when this buffer is empty.

A simple program for controlling the transmitter using polling follows:

```
I = 0
DO UNTIL I = N
    DO WHILE NOT XMT-READY
    END
    XMT-DATA = DATA(I)
    I = I + 1
END
```

In this case, the program will already know how many characters to transfer, so there is no need for an escape out of the loop, as there was for the receiver. In implementations using interrupts, this transmitter software is similar to the receiver software already illustrated.

Programming for Error Conditions

The previous illustrations assumed that there were no error conditions in the data being received. However, there are error conditions which can be detected on the receiver side of the interface, mainly overruns, framing errors, and parity errors.

An overrun condition results when the next character has been received but the previous character was not "read" from the receiver buffer by the program. A data character is lost.

A framing error is the result of a STOP condition (1 bit) being expected one bit timing after the last bit of the data character, but a zero bit being detected instead.

Parity errors occur when the parity of the received character is not what was expected (odd or even) by the interface (if parity checking is enabled).

If any of these error conditions are present, the error bit or condition in the interface is set to 1. Hence, upon receiving a character, the software should check the error status to determine if an error has occurred. If errors do occur, the type of error can be indicated by the value placed in RCV-FLAG. In a simple receiver implementation, the errors are merely reported to the calling program. No action is taken by the receiver routine, except that the receive operation may be prematurely terminated.

Additional Considerations

A framing error can be forced via the break key on terminals and via the transmit break facility of the interface itself. As mentioned earlier, many timesharing systems are programmed to recognize framing errors as exceptions or as attention signals to stop a program or enter a command. A break forces a 0 (space) condition on the line for longer than the combined time duration of the START, the data bits and the STOP, thus guaranteeing the setting of the framing error bit in the interface.

A break condition can be reported to the calling program using the same RCV-FLAG. More complex implementations might have a break "action routine" invoked to force some higher level action, like return to MENU or return to command mode.

Later it will be seen that some asynchronous interfaces have other capabilities which can be programmed. Such capabilities include the selection of character length and communications line speed. These capabilities are usually programmed by an initialization routine which selects the appropriate feature before the receiving and transmitting of data begins.

≡ Terminology ≡

asynchronous serial interface	polling
bit time	receiver data register
device handler	receiver status register
I/O page	transmit data register
interrupt	transmit status register
interrupt-driven	UNIBUS
interrupt service routine	

≡ Review Questions ≡

1. Why are interrupts used in controlling an asynchronous communications interface?

2. List the use of each of the following registers for asynchronous communications:
   a. Receiver Status Register
   b. Receiver Data Register
   c. Transmitter Status Register
   d. Transmitter Data Register

3. Program statements like

DO WHILE NOT RCV-FLAG

END

in most environments will result in an infinite loop. Why is this not an infinite loop in the example presented in Figure 17–3?

≡ Assignments ≡

1. On a local computer system, use polling techniques to display the following message on a terminal display:

TESTING THE POLLING CAPABILITY OF AN ASYNCHRONOUS INTERFACE

2. On a local computer system, use the ideas presented in Figure 17–3 to implement RCV and RCV-INT.

18

Programming Multiline Interfaces

Hardware Control/Status Registers

Chapter 5 presented **multiline asynchronous hardware interfaces**. Such interfaces are controlled by I/O instructions or memory-resident control and status registers. As in Chapter 17, whether these registers are implemented in hardware as memory locations (PDP-11) or as values retrieved or set using some I/O instruction (most microcomputers), the concepts of how a multiline interface is controlled do not change. Control registers such as those shown in Figure 18–1 will be assumed.

It also will be assumed that the multiline interface has a **Line Parameter Register** which can be used to activate a line and set its parameters. Note that interrupts can be enabled for the receiver and transmitter of the interface, but unless at least one line is enabled for transmit or receive, no interrupts will be generated. Thus, the multiline interface provides the interrupt facility, but the individual lines controlled by the interface trigger the interrupts when a character from a line in the FIFO of the receiver is present and when the transmit character-holding buffer of the transmitter is empty. Before a receiver or transmitter interrupt can be triggered by a line, the line must be enabled for receive and transmit, respectively.

Some multiline interfaces allow the processing of more than one character in the FIFO buffer on a given interrupt. In this case the hardware signals that at least one character is present in the FIFO, and the receiver interrupt handler can process all the characters or some fixed number of characters in the FIFO. Receiver interrupts will only be triggered if there is at least one character in the FIFO buffer. Hence, if a given interrupt is used to process all characters in the FIFO, if no more characters have arrived since the last character was processed by the receiver interrupt handler, and if the interrupt handler returns from the interrupt, no interrupt will be generated until a new character arrives from some line.

While the **status bits** and **control bits** shown for each register in Figure 18–1 might be implemented in a different register or by different I/O operations for some system architectures, the use of the status and control information remains conceptually the same. These status and control signals (bits) will now be discussed.

234

FIGURE 18–1   Device Control and Status Registers of a Multiline Interface

Transmitter Control/Status Register	Transmitter Ready
TCSR	Transmitter Interrupt Enable
	Transmitter Enable
	Transmitter Line Number

Transmitter Control/Status Register

TCSR

Transmitter Ready
Transmitter Interrupt Enable
Transmitter Enable
Transmitter Line Number

Receiver Control/Status Register

RCSR

Receiver Ready
Receiver Interrupt Enable
Receiver Line Number
FIFO Full Alarm Enable
FIFO Full Alarm

Line Parameter Register

LPR

Line Number
Receiver Enable
Parity Enable
Even/Odd Parity
Character Length (5, 6, 7, 8)
Receive Line Speed
Transmit Line Speed
STOP Length (1, 1.5, 2)

Transmitter Buffer Register

TBR

Character to be Transmitted
for Line Number in TCSR

Transmitter Line Control Register

TLCR

Transmit Enable for Lines

Transmitter Break Control Register

TBCR

Transmit Break for Lines

Receiver Buffer Register

RBR

Received Character for Line
 Number in RCSR
Error Bit
Overrun Error
Framing Error
Parity Error

Transmitter Control/Status Register

The **Transmitter Control/Status Register** is used to set control information for transmission and to determine transmit status for a line needing service. The **Transmitter Ready** status indicates that the line specified by the **Transmit Line Number** is ready for another character. If the **Interrupt Enable bit** is set, the Transmitter Ready condition will generate a hardware interrupt for service. The Transmitter Enable condition enables the entire multiline interface for transmitting characters. However, unless a line is enabled (via the Transmit Line Control Register), the Transmitter Ready condition will never occur.

Receiver Control/Status Register

The **Receiver Control/Status Register** provides information about data being received. The **Receiver Ready** condition indicates that a character is present from a line and that this line needs service. The FIFO is used as a buffer and the next line (on a first-in/first-out basis) requiring service has its character in the FIFO transferred to the Receiver Buffer Register. The Line Number in the Receiver Control/Status Register specifies the line requesting service. Some interfaces have this Line Number in the Receiver Buffer Register along with other information about the character being received rather than in the Receiver Control/Status Register. If the Receiver Interrupt Enable bit has been set, then the receiver will interrupt when the Receiver Ready condition occurs. The **FIFO Full Alarm** indicates that the FIFO buffer has overflowed and one or more characters have been lost from one or more lines. When the **FIFO Full Alarm Enable** is set, the FIFO Full Alarm will generate a hardware interrupt when a FIFO overrun occurs.

Line Parameter Register

The Line Parameter Register specifies the parameters for a given line on the multiline interface. The most general implementation would allow the setting of parity (odd or even), the enabling of parity checking, the character length (5, 6, 7, 8), the receive line speed, the transmit line speed, the STOP condition length (1, 1.5, 2.0) and whether or not the line is to have the receiver enabled. Some lines, e.g., one driving a printer, might not require that the receiver be enabled.

Transmitter Buffer Register

The **Transmitter Buffer Register** is used to send a character to a line needing service. The line receiving the character placed in this buffer is the one currently being serviced for transmit, i.e., the one whose line number is in the Transmitter Control/Status Register.

Transmitter Line Control Register

The **Transmitter Line Control Register** controls whether or not a line is to be enabled for transmission. Usually, a specific bit associated with a specific line permits each line to be enabled when this bit is set and disabled when it is cleared — for example, bit 0 for line 0, bit 1 for line 1, and so on.

Transmitter Break Control Register

Included in the **Transmitter Break Control Register** is a bit for each line to force a break condition on the line when the line is being serviced. This is necessary since the break condition is often needed as a normal attention signal, and this condition cannot be generated when an eight-bit character is sent. Setting the bit corresponding to a particular line will force the break condition for either a specified amount of time, or until the bit is cleared, depending on how the multiline interface operates.

Receiver Buffer Register

The **Receiver Buffer Register** is shown in Figure 18–1 to include both the error conditions associated with the character received and the received character itself. The character in the Receiver Buffer Register was in the FIFO buffer before it was placed in this register.

Logically, the following functions must be provided to control a multiline interface:

initialize device

enable line

read from line

write to line

disable line

clear device

The initialize device and clear device are often provided by the operating system when the operating system is loaded (**booted**). The enabling of a particular line is done upon request by either the operating system or by a particular user request.

An I/O driver for such an interface would likely consist of the following routines:

MLINIT

MLENABLE(LINE,EFLAG,SPEED,PARITY,CLEN)

MLDSABLE(LINE,EFLAG)

MLREAD(LINE,MODE,EFLAG,RBUFFER,RLEN)

MLWRITE(LINE,EFLAG,WBUFFER,WLEN)

MLRINT

MLWINT

MLCLEAR

The device initialization could be done by an application which has complete control of the interface via an **initialization routine**, say, MLINIT. Or the operating system could provide for this initialization either via a command or automatically upon initial loading of the operating system. In any case, initialization involves clearing the device, setting the addresses of the **receiver** (read) **interrupt handler** MLRINT and the **transmit** (write) **interrupt handler** MLWINT into the appropriate interrupt vector or first-level interrupt handler (this is machine-dependent), and then enabling the device for interrupts (both on the transmit and receive side). No interrupts can occur until a line is enabled using MLENABLE, i.e., when a particular application has enabled a line for use. The MLENABLE routine must specify the LINE to be enabled, and if programmable, the SPEED at which the line is to operate, the PARITY (if any), and the length of characters in bits (CLEN). The parameter EFLAG in this case will be a return code indicating the success or failure of the requested enabling of the line. Conditions under which enabling a line fails include: invalid parameters and a line that is already enabled.

The MLREAD and MLWRITE routines receive input from and put output to a particular line. The particular design to be illustrated assumes that the event flag EFLAG can be checked by the program during execution to see if the I/O operation to a particular line has been completed. This allows program execution and I/O operation to continue **concurrently** (in an interleaved manner).

The MODE parameter in the MLREAD is used to indicate if the routine is interacting with a terminal, in which case the receiver interrupt routine must process such things as backspace and delete characters and echo them appropriately on the terminal. This will be covered later. Also, the MODE parameter can specify if the terminal is to have echoing to a CRT or printer enabled on the transmit side, assuming the terminal is operating in full-duplex.

Software Design Techniques for Supporting Multiple Lines

Software controlling a multiline interface must initiate read and write requests to specific lines on the interface and keep track of the necessary parameters (buffer address, data count, etc.) associated with a particular I/O operation on a given line. The logic of the receiver and transmitter modules of a multiline interface I/O driver are similar to the corresponding modules of a single line asynchronous interface. What must be added is the multiple line support.

Using data structures (control blocks) concepts from operating system implementation, it is relatively straightforward to support multiple lines with common interrupt handlers using re-entrant coding techniques. The use of such control blocks will be outlined in detail. For every line supported on a multiline interface, there must be a **control block** which represents the "activity" of that line to the software controlling the interface. Figure 18–2 illustrates the structure of a **line control block (LCB)**, a data structure representing a line controlled by the software.

FIGURE 18–2   Structure of a Line Control Block (LCB)

Line Control Block Format	Symbolic Name*
Device Register (Line) (Address)	LINE
Receiver Buffer Register (Address)	IN-CHAR **
Transmitter Buffer Register (Address)	OUT-CHAR **
Event Flag (Address)	EFLAG **
Input Buffer (Address)	IN-BUFFER **
Requested Input Count (Address)	IN-LENGTH **
Pointer to Current Input Location	IN-POINTER
Current Input Count	IN-COUNT
Output Buffer (Address)	OUT-BUFFER **
Requested Output Count	OUT-LENGTH
Pointer to Current Output Location	OUT-POINTER
Current Output Count	OUTPUT-COUNT
Mode (Transmit or Receive; Block or Terminal; Echo or No-Echo)	MODE
Backspace Sequence Indicator	BS
Input Pointer for Ring Buffer	RING-IN
Output Pointer for Ring Buffer	RING-OUT
Size of Ring Buffer	RING-SIZE
Ring Buffer	RING
Ring Count	RING-COUNT

* Symbols designated by ** will likely be addresses and will require some form of indirect addressing when referenced in various modules in the following figures.

A mapping table is used by the MLREAD and MLWRITE routines and the interrupt handlers MLRINT and MLWINT to determine the control block representing the line being serviced. On any given interrupt, either the Transmitter Control/Status Register or the Receiver Control/Status Register, depending on whether it is a Transmit or Receive interrupt, contains the line number of the interrupting line. This line number can be used as an index into a table containing addresses of the respective Line Control Blocks for each line (in assembler language) or as an index into an array, each element being the control block for a line N (in higher level languages). Figure 18–3 illustrates this mapping.

FIGURE 18–3   Determining the Address of Line Control Block Using Address Table

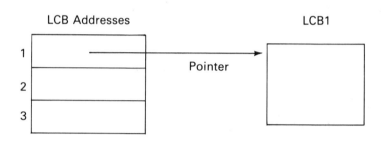

In the figures which follow, the logic is illustrated with pseudocode and this pseudocode will always use the symbolic names shown in Figure 18–2. Actual implementations will require indirect addressing to reference the parameters passed to MLREAD and MLWRITE in interrupt handler routines MLRINT and MLWINT. To simplify the notation in these figures, all references to variables use direct (address) references to the symbolic names listed in Figure 18–2, even though symbols designated with ** will be addresses stored in the LCB requiring indirect addressing.

Re-entrant coding techniques require that all data areas be located outside of the re-entrant module, i.e., must be pointed to by a register. The use of the LCBs provides the means for determining what line is being serviced by a given routine at a specific time, particularly in the interrupt handlers, so that the address can be placed in a register to be used by the common re-entrant portion of the interrupt handler.

Figure 18–4 provides pseudocode to illustrate how a multiline interface might be set up and controlled for a particular application. The variable names used in this figure are consistent with the symbolic names listed in Figure 18–2, i.e., a name $NAME$ is the same as the name of an element in the control block for a line L which is later referenced in the interrupt handlers MLRINT and MLWINT by using the form NAME(L). This should simplify the the association of parameters used in calling

FIGURE 18—4   Logic for Controlling a Line on a Multiline Interface

```
CALL MLINIT     /* Initialize Interface */
CALL MLENABLE(1,EFLAG,2400,"ODD",8)          /* ENABLE LINE 1 AT 2400 bps */
DO UNTIL OUT-BUFFER = "*STOP"
    IN-LENGTH = 80
    CALL MLREAD(1,EFLAG,IN-BUFFER,IN-LENGTH)
    DO WHILE EFLAG = 0                              /* LOOP ON BUSY */
    END

    OUT-BUFFER = IN-BUFFER
    OUT-LENGTH = IN-LENGTH
    CALL MLWRITE(1,EFLAG,OUT-BUFFER,OUT-LENGTH)
    DO WHILE EFLAG = 0                              /* LOOP ON BUSY */
    END
END

CALL MLCLEAR                                       /* CLEAR DEVICE */
```

MLREAD and MLWRITE with the references later in MLRINT and MLWINT using control block entries for a line L.

The CALL MLINIT in the program in Figure 18—4 is the initialization of the interface. Here it is assumed that the user has complete control of the interface and the interface is not initialized by the operating system itself. Had it been a function of the operating system at startup time, this call to MLINIT would not be necessary. MLINIT will set up interrupt vectors and reset the device for initial use.

Once the device is initialized, an application (or system) program cannot use a specific line unless it is enabled, just as a disk file cannot be used unless it is first opened. The MLENABLE routine activates a particular line, setting its characteristics upon enabling the line. If the capabilities exist, the line speed, character length, parity, and the length of the stop bits are set. Sometimes many of these characteristics are strapped (selected) on the hardware interface and cannot be changed by software. In this case, a specific line will always operate with fixed (hardware) characteristics, e.g., 1200 bps, odd parity, with 8-bit characters and a stop bit length of 1.5. Some software implementations associate a **logical unit** or line number with a particular line that is mapped to a physical line number. This allows more flexibility in dealing with lines, since the programmer can refer to them in I/O operations without knowing exactly what physical line is connected. This could be useful for supporting specific users who may be assigned specific **logical line numbers** with certain authority which can only connect to specific **physical line numbers** at specific locations.

Block Mode

There are two possibilities for data transmission and reception on one of the lines of an interface: either data is being sent to and from an interactive terminal, or data is being sent in fixed-length blocks (perhaps with a protocol) to another computer system or some specialized device. The simplest case is that of **block transmission**, because as will soon be discussed, controlling a terminal involves some special logic for handling corrections (backspaces or deletes) and variable-length input strings (usually terminated by a carriage return). The MODE parameter of MLREAD is used to specify if a line is operating in block mode or terminal mode.

Since using fixed-length blocks is the simplest, assume that the program in Figure 18–4 receives a block of data of length IN-LENGTH into a buffer IN-BUFFER using MLREAD. It then moves the received data into the output area OUT-BUFFER and transmits the same number of characters received back to the sending system using MLWRITE. Figure 18–5 illustrates the simple receive-a-block, send-a-block sequence.

Consider that the MLREAD routine must start the receive operation on the specific line being controlled. The progress of data received is hereafter controlled by the interrupt handler MLRINT. Hence, MLREAD must set up the parameters to be used by the interrupt handler, as shown in Figure 18–6, mainly the address of the receive buffer IN-BUFFER (2 in Figure 18–6), the number of bytes to read (3), IN-LENGTH, and the address of the event flag EFLAG (4) to be used to report the operation complete by the interrupt handler MLRINT. The MODE for the line must be set to indicate a receive is active in either block or terminal mode (5). If not already enabled, the receiver hardware must also be enabled. This enabling depends on whether or not the ring buffer concept discussed later is implemented.

FIGURE 18–5   Simple Send/Receive Program in Block Transfer Mode

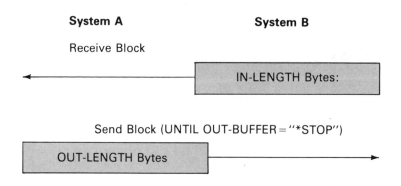

System A

Receive Block

← IN-LENGTH Bytes:

Send Block (UNTIL OUT-BUFFER = "*STOP")

OUT-LENGTH Bytes →

System B

FIGURE 18–6   Logic of Block Transfer Receive Routine

MLREAD

If LINE busy or Line Not Enabled		1
THEN RETURN to Caller with EFLAG = Error		
Save Buffer Address	(IN-BUFFER)	2
Save Read Length Address	(IN-LENGTH)	3
Save Event Flag Address	(EFLAG)	4
Indicate Receive in Progress	(MODE)	5
Return to Caller with EFLAG = 0		6

When a programmer uses the Line Control Block concept illustrated in Figure 18–2, every line has specific control block elements in which MLREAD saves these parameters. Once the parameters are saved, the MLREAD routine will show the receiver active in the control block (MODE) and possibly enable the line for receive in hardware. The line may or may not be enabled for receive depending on whether the ring buffer feature implied in Figure 18–2 is implemented. If so, the receiver side of a line is enabled in hardware whenever the line is enabled. Characters arriving prior to a read request are buffered in a ring buffer (circular FIFO buffer) RING, which helps to prevent loss of characters in software in a manner similar to the way the FIFO buffer does in hardware. While this is perhaps more useful in a terminal environment (to allow "key ahead"), it could be activated in block transfer mode. This is discussed in more detail later in this chapter.

The sample logic in Figure 18–4 shows the program looping when the value of the event flag EFLAG is 0. This looping represents **idle time**, when the computer system is doing no useful work. It is possible for "useful" work to be done during this period before this flag is checked, e.g., another message transmission could be started on another line. This illustrates the system's ability to do data transfer on several lines, do some processing, and then come back and service a read or write request started earlier on a line. The result of this is that data is received "simultaneously" from multiple sources. Later, when we discuss terminal control, users will appear to have simultaneous control of the system as they do in any timesharing system.

In block transfer mode, the event flag EFLAG will remain zero until set to a nonzero value by the interrupt handler MLRINT once it has received the number of characters specified by the parameter IN-LENGTH. Figure 18–7 illustrates the logic of the receive interrupt handler MLRINT.

Just how the appropriate control block is pointed to is language-dependent. In assembler language, a register is used. In higher level languages, pointers or subscripts might be used. In any case, the LCB data structure describes the state of a line to MLRINT — in particular, the number of characters received, the next location into which to place the next character and the maximum number of characters to receive.

FIGURE 18–7   Basic Logic of MLRINT

```
MLRINT
    Save All                                               1
    Determine Line Number L causing Interrupt             2
            (Point to Line Control Block)
    IF Error on line L THEN DO                             3
        Clear MODE(L)                                      4
        Set EFLAG(L) = ERROR                              5
        Restore All                                        6
        Return from Interrupt                             7
    END                                                    8
    Place IN-CHAR into IN-BUFFER(L,IN-POINTER(L))         9
    Advance IN-POINTER(L) by 1                            10
    Increment IN-COUNT(L)                                 11
    IF IN-COUNT(L) = IN-LENGTH(L) THEN DO                12
        Clear MODE(L)                                     13
        Set EFLAG(L) = 1                                  14
    END                                                   15
    Restore All                                           16
    Return from Interrupt                                 17
```

The last parameter used by the interrupt handler MLRINT is the event flag EFLAG, which is used to communicate the completion of the receive operation to the program using the line.

Referring to Figure 18–7, note that each receiver interrupt for this line signals the presence of another character to be placed in the user's input buffer. After the interrupting line number L has been determined (the pointer to L's LCB has been set), a check for an error on the received character is made (3); if an error occurred, the read is terminated (4–5) and a return from interrupt is done (6–7). If no error occurred, the received character is stored (9), the input pointer is advanced (10), and the input character count is incremented (11) and checked against the maximum count (12). If the input character count is equal to the requested count, then the requested operation is finished and the MODE is cleared (13), indicating no operation is in progress, the Event Flag is set (as pointed to by the control block) to communicate to the applications program that the read is complete (14), and a return is made to the interrupted program (16–17). If there is more data to receive and no error has occurred, a return is made to the interrupted program (16–17) with MODE and EFLAG still indicating a receiver operation is in progress. In the latter case, since the event flag has not been set, the sample program shown in Figure 18–4 will still be looping on the zero value in EFLAG.

Transmit Block Mode

The logic for the transmit block mode of MLWRITE is shown in Figure 18–8.

FIGURE 18–8   Logic of Block Transfer Transmit Routine

```
MLWRITE
    If LINE busy or Line Not Enabled,
     THEN RETURN to Caller with EFLAG = Error
    Save Buffer Address            (OUT-BUFFER)
    Save Write Length Address      (OUT-LENGTH)
    Save Event Flag Address        (EFLAG)
    Indicate Transmit in Progress  (MODE)
                 (Enable Transmitter)
    Return to Caller with EFLAG = 0
```

The logic of MLWRITE is similar to MLREAD because it basically sets up the transmit operation in a similar manner to the way MLREAD set up the receive operation. It is the interrupt handlers MLRINT and MLWINT that do all the I/O. Hence, MLWRITE returns to the caller with the appropriate value for the EFLAG.

The transmitter for the line which has been enabled for transmit will eventually interrupt, indicating it is ready for another character to be sent. The logic of MLWINT is shown in Figure 18–9.

FIGURE 18–9   Basic Logic of MLWINT

```
MLWINT
    Save ALL                                              1
    Determine Line Number L causing Interrupt             2
    IF OUT-COUNT(L) = OUT-LENGTH(L) THEN DO               3
      Clear MODE(L)                                       4
      Clear Transmit Enable for Line L                    5
      SET EFLAG(L) = 1                                    6
    END                                                   7
    ELSE DO                                               8
      Advance OUT-POINTER(L)                              9
      Move OUT-BUFFER(L,OUT-POINTER(L)) to OUT-CHAR      10
      Increment OUT-COUNT(L)                             11
    END                                                  12
    Restore All                                          13
    Return from Interrupt                                14
```

The transmitter interrupt handler MLWINT checks to see if all characters have been sent (3). If so, it clears the transmitter (MODE and transmit enable for this line) (4–5), sets the event flag (6) and returns from the interrupt (13–14). If another character is to be sent (8), the pointer is advanced (9), the character is sent (10), the the count is incremented (11), and MLWINT returns from interrupt (13–14).

Ring Buffer

As mentioned previously, it is possible to allow the receiver interrupt handler do software buffering of characters received from a line while the line has no MLREAD pending. To implement this, a simple **FIFO circular buffer** or **ring buffer** RING is set up for each line with two pointers: an input pointer RING-IN, used by MLRINT to place characters into the ring buffer, and an output pointer RING-OUT, which is used by MLREAD to take characters from the ring buffer. (Later it will be seen that in terminal mode, RING-OUT is also used by the transmitter interrupt handler MLWINT.) This ring buffer concept is illustrated in Figure 18–10.

Initially RING-OUT = RING-IN. There is also a ring buffer counter, RING-COUNT, which contains the number of characters in the ring buffer and a ring buffer size, RING-SIZE, which contains the size of the ring buffer. If RING-OUT = RING-IN and RING-COUNT = 0, then the ring buffer is empty. When RING-OUT = RING-IN and RING-COUNT = RING-SIZE, then the ring buffer is full. In the latter case, another character being received before a character is removed from the ring buffer results in a **ring buffer overflow**, which is similar to the hardware FIFO full condition.

If the ring buffer concept is implemented in MLRINT, then when MLREAD initializes for a read, it must check to see if characters have been previously placed in the ring buffer. If characters are in the ring buffer (RING-COUNT › 0) then any characters in RING up to IN-LENGTH should be taken from the ring buffer and placed into the receiver buffer (IN-BUFFER in Figure 18–4) before MLREAD indicates that a

FIGURE 18–10   Use of FIFO Ring Buffer for Receiver

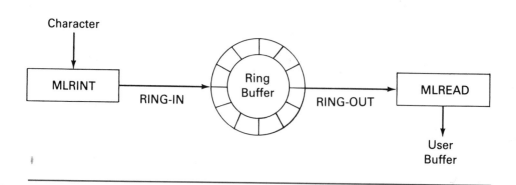

receiver operation is in progress on the line (by setting MODE). Note that the order in which RING-OUT is advanced and RING-COUNT is decremented in MLREAD is important, since interrupts can occur while instructions are being executed in MLREAD and these interrupts can result in the changing of RING-IN and RING-COUNT. In some cases, interrupts may have to be blocked for the line being serviced by MLREAD to adjust RING-OUT. If MLREAD uses the following:

> Move RING(L,RING-OUT(L)) to IN-BUFFER(L)
> Increment RING-OUT(L)(Modulo RING-SIZE(L))
> Decrement RING-COUNT(L)

where RING(I,J) is the Jth character of the ring buffer for line I. Assuming that the decrement of RING-COUNT is a single indivisible hardware operation (as on the PDP-11), then MLRINT can use

> IF RING-COUNT(L) = RING-SIZE(L) THEN ERROR
> Increment RING-IN(L)(Modulo RING-SIZE(L))
> Move CHARACTER to RING(L,RING-IN(L))
> Increment RING-COUNT(L)

so that the input pointer is advanced by MLRINT, the output pointer is advanced by MLREAD and the count is incremented and decremented by these two coroutines in a single indivisible operation. The result is that the counter will be adjusted correctly. Note that if the increment and decrement are interruptible in the middle of its execution, e.g., if a higher level language performs these operations with multiple hardware instructions, then a critical section problem exists in the operation of MLREAD and MLRINT, in which case the use of primitives P and V (LOCK and UNLOCK) will be necessary. Readers unfamiliar with such concepts should consult Deitel or Habermann [Deitel 1983, pp. 89ff; Habermann 1976, pp. 71–78].

The ring buffer concept has some use in the block transfer mode. However, it is in the terminal I/O mode that it is most valuable. This is discussed in the next section.

Controlling Terminals

Controlling interactive terminals on either a single line asynchronous interface or a multiline interface is not simply a matter of counting bytes transmitted or received, as was done in the block transfer mode. Users making errors and backspacing over previously entered characters and the need to be able to operate in a full-duplex environment in which characters keyed are received by the computer system and transmitted back to the screen or display are exceptions that require careful processing of the characters being transmitted and received. In a full-duplex environment, it is also desirable to be able to suppress the echo for security reasons during the entry of such fields as passwords.

Figure 18–11 illustrates the flow of data keyed from a terminal, processed by the receiver interrupt handler MLRINT, "echoed" back to the terminal, and processed by the transmitter interrupt handler MLWINT as a result of the echo.

FIGURE 18–11   Data Flow on Receive of Character from a Terminal

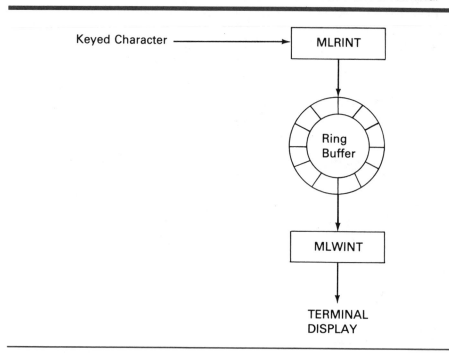

Figure 18–11 shows the received data flowing through the ring buffer prior to being handled for output on the **echo**. The design of the receiver interrupt handler is simplified if all output to the transmitter is handled by MLWINT. The receiver merely needs to enable transmit for the line requiring echoing of characters if transmit is not already enabled. In this case, MLRINT uses the RING-IN pointer and MLWINT uses the RING-OUT pointer. There is no critical section problem in manipulating the data in this buffer, because the manipulation of two different pointers by mutually exclusive routines cannot erroneously update these pointers. Again the increment and decrement of RING-COUNT by MLRINT and MLWINT must be single indivisible operations or MLRINT and MLWINT must not be able to interrupt each other while the increment and decrement is executing.

Use of Line Control Blocks

The use of line control blocks (LCBs) to represent the activity of a line simplifies the programming for controlling terminals. Once the line is determined, the routines proceed as if they were handling a single line. Whether interrupts occur at 300 or at 1200 a second, the programmer merely needs to think in terms of processing a single interrupt. The cpu will handle the invoking of the interrupt routines via the automatic interrupt mechanism.

A multiline interface I/O driver can be implemented so that it will support both block transfers and interactive terminals. The MODE indicator within each line control block can be added as a parameter in the MLREAD and MLWRITE routines to indicate if a given line is in block transfer or interactive mode. Note that for output, the operation is the same for block transfer and terminal mode. The MLREAD routine must set the MODE indicator in the LCB for the appropriate line. It must also save the buffer address, maximum read input data count address, and the address of the event flag in the LCB. If there are characters in the RING buffer, the MLREAD routine must enable transmit interrupts so that the input characters may be processed for echo, counted, and placed in the input buffer by the transmit interrupt handler MLWINT. Once this is done, all further processing is handled by the interrupt handlers MLRINT and MLWINT.

Design of Interrupt Handlers

Figure 18–11 illustrated the flow of data through the interrupt handlers: the processing of the input character by the receiver interrupt handler MLRINT, which places it into the ring buffer, and then the removal of the character from the ring buffer for echoing (if enabled) of the character and placement into the user buffer by the transmit interrupt handler MLWINT.

Figure 18–12 outlines the logic of the receiver interrupt handler MLRINT for processing in terminal mode using the ring buffer. It is assumed in Figure 18–12 that all received characters will be processed by the transmitter interrupt handler MLWINT before being placed in the user buffer.

Note that the processing in the receiver interrupt handler shown in Figure 18–12 is very simple. The transmit interrupt handler ends up doing most of the work when this ring buffer design is used for terminal mode. Notice that even for the case where echoing is not

FIGURE 18–12   Logic of Receiver Interrupt Handler for Terminal Mode

MLRINT

    Save All
    Determine Line Number L
    IF RING-COUNT(L) = RING-SIZE(L) THEN Error
    Increment RING-IN(L) (Modulo RING-SIZE(L))
    Move INPUT-CHAR to RING(L,RING-IN(L))
    Increment RING-COUNT(L)
    IF MODE(L) = TERM-ECHO OR MODE(L) = TERM-NOECHO
     Enable Transmit for Line L
    Restore All
    Return from Interrupt

desired, processing is still left to the transmit interrupt handler. This is so that common logic for both echo and no-echo modes can be used when processing terminal input. This is accomplished by echoing the NULL (000) character if NO-ECHO is specified. Terminals do not display the NULL character, but an interrupt will be generated by the interface exactly as if the character itself had been echoed. This decision to echo NULLs is made by the transmit interrupt handler, which checks the MODE to see if the code indicates TER-MINAL-ECHO or TERMINAL-NOECHO. Figure 18–13 illustrates the logic of the transmitter coroutine interrupt handler for **terminal mode**.

Once it is determined that the line is operating in terminal mode, the interrupt handler echoes some character (the character in the ring buffer [25 in Figure 18–13] or a NULL [26], depending on whether MODE indicates echoing is enabled or not). This echoing will cause another transmitter interrupt, which will be processed later. The input character is then taken from the ring buffer and placed in the user's input buffer in the location pointed to by the current input pointer IN-POINTER in the LCB (27). The count of the number of characters stored in IN-BUFFER is incremented (28), and the pointer to the next character position in IN-BUFFER is advanced (29).

Notice that the input of data in terminal mode will terminate when one of two conditions is reached: either the number of characters placed into the input buffer is equal to the maximum count specified (4), or the next character to be processed is a carriage return (15). In this specific example, carriage returns (octal 015) are not echoed to the screen, which allows a program to format the screen by leaving the cursor at the position of the last character entered.

Backspace/Delete Processing

On an interactive CRT terminal, some key is used to make the previous character "disappear" from the screen when echoing is enabled. (Normally, this is the backspace or delete key but it can be defined as another key on some systems.) The easiest way to make a character disappear is to have the transmit interrupt handler echo a backspace, space, backspace, i.e., three characters are echoed for each backspace (and/or delete) processed. The problem with this is that three interrupts must be processed, one for each of the echoed characters. The transmit interrupt handler must remember that it was in a backspace sequence and which of the three characters in this sequence it was processing. Perhaps the easiest mechanism for this is to use a BS indicator, which has three nonzero values if a backspace is in process: 1 means processing first backspace, 2 processing space, and 3 means processing the last backspace. A value of 0 in BS indicates no backspace processing is in progress.

The logic of the interrupt handler must take this into account prior to processing any further characters out of the ring buffer. Figure 18–14 illustrates the backspace processing sequence which must be added to the interrupt handler MLWINT illustrated in Figure 18–13.

The sequence is handled simply by not advancing the RING-OUT pointer until the backspace is fully processed and by having the appropriate statement or statements test BS (IF or CASE statements) to determine where the sequence is in handling the backspace. Echoing the last backspace results in the BS indicator being cleared and the

FIGURE 18–13   Transmit Interrupt Handler Logic for Terminal Mode
Processing

```
MLWINT
    Save All                                                              1
    Determine Line Number L                                              2
    IF MODE(L) = TERMINAL-ECHO or MODE(L) = TERMINAL-NOECHO             3
    THEN DO
        IF IN-COUNT(N) = IN-LENGTH(L) THEN DO                           4
            Disable Transmitter for Line L                              5
            Clear MODE(L)                                               6
            Move IN-COUNT(L) to IN-LENGTH(L)                            7
            Set EFLAG(L)                                                8
            Restore all                                                 9
            Return from Interrupt                                      10
        END                                                            11
    IF RING-COUNT(L)>0 THEN DO                                         12
        Increment RING-OUT(L)(Modulo RING-SIZE)(L)                    13
        Decrement RING-COUNT(L)                                       14
        IF RING(L,RING-OUT(L)) = Carriage Return                      15
        THEN DO                                                       16
            Disable Transmitter for Line L                            17
            Clear MODE(L)                                             18
            Move IN-COUNT(L) to IN-LENGTH(L)                          19
            Set EFLAG(L) = 1                                          20
            Restore All                                               21
            Return from Interrupt                                     22
        END                                                           23
        IF MODE(L) = TERMINAL-ECHO THEN                               24
            Move RING(L,RING-OUT(L)) to OUT-CHAR                      25
        ELSE Move NULL to OUT-CHAR                                    26
        Move RING(L,RING-OUT(L)) to IN-BUFFER(L,IN-POINTER(L))        27
        Increment IN-COUNT(L)                                         28
        Increment IN-POINTER(L)                                       29
    END                                                               30
    END                                                               31
    Restore All                                                       32
    Return from Interrupt                                             33
```

RING-OUT pointer being advanced past the current backspace (or delete), which will
have been completely processed upon the occurrence of the interrupt from the echoing
of this last backspace character.

Obviously, the logic for processing for block transfer and terminal mode should be
combined in the driver being discussed. The reader is left the task of figuring this out.
Appendix E outlines a project to do just that.

FIGURE 18–14   Logic for Backspace Processing Routine for Transmit
Interrupt Handler

```
IF RING(L,RING-OUT(L)) = BACKSPACE THEN DO
   BS = BS + 1
   IF BS = 1 THEN Move BACKSPACE to OUT-CHAR
   IF BS = 2 THEN Move SPACE      to OUT-CHAR
   IF BS = 3 THEN DO
      Move BACKSPACE to OUT-CHAR
      BS = 0
      Increment RING-OUT(L)(Modulo RING-SIZE(L))
   END
END
Restore All
Return from Interrupt
```

Applying Techniques to Single Line Interfaces

The techniques for implementing the software for asynchronous multiline interfaces described in this chapter can be applied to multiple single line interfaces. Once the device causing the interrupt is determined (using an interrupt vectoring technique to a first level handler) control can be passed to a second level interrupt handler with a register (in assembler language) or a line number N (in "C," Pascal, etc.) pointing to the LCB representing the line (interface) being serviced. Added to the LCB will be the address of the device being serviced (e.g., for the PDP-11, the address of its receiver and transmit control registers). Hence, the second level interrupt handlers are re-entrant routines implemented using the techniques described previously.

Modem Control

Many asynchronous interfaces provide modem control. Minimum capability for controlling modems usually includes being able to set and/or detect Data Terminal Ready, Clear to Send, Carrier, and Request to Send. A line status register for each line must be able to provide information on these RS-232 signals and allow the setting of conditions such as RTS.

Direct Memory Access (DMA) Capability

Multiline interfaces could be implemented with **Direct Memory Access (DMA)** capability. In this case, two additional registers would be needed in servicing a line: an address register and a byte-count register. Normally these would be implemented on the receive side, because it is usually necessary to monitor characters on the receive side as they arrive. If a memory address were updated to indicate the last character stored in memory via a DMA receive transfer, then a periodic monitoring (timer interrupt/task dispatch) could be done and DMA could indeed be supported on the receive side.

≡ Terminology ≡

block transmission
boot
concurrently
control bits
control block
direct memory access
DMA
echo
FIFO circular buffer
FIFO full alarm
FIFO full alarm enable
idle time
initialization routine
interrupt enable bit
interrupt handler
LCB
line control block
Line Parameter Register
logical unit
logical line number
multiline asynchronous hardware
    interface

physical line number
receiver interrupt handler
Receiver Buffer Register
Receiver Control/Status Register
Receiver Ready
ring buffer
ring buffer overflow
status bits
terminal mode
transmitter interrupt handler
Transmit Line Number
Transmitter Break Control
    Register
Transmitter Buffer Register
Transmitter Control/Status
    Register
Transmitter Line Control
    Register
Transmitter Ready

≡ Review Questions ≡

1. List five device registers for a multiline asynchronous interface. What are the purposes of each?

2. Why is it generally not possible to use a FIFO on the transmit side of a multiline asynchronous interface?

3. What is a FIFO overrun? What is the cause of it?

4. How are data structures used to implement a multiline interface software driver? Use a high-level language like Pascal or "C" to represent such data structures.

5. How does the control of a line attached to a terminal differ from the control of a line attached to another computer which is sending and receiving data files?

6. What is a ring buffer? What is its primary purpose in implementing software for a multiline interface?

7. How can the concepts presented in this chapter be applied in supporting multiple single line interfaces? Be specific.

═══ Assignment ═══

Implement the project for supporting a multiline interface described in Appendix E. Be sure to used data structures, interrupt handlers, and modular design in implementing this project.

References

Deitel, Harvey M. 1984. *An Introduction to Operating Systems.* Reading, Massachusetts: Addison-Wesley.

Habermann, A. N. 1976. *Introduction to Operating System Design.* Chicago: Science Research Associates.

19

Asynchronous Terminal Emulators

Introduction • Background • Options Available in Terminal Emulators •
Selecting Line Speed • Character Length • Parity • Duplex • XON/XOFF
• Command vs. Interactive Mode • Sending and Receiving Files •
Implementing Terminal Emulators

Introduction

The term "emulate" deals with "the ability of one system to imitate another, with the imitating system accepting the same data and programming and achieving the same results as the imitated system, but with possibly a different time performance" [Sippl and Sippl 1972]. As a result of the microcomputer revolution, a common software product has become available on most small computers — the **terminal emulator**.

A terminal emulator allows a given computer to "look like" a computer terminal, thus eliminating the need to purchase another piece of equipment to communicate to other computers. The term "terminal emulator" implies that the software allows a computer to replace a terminal. While this is indeed the case, many additional functions are provided in such emulators. The most important feature is the ability to transmit and receive files between computers. This is particularly useful in moving data from one computer system to another during a conversion to new hardware.

The purpose of this chapter is to provide information on how such an emulator can be implemented. The flow of information within such an emulator is of particular interest.

Background

The terminal emulator is indeed one of the most useful software packages which exists for microcomputers today. While called by different names, these packages all provide the same basic functions for communicating to other computer systems.

Just ten short years ago, conversion of data from one system to another was a very difficult task because of the incompatibility of computer media available on many systems. It was often necessary to write specialized communications software to use a communications link to move data from one computer to another.

Such is not the case today. Virtually all microcomputers available provide an **RS-232 serial interface** and some terminal emulation software package to make the computer look like a terminal to another computer system. Being able to access various computing services, like timesharing, investment systems, Western Union telex, etc., is obviously a valuable capability. What makes the emulators even more valuable is their ability to receive and transmit data files from disk or diskette. Hence, the ability to move or "convert" data from one system to another becomes relatively simple with the use of such emulator packages. Figure 19–1 illustrates how a terminal (keyboard and display) is interfaced to a microcomputer so that information entered on the keyboard is sent over an asynchronous communications line to another computer and is received back to the CRT display on the microcomputer (operating in full-duplex with echoing).

While the terminal emulators do provide a wide variety of capabilities, it is necessary to properly **configure** (set up) these programs to be compatible with the computer system to which the emulator will be communicating.

Options Available in Terminal Emulators

Terminal emulators provide for a setup or configuration process to set various parameters for communications. Included in the setup options are such things as speed, number of bits per character, parity, duplex, and **XON/XOFF** transmission control.

Selecting Line Speed

The communication speed between two systems is specified in bits per second (and sometimes baud — see Chapter 7). The selection of speed is usually one of the following: 110, 300, 600, 1200, 2400, 4800, 9600, 19,200 bits per second. Be sure you select the appro-

FIGURE 19–1   Data Movement Using Terminal Emulator Operating in Full-Duplex With Echoing

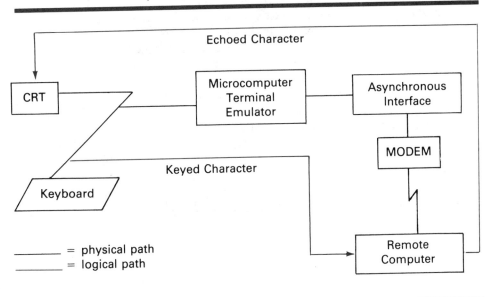

priate speed, which must be identical to the speed of the system (and modem, if one is being used) to which the emulator and microcomputer will communicate.

Character Length

The choices for character length indicate the number of bits in a data character (not counting parity). The choices are usually 5, 6, 7, or 8, with 7 and 8 being the most common selections today. Since ASCII is a seven-bit code and usually uses a parity bit (see next section), systems using ASCII usually require 8 bits per data character. ASCII-based systems usually use parity so that a high-order eighth bit is appended (see next section).

IBM mainframe systems use EBCDIC (Extended Binary Coded Decimal Interchange Code), which is an eight-bit code, and hence require the use of 8 bits per data character.

Parity

As indicated in Chapter 4 on error detection, parity allows the high-order bit of a character to be set to a specific parity (even or odd). Recall that in even parity, the sum of the one bits in a character including the parity bit must be even. In odd parity, this sum must be odd. The parity bit in each case is set to the appropriate value to yield the desired parity. The receiving system and software will check this parity bit if parity checking is enabled. Hence, the parity must be set correctly if either system checks parity.

The choices for selecting parity are: EVEN, ODD, NONE, MARK, SPACE, and IGNORE. If EVEN, ODD, MARK, SPACE, or IGNORE is selected, the number of bits transmitted and received for each character is one more than the number of bits in a data character. For example, if the data character length is seven, a high-order bit is appended to the character for parity. In the case of EVEN or ODD parity, the parity will be set even or odd, respectively. In the case of IGNORE, it is undefined but usually zero. Some emulators allow the setting of the parity bit to always one (MARK) or always zero (SPACE).

The other option is NONE, which yields no parity bit at all. Note that the use of 8-bit characters with no parity is more or less equivalent to the use of 7-bit characters with parity ignored or always set to either zero or one.

If uncertain of the parity required by a specific system, a user can start with 7-bit characters with odd parity. If this yields incorrect communication (strange characters), try 7-bit with even parity. One of the two will usually work correctly. If this fails, the best choice is either 7 bits ignore parity or 8 bits no parity. Note that if the remote system is using a different character code (e.g., EBCDIC instead of ASCII), the character codes, not the parity, are incompatible.

Duplex

The selection of duplex is usually done by choosing one of: **full-duplex**, **half-duplex**, or **full-duplex with local echo**. In a full-duplex environment, the characters transmitted from a terminal are received by the remote computer system and transmitted back to the display of the terminal or microcomputer. This is possible since the communications link supports simultaneous data transmission in both directions. The computer system, therefore, controls the display of the local terminal or microcomputer. This is best, since then the appropriate backspace (delete, backspace, etc.) will echo correctly by backspacing over the previous character, printing a blank, and then backspacing again so that the deleted character is erased from the display.

Another advantage of full-duplex is that echoing can be suspended at certain times for security reasons. For example, it would be best if a password were not echoed to a display. The logon software of a remote computer can suspend echoing when a password is being entered and turn echoing back on after the password has been accepted.

Half-duplex and full-duplex with local echo have the characters displayed locally by the microcomputer on its display. Hence, if a backspace character is entered, the local terminal will back up to the previous character but not erase it. However, the computer system to which the emulator is communicating may not use backspace to delete a character (e.g., it may use delete [DEL]), and although it appears on the screen that the character was deleted, the computer system will have a command which includes a backspace character and will likely reject it.

Half-duplex and full-duplex local echo differ in that the former allows either transmission or reception of information at any given time, but not both at the same time. Full-duplex local echo will allow transmission of characters while receiving characters from the other computer system. Note that both half-duplex and full-duplex with local echo will always result in passwords being displayed on terminals, which makes security in entering passwords difficult.

Choosing full-duplex with a system which does not echo back the characters results in characters not being displayed on a CRT display when a character is entered in characters on the keyboard. Choosing half-duplex or full-duplex local echo when the system does echo back characters will result in each keyed character being displayed twice on the display. If either of these conditions result, change the duplex accordingly.

XON/XOFF

In communicating between one computer and another and between a computer and a terminal, it is possible that the receiving computer or terminal may not be able to handle data coming over the line fast enough to prevent the loss of data (e.g., data is being written to a printer or disk which cannot operate as fast as arrival rate of the data). Many systems provide for the suspension of data transmission by having the receiving system send an **XOFF** (^S — octal 023) to the other system when it is unable to continue receiving data and then transmitting an **XON** (^Q — octal 021) when it is once again able to receive information. A full-duplex environment is required to accomplish this. Selection of XON/XOFF will provide for an emulator sending XOFF and XON to control the data being received and for recognizing XOFF to suspend and XON to resume data transmission.

The use of XON/XOFF is required for the successful transmission and receiving of data from disk files, since the emulator and the remote computer system may not be able to keep up with the arrival rate of data being received. Note that even in a full-duplex environment, the ˆS and ˆQ are not echoed on the display.

Command vs. Interactive Mode

Most terminal emulators have a command mode which controls various functions available in the emulator. Commands usually available include the following:

Enable Printer:	Enables the printer to print data received by the emulator
Disable Printer:	Suspends the printing of data received
Specify Receive File:	Allows the selection of the file to which data is to be received when enabled
Enable Receive File:	Starts the writing of data received to the receive file
Disable Receive File:	Suspends writing of data to the receive file (does not close file)
Terminate Receive File:	Closes receive file
Specify Transmit File:	Allows selection of file to be used for data transmission when enabled
Enable Transmit File:	Enables transmission of data
Disable Transmit File:	Suspends data transmission
Terminate Transmit File:	Terminates transmission of data and closes transmit file
Enter Configuration Mode:	Allows reconfiguration of emulator
Terminate Emulator:	Returns to operating system
Enter Interactive Mode:	Enters mode where true emulation of a terminal takes place (keyboard and display)

There is always a special mechanism which allows the return to command mode from interactive mode. This can be a function key, an escape key or a control sequence. Hence, the user has the ability to transmit information interactively, enter command mode to send a data file, return to interactive mode to send more data interactively, etc. The same is true on the receive side of the terminal emulator.

Sending and Receiving Files

There are some simple ways to transmit a file to and receive a file from a remote computer system. These are illustrated in this section.

Most systems have an editor which has an input mode to collect lines of information keyed by a terminal. A user can invoke such an editor using the interactive mode of the terminal emulator with a sequence similar to the following:

$RUN EDIT
*FILE = TEST$$
*INSERT$$
#

This sequence specifies that a file TEST is being edited and the editor is in insert mode ready to collect information. The user can then select command mode in the terminal emulator, specify a transmit file name (say TEST1), enable file transmission and wait for end-of-file on that file. Upon indication of end-of-file by the terminal emulator, the user returns to interactive mode to enter the terminating character necessary to exit from the insert mode of the editor. For example, this might require

#^Z
*END$$
$

The file named TEST on the remote computer will contain the data from the file TEST1 transmitted by the terminal emulator.

Most computer systems with dial-up terminal capability have a simple TYPE or LIST command. To receive a file from the remote system, proceed as follows:

1. Use interactive mode of the terminal emulator to log on to remote system.
2. Type the command TYPE TEST without the carriage return.
3. Select command mode in the emulator, specify the RECEIVE FILE as TEST2 and enable it.
4. Return to interactive mode and type the carriage return (enter). Data received will also be written to the receive file named TEST2.
5. When receiving of data completes and the remote system types its command prompt select command mode in the terminal emulator and terminate the receive file. The data received from file TEST will be stored in TEST2 on the microcomputer system (including the last operating system prompt from the remote system which can be edited out of the file TEST2 later).

Another technique which works is to use a standard "copy" utility from the terminal or communications line to a disk file and vice versa. For example, the command

CAT › TEST

in UNIX takes information from the terminal and places it in the file TEST. The emulator can transmit the file, and the end-of-file character can be entered interactively from the keyboard on the microcomputer. The commands

COPY COM1:	TEST	(MS-DOS)
COPY TEST	COM1:	(MS-DOS)
PIP COM:	TEST	(CP/M)
PIP TEST	COM:	(CP/M)

FIGURE 19–2   Overview Structure of a Terminal Emulator [Osborne 1983, p. 16]

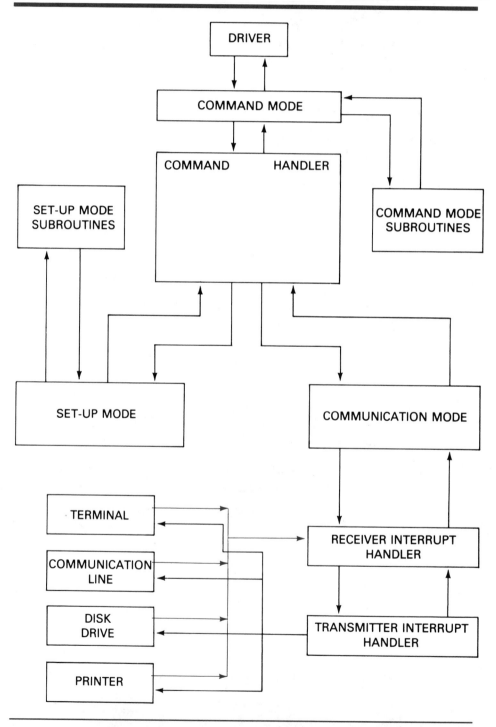

used on today's microcomputers are similar to the UNIX CAT command above and can be used to transfer files between computers. (MS-DOS is a trademark of Microsoft Corporation; CP/M is a trademark of Digital Research Corporation.)

When transferring files between two small computers, the use of a terminal emulator on each proves to be the most successful method of transferring files. A terminal emulator can be run on each microcomputer, with one being set to receive a file while the other is set to transmit a file.

While the above sequences may differ slightly on different computer systems and with different terminal emulators, the basic procedures remain the same. As long as the parameters are set correctly and one system does not outrun the other (by having XON/XOFF enabled), file transfer between systems should be successful.

Implementing Terminal Emulators

Figure 19–2 illustrates an overview of a possible structure for the implementation of a terminal emulator. The receiver and transmitter interrupt handlers become the "work-

FIGURE 19–3   Transfer of Data Character from Receiver Interrupt
Handler to Transmit Interrupt Handler of Another Line

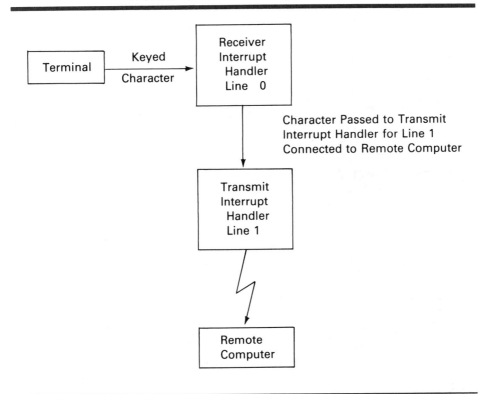

horses" of the emulator. A terminal emulator can be implemented using a multiline interface driver such as discussed in Chapter 18 if the interrupt handlers are modified slightly. The reason modifications are required is that information which is received by the interrupt handler from the line connected to the terminal on the microcomputer must be sent over the line connected to the remote computer, and information received from the line connected to the remote computer must be transmitted to the line connected to the terminal display on the microcomputer.

Hence, information received from one line must now be echoed on another line, i.e., characters received via interrupts from one line on receive must be sent to another line via the transmit interrupt handler for that second line. Figure 19–3 illustrates such data transfer between interrupt handlers.

The use of interrupts allows rapid transfer of data from one line to another. Also, data to be read or written to printers and disks can have the I/O operation to these devices started and monitored by the interrupt handlers.

If a polling technique is used to implement the terminal emulator, it is more likely that data might be lost because of the speed of the transfer of information from the receiver of one line to the transmitter of another and the inability to immediately service data on either line without interrupts. Some architectures may not allow a totally interrupt-driven terminal emulator to be implemented. In such cases, the support of XON/XOFF helps to solve the problem of lost data.

≡ Terminology ≡

configure	terminal emulator
full-duplex	XOFF
full-duplex with local echo	XON
half-duplex	XON/XOFF
RS-232 serial interface	

≡ Review Questions ≡

1. What is a terminal emulator? Describe what must be done to correctly configure a terminal emulator.

2. What will be the result of setting the parity to odd in a terminal emulator when the parity used by a remote computer is even?

3. Trace the path of a character keyed on a keyboard attached to a computer controlled by a terminal emulator which is communicating with a remote computer in full-duplex.

4. The character length is most commonly set to _____ and _____ when using a terminal emulator.

5. The choices of parity setting in a terminal emulator are:

_____

_____

_____

_____

_____

_____

6. What might be the result of setting the terminal emulator line speed to 1200 bps when the speed of the communications line to the remote computer is 300 bps?

7. How is a computer transmitting data using a terminal emulator prevented from outrunning the computer receiving this data?

≡ Assignment ≡

Add XON/XOFF support to the project described in Appendix E.

References

Osborne, Mark Craig. 1983. "An Asynchronous Communications Terminal Emulator." Master's Project Report, West Virginia University.

Sippl, Charles J., and Charles P. Sippl. 1972. *Computer Dictionary*. Indianapolis: Howard W. Sams & Co.

20

Programming Synchronous Communications Hardware Interfaces

Introduction • Initialization • Transmit Mode • Direct Program Control Interfaces — Transmit • Direct Memory Access Interfaces — Transmit • Transmit Exceptions • Receive Mode • Direct Program Control Interfaces — Receive • Direct Memory Access Interfaces — Receive • Receiver Overruns

Introduction

A typical **synchronous communications hardware interface** provides the capability of transferring data from computer memory to a modem using **synchronous transmission**, as described in Chapter 6. The software controlling such synchronous interfaces must provide certain initialization and "line driving" procedures. The most common procedures will be described in relation to the conditions or status set or used in the appropriate status registers of the interface. [Lane, 1984]

It is assumed that individual registers of the synchronous interface provide capabilities for:

1. determining (device/interface/line/modem) status
2. controlling the interface
3. receiving and transmitting data
4. setting parameters

As with asynchronous interfaces, some synchronous interfaces provide this information and control in unique device control and/or status registers, while others provide this capability by specific I/O instructions. In either case, again the concepts of programming and controlling the device are similar. Hence, such an assumption will not interfere with the basic concepts of controlling and programming a synchronous communications interface.

Since data communications involves both the transmitting and receiving of data, a synchronous interface must provide a means for controlling both data transmission and receiving. Full-duplex communication provides for simultaneous communication in both directions on a communications medium. This means that the synchronous communications interface must be capable of being in receive mode and transmit mode simultaneously. This requirement dictates a need for independent control and data registers for transmit and receive modes.

Interface control mechanisms can be divided into the following categories:

1. Device Initialization and Control (Not specific to transmit or receive mode)
2. Receiver
   status

control
data transfer (read)
3. Transmitter
status
control
data transfer (write)

For the purpose of discussing the synchronous communications hardware interface, a protocol defining a data transmission technique using two consecutive synchronization (SYN) characters to frame a message being transmitted or received (as discussed in Chapter 6) is assumed. Protocols and techniques which synchronize using FLAG characters use similar procedures for controlling the hardware interface by the software.

Chapter 7 dealt with the signals on an RS-232 interface. Recall that the following signals are set by the modem according to certain conditions monitored and/or controlled by the modem:

Data Set Ready
Indicates the modem is powered up and ready

Carrier Detect
Indicates that the carrier signal is present on the communications medium (required for successful transmission)

Clear to Send
Indicates conditions on the communications line are okay for data transmission

Ring
Indicates the phone is ringing (new call — for auto answer modems)

These signals must be checked by the software driving the synchronous interface during initialization and/or communication.

The computer system indicates it is ready for synchronous communications to begin by turning on **Data Terminal Ready** (DTR). This signal is usually required when controlling dial-up lines with auto-answer capability. The other control signal that the computer system sets and controls via software is **Request to Send** (RTS). This informs the modem that transmission is desired. Only when **Clear to Send** (CTS) is set by the modem can the computer software begin the transmission of data.

Initialization

Certain procedures must be followed to initialize a synchronous communications hardware interface via software before data communications can commence. These procedures are outlined below:

1. Select half-duplex or full-duplex, depending on the type of communications to be provided.
2.a. If on a lease line (permanent connection),
    (1) Check for Data Set Ready and **Carrier Detect**. If on, set Data Terminal Ready. If not, inform "operator" with appropriate message.
  b. If on dial-up line,
    (1) Wait for Ring.
    (2) After Ring is detected, set Data Terminal Ready (answer phone).
    (3) Check for Data Set Ready and Carrier Detect. If on, set Data Terminal Ready. If not, inform "operator" with appropriate message.
3. Select character length desired (if programmable).
4. Select Parity enable, Even/Odd Parity, and Automatic CRC generation if it is supported by the interface and desired.
5. Set the synchronization (SYN) character value in the interface.
6. System is ready for communications (transmitting and receiving by setting appropriate control bits in registers to read and write data to the line).

Software must often check the Data Set Ready, Carrier Detect, and **Ring indicators** during operation of the communications software. The primary purpose of this is to determine if a line has been lost, a modem turned off, or a line disconnected and a new call is coming in. Such conditions are often controlled in software by having such changes (often called **Data Set Change**(s)) cause a "hardware interrupt." This interrupt is just one more asynchronous event which must be serviced by the communications software (see Chapter 15).

Transmit Mode

Before data transmission can begin, the transmit modules of the communications software must set Request to Send and wait for Clear to Send to be set by the modem. This setting of Clear to Send can be instantaneous (always set — full-duplex) or can take up to 250 milliseconds. This is referred to as **modem turnaround time** and is dependent on the environment for communications (modems, etc.). If the software begins transmission before Clear to Send is set, data will be lost. This turnaround time is basically the time required by a modem and a communications medium to go from receive to transmit mode. The detection of the Clear to Send condition by the software can be accomplished by periodic "polling" of the communications status register or by the use of the interrupt mechanism of the hardware on which the software is running. One should note that other processes should not be blocked while waiting for Clear to Send, since in some environments this "wait" could take over .2 second. Other devices which are time-dependent could have a character overrun should such blocking occur.

Once Clear to Send is set, data transmission can begin. The software must already know the address of the data buffer to send and the length of the message in the buffer. How the data is transferred to the hardware interface and subsequently over the communications medium depends on the type of hardware interface being used. Different interfaces provide for data transmission in different ways. Some require that all characters be put into a transmitter buffer one at a time by the software (**direct program control**) while others "automatically" fetch data from the appropriate data buffer location when needed (**direct memory access [DMA]**). The former requires that the software process each character transmitted, advance the data pointer, and reduce the count of characters to be sent. The latter requires that the software set the buffer address and message length into special registers before the beginning of transmission; the hardware interface will keep track of the current data character address and the count and automatically transfer data into or from the correct memory location. The procedures for each are in the next sections.

Direct Program Control Interfaces — Transmit

Once Clear to Send has been detected, transmission can begin. The procedures for starting and controlling this data transmission using a direct program control interface are outlined below:

1. Set the Send mode into the interface (in half-duplex mode, this will usually disable the receiver logic of the interface).
2. The transmitter will go "Active" (usually indicated by a status bit in a transmitter control register).
3. Wait for the Transmitter to indicate it needs data. This can be done by polling a status bit (transmit complete, done, etc.) which indicates that the next character must be placed into the transmitter buffer. This polling could be replaced by a transmit interrupt handler, which would get control only on a hardware interrupt generated when this status bit is set by the interface. Note that the clocking for the setting of this status bit, which indicates the next character is due, is usually controlled by the modem itself. The term **external clocking** is used to describe the type of clocking used in a synchronous environment. The term itself is often confusing, however, because some manuals use it to describe clocking external to the modem, while others use it to describe clocking external to the data terminal equipment (communications interface). Therefore, it is best to use the terms **modem clocking** and **nonmodem clocking** for the sake of preciseness and to prevent confusion [McNamara 1982, p. 211]. Pin 15 (TT — Transmitter Signal Element Timing) and pin 17 (RT — Receiver Signal Element Timing) are the clock leads in modem clocking (see Figure 7-7).
4. Place the next data character into the hardware transmitter buffer, advance the buffer pointer, and decrement the transmit data count.
5. Continue in steps 3 and 4 until the count goes to zero. When the count is zero, turn off the Send request to disable the transmitter. (It is usually recommended that one extra "PAD" character [usually 377 octal or FF hexadecimal] be sent after the data buffer to guard against data loss during line "turnaround.") Finally, disable interrupts if they are being used.

The above procedures will result in data being sent to the computer system on the "other end of the line."

Direct Memory Access Interfaces — Transmit

The direct memory access interfaces are simpler to control than the direct program control devices. Once Clear to Send is detected, transmission can begin. The procedures outlined below indicate the steps required for most DMA interfaces:

1. Set the buffer address into the appropriate device register (transmit buffer address).
2. Set the byte count into the transmit count register.
3. Set the Send request to activate the transmitter (the receiver logic will be disabled if half-duplex mode is selected in the interface).
4. Wait for an indication that the transmit operation is complete by polling the status bit or processing an "operation complete" interrupt.
5. Clear the Send request and turn off interrupt enable for the device if interrupts are being utilized.

Transmit Exceptions

Most interfaces will send SYN characters over the line if the software or hardware is too slow in placing a character into the transmit buffer when it is required for transmission. This idling of SYNs can create an error condition for the receiving computer system if the protocol does not allow this. The **idling of SYNs** is usually indicated by some status bit or condition in a status register for the device so that the transmit software can be made aware of this condition.

Receive Mode

Assumption that the protocol being used requires the recognition of two SYN characters before the receiving of data begins, the receiver is enabled to start searching the data coming over the line for these SYNs. Framing is done as indicated in Chapter 6 until this "SYN SYN" sequence is detected. If the receiver is set to strip (throw away) subsequent SYNs which immediately follow the initial SYNs, the receiver will not go "active" until the first nonSYN character is detected. Once the receiver goes active, data is being received; most protocols require the resetting of the Strip SYN mechanisms so that intermediate data characters with the same bit pattern as SYNs are not deleted from the data being received. This is particularly true for protocols which provide transparency. As with the transmitter, the procedures followed by the software depend on whether the synchronous interface is a direct program control interface or a direct memory access interface.

Direct Program Control Interfaces — Receive

Before the enabling of the Receiver to search for SYNs, the software which controls a direct program control synchronous interface must save the receiver buffer address and the count of the maximum number of data characters to be received. Once the receiver is active (SYNs detected and perhaps leading SYNs thrown away), data will be transferred by the software one character at a time. The procedure is as follows:

1. Wait for the status indication that a character has been received into the hardware buffer. As before, this waiting could be accomplished by polling or by the use of interrupt mechanisms.
2. When the next character is available, the software must transfer it from the hardware receiver buffer to the data buffer in memory. The buffer address is advanced and the count decremented. The count could be an exact count (as in a byte-count-oriented protocol) or a maximum count (as in a character-oriented protocol). In the latter case, the software must also monitor the received data for the occurrence of the "ending character" (ETX, EOT, etc.).
3. Cycle in steps 1 and 2 until the count goes to zero or the ending character (if any) has been detected. Then disable the receiver in the appropriate manner. If polling is being used, the receiver must be reactivated in order to receive more data. If interrupts are being used, receiver interrupts should be disabled. Check for any errors which are indicated by certain bits in the receiver status register (parity error, CRC error, etc.), if such error-detection mechanisms exist and are being utilized.

The protocol will determine when the receiver should be enabled and when it should be disabled. It will also specify if the receiver can be active when the transmitter is active (full-duplex).

Direct Memory Access Interfaces — Receive

As with transmit, the procedure for programming to receive data using a direct memory access interface is simpler than that of the direct program control interface. The procedure outlined below begins before the receiver is enabled.

1. Set the receiver buffer address into the interface (receiver buffer address).
2. Set the receiver count (usually a maximum count).
3. Enable the receiver.
4. If a byte-count–oriented protocol is being supported, wait for the receiving of data to complete. If a character-oriented protocol is being supported, monitor the characters already received for an ending character. The DMA interfaces provide a mechanism (usually a register indicating the current or next data address) for the software to determine what data has already been placed in memory. This monitoring must be done periodically by the software.
5. Once the character count goes to zero or the ending character has been detected (through periodic monitoring of the data stream), disable the receiver (and the receiver interrupts if they are being used).
6. Check for any errors indicated by the hardware (if any error detection mechanisms are enabled).

How error conditions are processed is dependent on the protocol. Once the overall communications software structure is presented (in Chapter 22), the posting of errors to certain modules in this structure will be discussed.

Receiver Overruns

It is possible that the software (and possibly the hardware for DMA devices) may not respond fast enough to get the previous data character from the receiver hardware buffer before the next character is placed into the buffer. This is known as an **overrun error condition** and data is lost. An indication of this is provided in the receiver status register.

≡ Terminology ≡

carrier detect
clear to send
data set change
data terminal ready
direct memory access [DMA]
direct program control
external clocking
idling of SYNs

modem clocking
modem turnaround time
nonmodem clocking
request to send
ring indicator
synchronous communications
hardware interface
synchronous transmission

≡ Review Questions ≡

1. What is the purpose of the Ring Indicator?
2. List four aspects of controlling a synchronous communications interface:

_____

_____

_____

_____

3. What is meant by the term "idling of SYNs"?
4. Should transmission begin if Clear to Send is not set? Why or why not?
5. Outline the sequence for beginning data transmission for a direct program control synchronous interface.
6. How can an overrun condition occur in a synchronous communications interface?

7. How does control of a synchronous communications interface with direct memory access (DMA) capability differ from one requiring direct program (character-by-character) control?

References

Lane, Malcolm G. 1984. "Data Communications Hardware and Software." In *Advances in Data Communications Management.* Edited by Jacob Slonim, E. A. Unger, and P. S. Fisher. Volume 2. Chichester, Great Britain: John Wiley & Sons.

McNamara, John E. 1982. *Technical Aspects of Data Communication.* Second Edition. Bedford, Massachusetts: Digital Press.

21

Finite State Logic in Protocol Implementation

Representing State Diagrams with State Control Blocks • Higher Level
Language Implementations of Finite State Machines

Representing State Diagrams with State Control Blocks

As outlined in Chapter 10, the use of states and transitions from state to state determined by an event (often a data character or complete message received) can simplify programming for implementing a protocol. **State diagrams** used for **finite state machine** implementations are represented with data structures. In assembler language, control blocks are used, with the address of each control block representing a state. A new state for a given input is identified by the address of the new state's control block. Each **state control block** consists of one or more 3-tuple element, each element representing an event (input) which is valid for the current state, an action routine (address), and a new state (address). For **data link control protocols**, these events might be messages which have arrived (**procedural rules** of protocol) or input characters (**syntax of protocol**). Figure 21–1 illustrates events as input characters. [Lane 1984]

Figure 21–2 illustrates a *portion* of a state diagram for receive mode of transparent of the Binary Synchronous Communications Protocol (see Chapter 12). The corresponding format for the control blocks which represent these states are given in Figure 21–3. Note how simply the mechanism provides for the processing of data (text) being received in state S3. In this state, anything other than a DLE results in the data being processed and a cycle in the same state. Note also that it is necessary to use a counter in the action routine DATA to avoid overflowing the receiver software buffer with a

FIGURE 21–1   Use of (Assembler Language) Control Blocks for Implementing Protocol Syntax

---

A state control block containing one or more elements represents a State. Each element of a given state consists of a 3-tuple, containing:

1. A valid EVENT for the state (a received character)
2. An ACTION ROUTINE (address) for processing current character
3. The NEXT STATE for the event (address of state control block)

FIGURE 21–2   Partial State Diagram for BSC Transparent Protocol

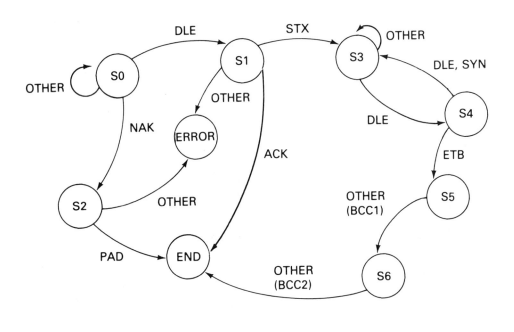

message which is longer than the maximum message length (probably due to the ETB being garbled).

A DLE causes a transition from state S3 to S4 (DLE found) where searching for control characters of a DLE following the detected DLE takes place. A DLE detected in state S4 is processed as data (DATA action routine) and causes a transition back to state S3, the data state. Comparing the other states in Figures 21–2 and 21–3 should clarify how such mechanisms work. Figure 21–4 lists the pseudocode for a finite state machine (oriented towards assembler language) which uses the control block format of Figure 21–3 to interpret the syntax of a BSC data message with CRC-16 error checking (BCC1 and BCC2 characters are the 16-bit CRC error check character).

Higher Level Language Implementations of Finite State Machines

Using arrays and indices, the EVENTs, the ACTION routines, and the NEXT-STATEs illustrated in Figures 21–3 and 21–4 can be implemented in languages like Pascal and "C." Appendixes C and D contain finite state machine implementations for the BSC protocol implemented in C and in Pascal [Jones 1981; Gesalman 1983]. Readers familiar with one or both of these languages can compare the implementations with the assembler-language-oriented logic of Figure 21–4.

FIGURE 21–3 Format of State Control Blocks for BSC Protocol Receiver

STATE	EVENT (Character)	ACTION ROUTINE	NEXT STATE
S0	DLE	CTRLMSG	S1
	NAK	CTRLMSG	S2
	OTHER	ERROR	S0 (same)
S1	STX	DATAINIT	S3
	ACK	ACKMSG	END
	OTHER	ERRORRTN	ERROR
S2	PAD	NAKMSG	END
	OTHER	ERRORRTN	ERROR
S3	DLE	CTLCHAR	S4
	OTHER	DATA	S3 (same)
S4	DLE	DATA	S3
	ETB	ENDMSG	S5
	SYN	IGNORE	S3
	OTHER	ERRORRTN	ERROR
S5	OTHER	BCC1	S6
S6	OTHER	BCC2	END

S0 — Looking for DLE-STX, DLE-ACK, or NAK
S1 — Looking for ACK or beginning of text (STX)
S2 — Looking for PAD after NAK
S3 — Receiving data monitoring for DLE
S4 — Looking for DLE or control character after DLE in data
S5 — Looking for BCC1 after ETB
S6 — Looking for BCC2 after BCC1 (error check character)
END — End of message
ERROR — Error state

FIGURE 21–4   Pseudocode for Receiver Finite State Machine Using Control Block Formats of Figure 21–3 (Assembler Language Control Blocks Assumed)

* RECEIVER FINITE STATE MACHINE (FSM) *

```
FSM:
    Set S to point to current STATE
    Initialize EVENT Index I = 0
    EVENT-FOUND = FALSE
    DO UNTIL EVENT-FOUND
        IF EVENT(S,I) = INPUT-CHARACTER OR EVENT(S,I) = OTHER
                THEN EVENT-FOUND = TRUE
        ELSE I = I + 1
    END
    CALL ACTION(S,I)
    Set STATE = NEXT-STATE(S,I)
    RETURN
```

(Assembler Language) Variables

INPUT-CHARACTER — Character received
S — Register pointer to current STATE
I — EVENT (element) index within current STATE
EVENT(S,I) — Ith EVENT (character) in STATE pointed to by S
OTHER — Special Indicator for any other EVENT (character)
EVENT-FOUND — TRUE/FALSE indicator for EVENT found
ACTION(S,I) — Action Routine for Ith EVENT of STATE S
NEXT-STATE(S,I) — Next State for Ith EVENT of STATE S

Terminology

data link control protocol
finite state machine
procedural rules

state control block
state diagram
syntax of protocol

Review Questions

1. What rules of a protocol can be implemented using finite state machine concepts?

2. What is a state control block? Illustrate the format of a state control block which can be used to analyze the syntax of SDLC information transfer messages.

3. What are the differences in the structure of state control blocks when assembler language and a high-level language like "C" or Pascal are used?

≡ Assignment ≡

Using a local computer system, set up the state control block for 2 above for interpreting the syntax of an SDLC information transfer message. Implement the finite state machine illustrated in Figure 21–4 and test it with test data set up in the correct format for SDLC information transfer messages.

References

Gesalman, Paul W. 1982. "Table Driven Implementation of Multiple Data Communication Protocols." Master's Project Report, West Virginia University.

Jones, James Kenneth, II. 1981. "Implementing Hasp Multileaving Data Communications Protocol Using Finite State Logic." Master's Project Report, West Virginia University.

Lane, Malcolm G. 1984. "Data Communications Protocols." In *Advances in Data Communications Management*. Edited by Jacob Slonim, E. A. Unger, and P. S. Fisher. Volume 2. Chichester, Great Britain: John Wiley & Sons.

22

Modular Software Structure for Data Link Control Protocols

Overview • Interface Control Transmit Monitor (ICXMT) • Data Link Control Transmit Monitor (DLCXMT) • Interface Control Receive Monitor (ICRCV) • Data Link Control Receive Monitor (DLCRCV) • Interface Control Monitors and Interrupt Processing • Circular List of Receiver Buffers • Command Handler Dispatcher/Communications Controller

Overview

This chapter presents a **modular software structure** which shows more of the detail functions of various modules in a typical communications data link control protocol. The detail will show major functions performed by various modules. The interrupt handlers which are part of the design are also outlined and are similar to those in any operating systems environment.

No particular programming language is assumed for the prototype structure being presented. However, certain "systems-programming-like" capabilities must be provided. Much communications software is still implemented in assembler language, particularly on small computers. If the language used is assembler language, then the proposed structure will indeed make implementation and debugging far easier. Other languages, such as "C" (available under UNIX, a trademark of Bell Telephone Laboratories), are also excellent for implementing the proposed structure.

Figure 22–1 presents an overview of a simple structure for implementing point-to-point data link control protocols. The **RECEIVER** and **TRANSMITTER** tasks have each been separated into two tasks — an **interface control task** designated **IC**, and **data link control task**, designated **DLC**. This software structure limits the dependence on the specific protocol being implemented to the DLC modules for transmit and receive. The interface modules then depend almost entirely on the hardware interface. [Lane 1984]

In many implementations of data link control protocols, the protocol logic is entangled with the communications interface driver, particularly the interrupt handlers. Experience has proved that such implementations are difficult to modify, even if only the data link control protocol changes or the communications interface is replaced by a different interface.

The modular structure shown in Figure 22–1 lends itself to implementing support for different hardware interfaces without having to modify the data link control routines, i.e., the interface control modules for receive and transmit theoretically are all that need to be changed. Similarly, it should be possible to change the protocol by changing only the data link control level modules, and it should also be possible to modify the higher level protocols without affecting the data link control protocol modules. Figures 22–2 and 22–3 illustrate that such a software structure will allow replace-

284

FIGURE 22–1 A Simple Modular Communications Software Structure

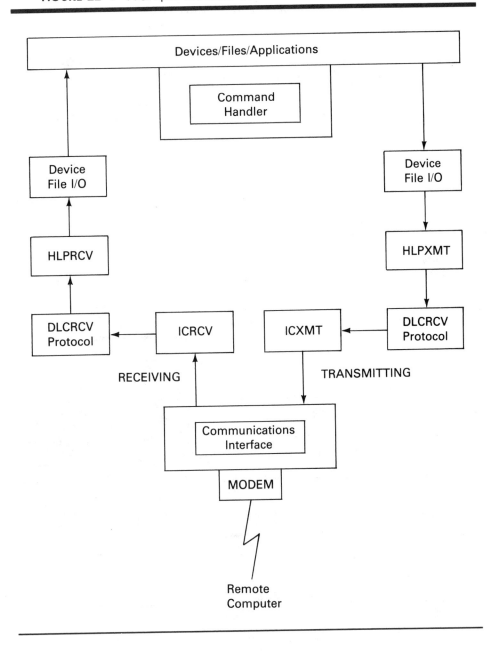

FIGURE 22–2   Communications Software in Configuration I

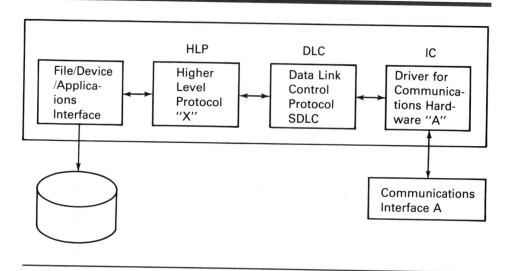

FIGURE 22–3   Communications Software in Configuration II

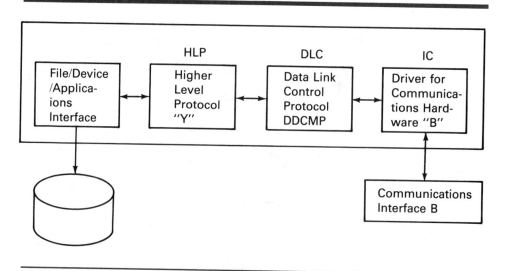

ment of the data link control protocol (high-level) modules without modifying the remainder of the communications software. In practice, minor changes to the interface control receiver are often needed because of problems in maintaining strict independence of this module from the protocol, but the implementation of a new data link control protocol can be undertaken with relative ease when compared to other nonstructured implementations of communications software. This is particularly true if a finite state machine and state diagrams are used to implement the data link control modules (see Chapter 21 and Cypser 1978).

Interface Control Transmit Monitor (ICXMT)

The **interface control transmit monitor (ICXMT)** is essentially the driver for the synchronous communications interface. It is "fed" messages to send by the data link control transmit monitor (DLCXMT) and does minimal processing of the messages before transmitting them over the communications line. Since the purpose is to have DLCXMT be the implementation of the protocol, most protocol-specific processing of the data has already been done by DLCXMT before it is passed to ICXMT. This also means that decisions as to whether to send a control message (such as ACK or NAK) or a data message are made by DLCXMT.

FIGURE 22–4 Functions of Interface Control Transmit Monitor (ICXMT)

Initiates transmit mode in the hardware

Saves parameters for use by transmit interrupt handler

Provides transmit interrupt handler for interface

Monitors progress of transmission

May control calculation of error check characters via hardware

The major functions provided by ICXMT are outlined in Figure 22–4. ICXMT "sees" a maximum of one buffer in its input queue at any one time. This is because DLCXMT may have to send an "immediate" request like a NAK or TIMEOUT message, before sending the next data message, since data messages are ordered first-in/first-out (FIFO). Hence, ICXMT can never be allowed to "see beyond" the current message to be sent.

ICXMT will initiate the transmit function in the hardware. Obviously, how this is done depends on the specific interface and will depend heavily on whether the interface is a direct program control interface or a Direct Memory Access interface. Sometimes it is advantageous to introduce some protocol-dependent functions into the ICXMT because of hardware features provided by the interface (e.g., automatic CRC generation, SDLC vs. character-oriented modes). This can often be done by using data structures (control blocks) defined in DLCXMT which specify bit patterns or codes to be used in initializing the transmit function in the hardware. If this is done, new protocols can be defined in the DLCXMT which also imply hardware modes in control blocks defined in DLCXMT and referenced by ICXMT. Hence, protocol-independence can still be maintained. [Lane 1984]

Data Link Control Transmit Monitor (DLCXMT)

The **data link control transmit monitor (DLCXMT)** provides the procedural rules for the protocol being supported. Messages are formatted according to the syntactical rules and "posted" to the ICXMT when the ICXMT has completed a transmission and is eligible to send the next message. (In half-duplex, the transmitter software may have to wait for the receiver to finish; this is signaled by an event flag indicating the receiver is not active.)

Figure 22–5 outlines the functions of the DLCXMT. The DLCXMT must keep track of the next message number to use for a (data) message and must also keep track of the number of the last "good" message received (often called the **ACK number**). The DLCXMT will build headers and trailers when necessary, insert control characters if required, and calculate and insert error control characters (unless this function has been passed on to ICXMT because of hardware features). DLCXMT decides if an immediate control message must be transmitted because of conditions being monitored by DLCXMT (e.g., timeout and error detected). If a control message must be sent,

FIGURE 22–5   Functions of Data Link Control Transmit Monitor (DLCXMT)

Schedules immediate control messages ahead of data messages to be transmitted

Passes messages from transmit Scheduler List one at a time to ICXMT on a FIFO basis

Moves messages posted to ICXMT to History List

Calculates CRC, LRC, VRC if Calculations not provided in hardware by ICXMT

Keeps track of the number of the next message to transmit and the number of the last message received correctly (ACK Number)

Places control information such as message number and ACK number into message buffers before posting it to ICXMT

Processes messages passed to it by higher level protocol

FIGURE 22–6   Transmit Message Scheduling with History List in Full-Duplex Environment

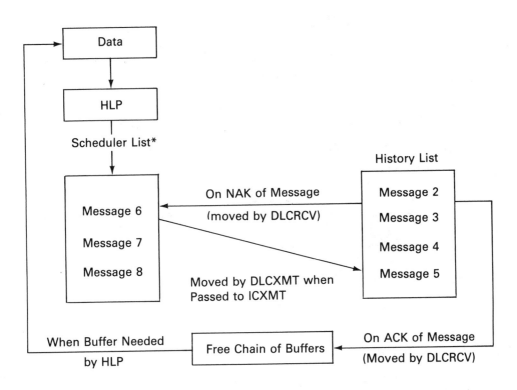

* Message Numbers Shown in Scheduler List Are Not in Message Until Passed to ICXMT by DLCXMT.

DLCXMT schedules this message to the ICXMT. Data messages are passed one at a time to the ICXMT on a FIFO basis if no control message is to be transmitted.

If full-duplex is to be supported, DLCXMT must also move the message posted to the ICXMT for transmission to a **History List**, in case the message must be retransmitted later due to an error during transmission of the current or a prior message. Figure 22–6 illustrates the movement of a data message to the History List and back to the **Scheduler List** (FIFO list of messages to be sent) or the freeing of the buffer containing a message in the History List. Messages are moved back to the Scheduler List by DLCRCV if it determines that message retransmission is necessary. In this case, a NAK would be sent by DLCXMT indicating the last good message number. Messages beyond this number are rescheduled by DLCRCV being moved to the top of the Scheduler List. This is most easily done by manipulating linked list pointers. State diagrams should be used to implement the DLCXMT. [Lane 1984]

Interface Control Receive Monitor (ICRCV)

The **Interface Control Receive Monitor (ICRCV)** is the driver for the receiver mode of the synchronous interface (see Figure 22–7). It must obtain a free buffer from a **buffer pool** and initiate the receive mode in the hardware to begin receiving data into the buffer. As in the case of the low-level transmit monitor, the ICRCV can provide error check calculation and error checking of a received data message. However, the less it does which is protocol dependent, the more the protocol definition is restricted to the Data Link Control Receive Monitor. Any errors detected by ICRCV must be **posted** to DLCRCV, including long blocks received (i.e., end of message not detected before buffer fills up).

FIGURE 22–7 Functions of Interface Control Receive Monitor (ICRCV)

Initiates receive mode in the hardware

Saves parameters for use by receiver interrupt handler

Provides receiver interrupt handler for interface

Monitors for end-of-message indicator (protocol-dependent) when operating on character-by-character basis

Posts buffers to DLCRCV with an indication of whether they were correct or in error

May control hardware error checking

Since ICRCV must know the end of the message, it inherently depends on the protocol. This is because a character-oriented protocol might define the end of message with one character (ETX) or a two-character sequence (DLE ETX), while a bit-oriented protocol defines the end of a message by a FLAG character. A byte-count-oriented protocol will determine the end of message by a count received from a header. In all cases, a maximum buffer size must be assumed.

Hence, ICRCV must monitor the data being received on a character-by-character basis in the cases where a software search is necessary to find the end of the message. In cases where the hardware can determine the end of a message, such as in SDLC, then this software search is not necessary. However, there is protocol dependence even in this latter case, since the hardware will likely be driven in a different mode than when a software search was necessary.

Once the message has been received, it is posted to DLCRCV for processing. DLCRCV must interpret messages according to the protocol being supported. Clearly it is difficult to make ICRCV totally protocol independent. One way to accomplish this is to define various parameters and definitions of end-of-message sequences in the DLCRCV data areas and let these control blocks drive ICRCV. While it is not mandatory to remove all protocol dependence of ICRCV, the communications software will be more easily modified later when new communications interfaces and/or communications protocols are to be supported. [Lane 1984]

Data Link Control Receive Monitor (DLCRCV)

The **Data Link Control Receive Monitor (DLCRCV)** will monitor data on a message basis (see Figure 22–8). It should rely on a finite state machine structure driven by state diagrams which define the protocol being supported (see Chapter 21). DLCRCV interprets the message according to the data link control protocol and determines if messages are valid (correct format, CRC/LRC/VRC okay, etc.). Received messages which are correct will be posted to a higher level protocol (e.g., decompression) module for processing. An erroneous message is thrown away and DLCXMT must be informed that a control NAK message must be sent with the last successful message number (ACK number) in it. This can be done by merely having an "immediate message" pointer which, if nonzero, indicates the address of the control message to be sent.

FIGURE 22–8   Functions of Data Link Control Receive Monitor (DLCRCV)

Checks for errors posted from ICRCV

Calculates error check character if not provided in hardware by ICRCV

Checks syntax of received buffer according to protocol rules

Posts message number (ACK number) of correctly received messages to DLCXMT

Informs DLCXMT of errors in received messages so that DLCXMT can schedule a NAK message

Reschedules messages to be Transmitted from History List to top of Transmit Scheduler List when NAK received

Frees buffers of messages in History List which have been ACKed

Posts correct data messages to higher level protocol (HLP)

FIGURE 22–9   Queue and Task Control in Communications Software

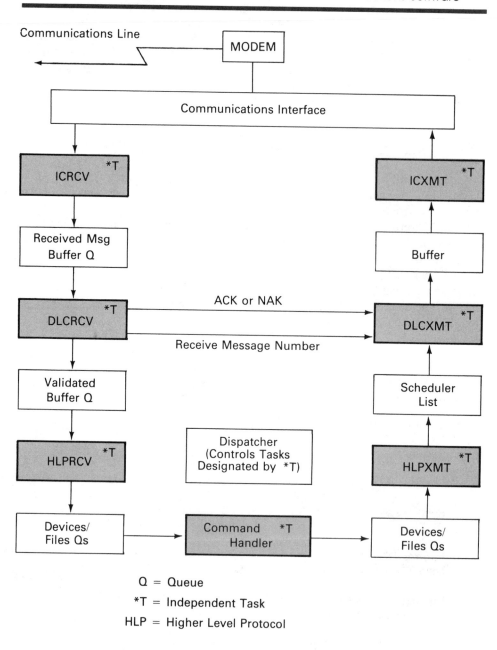

Communications Line

MODEM

Communications Interface

ICRCV *T

Received Msg
Buffer Q

DLCRCV *T

ACK or NAK

Receive Message Number

Validated
Buffer Q

HLPRCV *T

Dispatcher
(Controls Tasks
Designated by *T)

Devices/
Files Qs

Command *T
Handler

Devices/
Files Qs

ICXMT *T

Buffer

DLCXMT *T

Scheduler
List

HLPXMT *T

Q = Queue
*T = Independent Task
HLP = Higher Level Protocol

If a NAK is processed by DLCRCV, it must reschedule the transmit messages not correctly received, as indicated by the "ACK number" in the NAK message (see Figure 22–6). These messages are moved from a History List back to the Transmit Scheduler List so that DLCXMT will automatically select the first message to retransmit from the top of the Scheduler List. DLCRCV must reset the transmit message number back to the message number which follows the last transmitted message which was successfully received.

Figure 22–9 illustrates the ACK or NAK information being provided to DLCXMT by DLCRCV. This figure also indicates how buffers are processed and posted from module to module. Tasks, designated *T, in this figure are independent of each other, although task "synchronization" is periodically required. These tasks are driven by an input queue from another task and produce entries in an output queue, which is in turn input to another task. The task control through the use of input and output queues resembles that of a large (batch) multiprogramming system. Any higher level protocol (above DLC) is designated by HLP in Figure 22–9. [Lane 1984]

Interface Control Monitors and Interrupt Processing

The interface control monitors do indeed monitor data transmission and reception. However, it is the interrupt handler portion that does the work, just as it did in the implementation of the multiline asynchronous interface software presented in Chapter 18.

The ICRCV and ICXMT each has one interrupt handler associated with it: RCVINT will asynchronously post the status of the receive operation to ICRCV, and XMTINT will asynchronously post the status of the transmit operation to ICXMT (see Figure 22–10).

One technique for communicating the status of a receive event to ICRCV is to use a status byte or word at the beginning of each receive buffer. ICRCV must set up the parameters passed to it when it is dispatched. The address of the receiver buffer is all that is necessary if the structure is as shown in Figure 22–11. Since ICRCV operates on only one buffer at a time, it will be "waiting" for receive complete if the status byte is zero.

Similarly, there is a costructure for ICXMT and XMTINT as shown in Figure 22–12. In this figure, ICXMT is idle under two conditions: if XMT is busy and EFLAG is zero, or if XMT is not busy and no buffer is ready to send.

Whether the interface interrupts on every character or is a direct memory access interface, the operation of RCVINT and XMTINT appears the same to the modules ICRCV and ICXMT, respectively. The major difference is the number of interrupts that must be processed by the interrupt handler before the event flag is set.

Circular List of Receiver Buffers

Data processed by ICRCV is in on a FIFO basis. Most protocols require that subsequent messages received after an error is detected (in full-duplex mode) must be ignored. Hence, the status byte in the receiver buffer could have multiple values, say,

FIGURE 22–10   Operation of ICRCV and RCVINT

```
ICRCV
    IF RCV Not Busy THEN DO
        Save Parameters
        (Buffer Address
        Event Flag Address
        Byte Count Address)
        Set RCV Busy
        Initiate Receive in Hardware
        Return
    END
    IF EFLAG = 0 THEN Return
    Set RCV Not Busy
        .
        . (Process End of Operation)
        .
```

Event Flag EFLAG
(Set by RCVINT, Checked by ICRCV)

```
RCVINT
    Process Interrupt
    Check for errors
    Store Character
    IF END DO
        Disable Receiver
        Set EFLAG
    END
    Return from Interrupt
```

FIGURE 22–11   Structure for Receive Buffers

RCVBUF Format

Pointer to next buffer
Status
Buffer size
Current count
Data area

FIGURE 22–12   Operation of ICXMT and XMTINT

```
ICXMT
  IF XMT Not Busy THEN DO
  IF No Buffer to Send THEN RETURN
    ELSE DO
    Save Parameters
      (Buffer Address
      Event Flag
      Count)
      Set XMT Busy
      Initiate Transmit in Hardware
      Return
      END
  END
    IF EFLAG = 0 THEN RETURN
    Set XMT Not Busy
    .
    . (Process XMT Operation Complete)
    .
```

```
                    Event Flag
        (Set by XMTINT, Checked by ICXMT)
```

```
XMTINT
  Process Character
  Decrement Count
  IF last character THEN DO
    Disable Transmit
    Set Event Flag
    END
  Return from Interrupt
```

0   Free or in process by ICRCV
1-10   Finished processing by ICRCV, waiting for processing by DLCRCV
100-110 Finished processing by ICRCV, waiting for processing by next level
                              protocol.

Using this technique, ICRCV may initiate a receive (in full-duplex) whenever there is a buffer available. Because each module keeps its own pointer to the **circular list of receiver buffers,** each routine can determine if it has something to do, i.e., ICRCV can receive if next buffer has STATUS = 0, DLCRCV can process buffer if 0 < STATUS < 100, the next level protocol can process buffer if 100 < STATUS < 200, etc. If 1,

101, 201, etc. are used to designate that data in the buffer has been successfully interpreted according to the appropriate module, then other values 2, 3, 102, 103, etc. can be used to pass error information on to the next level if required. Note that when an error is detected by DLCRCV-checking error check characters or syntax, the buffer will not be passed on to the next highest level routine.

In many ways, this circular list of receiver buffers operates just as the FIFO hardware buffer did in hardware in the asynchronous multiline interface. Figure 22–13 illustrates the technique:

FIGURE 22–13   Circular Receiver Buffer Queue with Multiple Pointers

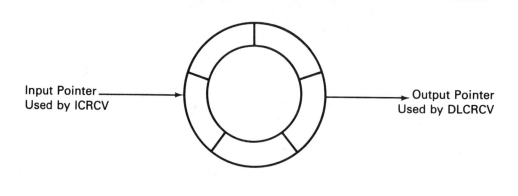

Command Handler

There must be some method to control the communications software. This is usually done by some type of command handler software with commands which can be local to the communications software or which can be placed into the communications buffers for transmission to a remote computer.

There is nothing particularly unique about the command interpreter itself. The types of commands which would be provided would likely include commands such as those shown in Figure 22–14.

Dispatcher/Communications Controller

A simple round-robin dispatcher could be used to pass control to each module in the system one at a time. Each module could check the appropriate event flag(s) to determine if it has any work to perform. If so, it performs it and returns to the dispatcher. If not, it returns immediately, giving up the CPU control for the next task. Hence, a

FIGURE 22–14   Typical Commands Supported by a Communications Software Command Interface

INIT	Initialize Communications
STATUS	Display status of line, error counts, Etc.
RESTART	Restart communications startup sequence
SUSPEND	Suspend communications
RESUME	Resume communications
*CCC	Send remote command CCC to other system
LOG	Log communications traffic to a disk (tape, etc) file
TIME = n	Set timeout interval

waiting task will quickly give up control to a task which is ready. Figure 22–15 illustrates a simple dispatcher of this nature.

The tasks shown in Figure 22–15 are ordered for receive according to the data flow, i.e., an input buffer is first processed by ICRCV, then by DLCRCV, and finally by HLPRCV. Similarly, the ordering on the transmit side is according to the order in which transmit modules process data.

A more sophisticated approach would be to implement a dispatcher which checked event flags for each task, had priorities assigned for certain (I/O bound) tasks, and dispatched the highest priority ready task. Since the communications line itself is often the bottleneck in a computer system, the receive and transmit tasks, particularly ICRCV and ICXMT should have highest priority. The device, file and/or application

FIGURE 22–15   A Round-Robin Dispatcher with Event Flag Checking by "Tasks"

```
DO UNTIL END
CALL    ICRCV
CALL    DLCRCV
CALL    HLPRCV
CALL    HLPXMT
CALL    DLCXMT
CALL    ICXMT
CALL    COMMAND
END
```

program interfaces are assumed to be handled in the higher level protocol modules, which in Figure 22–15 are called HLPRCV and HLPXMT.

=== **Terminology** ==

ACK number	ICRCV
buffer pool	ICXMT
circular list of receiver buffers	interface control receive monitor
data link control receive monitor	interface control task
data link control task	interface control transmit monitor
data link control transmit monitor	modular software structure
DLC	posted
DLCRCV	receiver
DLCXMT	scheduler list
History List	transmitter
IC	

=== **Review Questions** ==

1. Given the functions on the left, which of the modules DLCXMT, DLCRCV, ICXMT, and ICRCV provides each function:

    a. passes the ACK number to transmit side of software

    b. monitors progress of transmission

    c. schedules immediate control messages ahead of data messages

    d. posts messages to DLCRCV

    e. monitors for end of message for messages being received

    f. keeps track of message sequence numbers for messages to be sent

    g. initiates receive mode in the hardware

    h. may control error check character computation in hardware for messages to be sent

    i. reschedules messages to be transmitted upon detection of a NAK

    j. frees buffers in History List after messages in them have been acknowledged

2. Explain how a circular list is used in the implementation of a data link control protocol.

3. How do higher level protocols (above the data link control layer) fit into a modular structure like the one presented?

═ Assignments ═

1. Implement the SHDP protocol presented in Chapter 10 according to the specifications given in Appendix G. Use a modular structure and finite state logic for the project. Choose either asychronous or synchronous communications, depending on your computer laboratory environment for data communications.

2. Implement the subset of DDCMP described in Appendix F using synchronous communications. Refer to Appendix B for more detail about DDCMP, in particular the formal grammar. Use finite state logic and a modular software structure for this project. Thoroughly document the DDCMP software that you implement.

References

Cypser, R. J. 1978. *Communications Architecture for Distributed Systems.* Reading, Massachusetts: Addison-Wesley.

Lane, Malcolm G. 1984. "Data Communications Hardware and Software." In *Advances in Data Communications Management.* Edited by Jacob Slonim, E. A. Unger, and P. S. Fisher. Volume 2. Chichester, Great Britain: John Wiley & Sons.

23

Timing Considerations

Hardware and Software Clocks • Receiver Timeouts • Handshaking •
Line Turnaround • Half- and Full-Duplex Considerations

Hardware and Software Clocks

One critical aspect in the design of data communications link control software is the need to time certain events within the communications system. There are three specific areas where timing is critical: receiver timeout, handshaking sequence, and line turnaround time. It is necessary that a hardware clock be present in the system for communications software to be supported. It is ideal if the operating system under which the data link control protocol operates has timer service support for this hardware clock. This timer service support creates software clocks to time receiver timeout, handshaking sequences, and line turnaround in a communications environment. If the operating system under which the communications software will be run does not provide timer service support, the communications software must provide its own timer support.

One of two types of hardware timers is generally available: an **interval timer** or a **crystal (line) clock**. The interval timer is set to a specific value, which is decremented at specific intervals, e.g., every 60th of a second, depending on the resolution of the clock (which is sometimes programmable). When the interval is decremented to zero, an interrupt is generated, signalling the expiration of the interval to be timed. A timer action routine will be invoked or an event flag can be set upon the occurrence of this timer interrupt.

A line clock interrupts at a specific interval, e.g., every 60th of a second. Using such a hardware clock, the software must maintain a counter (software clock) which will be decremented on every interrupt. When the software counter becomes zero, a timer action routine can be invoked or an event flag set, depending on how the software is implemented. Figure 23–1 contains the pseudocode logic of a software timer interrupt handler for a line clock.

Receiver Timeouts

In a synchronous communications environment, an interface which is set to receive will remain in receive "forever," searching for synchronizing characters if the synchronizing characters are garbled in transmission. In full-duplex, it is possible that the next message to be transmitted will force the synchronization to occur, but a message will have

FIGURE 23-1   Pseudocode Logic of Timer Interrupt Handler with
Software Clock Interval

Timer Interrupt

TIMEINT
    Save All
    Decrement INTERVAL
    IF INTERVAL = 0 THEN DO
        CALL TIMER-ACTION
        DISABLE Clock
    END
    Restore All
    Return from Interrupt

been lost. The sequencing mechanism within the data link control protocol will provide for the detection of the lost message, and error recovery procedures will be invoked to inform the transmitting station of the lost message.

In the half-duplex case, the receiver will remain locked in receive mode, searching for synchronizing characters which will never be received. In this case it is necessary to have some way of forcing the receiving station out of receive mode and placing it into transmit mode. This is done via a **software clock**, which signals when a receiver timeout interval has expired. Controlled by either the appropriate operating system software or a communications software timer facility, the **hardware clock** will generate an interrupt upon the expiration of the receiver timeout interval, which will then asynchronously branch to the receiver timeout service routine. The operating system directive, or call, to the time module of the communications software which sets the timer requires parameters, which include the duration of the interval being timed and the address of the service routine which will get control when the interval expires.

The **receiver timeout service routine** will disable the receiver and change the communications mode from receive to idle. It also must flag a timeout condition to the link control protocol transmit routine so that a (timeout) NAK message can be transmitted when this routine is dispatched.

The **receiver timer interval** should be set just before the the receiver in the hardware is enabled. Upon synchronization (usually in the receiver interrupt handler), the receiver timer should be cancelled, since in a synchronous environment, characters will be clocked and received continuously until the receiver is disabled. Some protocols specify a receiver timeout interval which is long enough to include the time it takes for the data be received before the interval expires — in which case, the receiver timer can be cancelled as part of the completion routine in the receiver interrupt handler.

Handshaking

Most protocols specify a **handshaking sequence**, which depends on a timeout interval to trigger the handshake on one system or the other in a point-to-point environment. In this case, a station which is to transmit will usually delay for a predetermined (protocol-dependent) period of time if there is no data transmit until this "handshake" interval expires. This interval is considerably shorter than the receiver timeout interval so that the handshake is invoked before the other station triggers a timeout NAK for transmission. In this case, the handshake timer is set whenever the transmit mode is entered, but there is nothing yet to send. The expiration of this interval will result in the handshake message (usually an ACK) being transmitted.

Some protocols have allowed a timeout NAK to serve as the normal handshake sequence (UNIVAC NTR). Using this principle, there is no special handshaking sequence, since the normal receiver timeout triggers a NAK-ACK-ACK sequence.

Line Turnaround

In a half-duplex environment, modems require that there be a delay between receiving information and transmitting information. As discussed in Chapter 20, the interface control software must set Request to Send (RTS) and wait for Clear to Send (CTS). The wait for CTS is usually between 50ms and 200ms. Transmitting data before the CTS condition is set results in lost data.

The delay required for **modem turnaround** from receive mode to transmit mode is clocked by the modem itself. Most synchronous interfaces provide modem control and will interrupt whenever the CTS condition is set by the modem. This interrupt can be used to enable the transmitter to begin data transmission rather than waiting for CTS via polling (which will waste valuable time in the data communications system).

Full-duplex modems do not have this turnaround time requirement, and even if the protocol itself operates in half-duplex, the turnaround time delay is eliminated. Since this modem turnaround time can be as long as 200ms, a significant amount of time can be saved if it is eliminated, which means that throughput of the data communications line will go up.

Half- and Full-Duplex Considerations

Most of the timing considerations mentioned previously are most critical in half-duplex environments. However, receiver timeouts are still required even in full-duplex environments, since a break in the line connection or some other condition could result in the software locking in receive mode. Also, handshake sequences require timing to operate correctly.

☰ Terminology ☰

crystal
handshaking sequence
hardware clock
interval timer
line clock

modem turnaround
receiver timeout service routine
receiver timer interval
software clock

☰ Review Questions ☰

1. Why are timers needed in the implementation of data communications software?

2. If the hardware clock on a computer interrupts every 60th of a second, how must the software time intervals for a data communications environment (assuming no operating system timer support)?

3. Timing is required to trigger the _____ when communications software is in an idle (no data to send) state.

4. What is modem turnaround time? Why is it required?

24

Review of Data Link Control Protocol Software

Review • Startup Control • Line Control • Timeout Control • Error Control • Sequence Control • Transparency • Exceptions • Protocol Definition

Review

The primary purpose of this book has been to provide a firm understanding of data communications principles, data link control protocols, and most important, the principles for implementing data communications protocols. Implementation and maintenance of data communications software is far easier with such appropriate design techniques as finite state machines and modular structures, which isolate protocol functions in appropriate modules and separate the data link control protocol from the communications interface driver. Of course, proper documentation of all software is still a requirement for successful implementation and maintenance of such software.

This chapter will review the various aspects of data link control protocol definition and how it relates to the implementation techniques presented and discussed in Chapters 21 and 22.

Startup Control

Startup control deals with the initial communications message exchanges which take place when one system or another wishes to first begin data communications on an idle line. **Procedural states** can define when the communications software is idle with appropriate commands triggering a change of state to the initial sign-on state.

The sign-on state action routine will begin the sequence which identifies the message to be transmitted for sign-on, changes the state to receiving sign-on response, and, when a response is received from the other system, finally moves the software to the signed-on idle (handshaking) state.

Line Control

Line control includes the **handshaking sequence** and the message transfer sequences which are defined in a given protocol. **Finite state logic** once again can be used to determine when the software is sending and when it is receiving, changing the appropriate state control blocks to indicate the appropriate state. When sending data messages, substates will represent the syntax of data messages and control messages being received.

Part of line control will involve timers which are part of timeout control. In addition to the timeout control, which will be covered in the next section, there are timed delays in line turnaround which are a part of most data link control protocol handshake procedures. Such delays are controlled by software clocks, which are set when the line goes from receive to idle (usually in a half-duplex environment) and there is no data message to transmit. In this case, the line is not set to the transmit state (represented by the appropriate state control block) until the timer interval expires or a data message becomes available for transmission, in which case the software clock for the idle-to-transmit-state delay is cancelled prematurely. Hence, line control involves manipulation of state control blocks and the controlling of timers.

Timeout Control

In addition to the **timer control** necessary in many handshake sequences, there is a requirement for detecting when a line has remained in receive mode for too long a period of time. In this case, the software (protocol) specifies that data being received was either garbled (no synchronization) or something has happened to the line or other computer system. In either case, there must be a way to detect this and force the software from receive state to the state which forces the transmission of a (timeout) NAK message.

The software which begins the receive sequence must set a software clock to time how long a line is in receive without receiving data. If the interval expires before the message is received, then a timeout error has occurred, the state of the software must change, with the action routine in the new state scheduling a NAK message for transmission.

Error Control

Error control for all protocols studied in Chapter 12 used some form of a cyclic redundancy check (CRC) algorithm, with the error check character being added to the end of a data message (in SDLC before the final FLAG). How the CRC error check characters are computed depends on whether hardware or software is being used. If hardware is used and the CRC is calculated correctly by the hardware interface as data is received and transmitted, then the ICRCV and ICXMT modules must enable this checking and calculation in the hardware.

If software is used to compute the CRC, then part of the action routine for storing a data character will likely include the "addition" of the data character to the CRC calculation. Depending on how the interrupts work (character-by-character or direct memory access), the calculation may be done as the characters are received by the interrupt handler or after the fact, when the total data message has been received. In the former case, the interrupt handlers have protocol-dependent error check algorithms embedded within them, which violates the recommendation that the interface control modules be isolated from the data link control protocol modules. This is usually done to improve the performance of communications software, and if state-driven logic is used, will still allow the interface control modules to be modified fairly easily.

Sequence Control

Sequence control is part of the data link control (and higher level) protocol modules. During the protocol checking of a received message, the sequence numbers must be checked, and during the building of a message to be transmitted, the sequence numbers must be added. Part of the action routines for the receive and transmit modules for the protocol will provide for this sequence control. Note that the sequence information about messages received and ACKs received needs to be passed from the receiver DLCRCV module to the transmit DLCXMT module. This is usually done by global control variables **ACK#** and **SEQ#**, which contain the number of the last message received and the number of the next (or perhaps, the last) message to be transmitted. Some protocols, like DDCMP, even specify by name in the data link control definition what variables are to be used to maintain such sequencing control information.

All sequencing and sequence checking is done modulo some number (8 for SDLC, 256 for DDCMP). The sequence checking routines must use the proper modulus in performing additions and checking proper sequence numbers (e.g., message 0 follows message 7 in SDLC).

Transparency

In cases where **transparency** is built into the protocol, e.g., DDCMP and SDLC, no special considerations are needed to provide transparency. In a protocol like BSC, different state control blocks can be maintained, one set for receiving and transmitting nontransparent data messages, one set for receiving and transmitting transparent data messages. Primarily because such finite state logic greatly simplifies the implementation of a protocol like BSC, examples in this book have used the transparent BSC protocol to illustrate how a protocol's syntax can be represented.

Exceptions

Protocol exceptions or special cases are built into both the state-driven logic (via the state control blocks) and the action routines. The performance of the software in such exceptions may be totally different. The best example of such an exception might be a download of software into a remote computer under DDCMP. In this case, a new program will be received, and this new program will eventually receive control after it is loaded into the memory of the remote computer.

Protocol Definition

As long as **formal grammar** and **finite state machine** definitions of protocols exist, protocol implementation will become far easier. The information presented in this book has dealt with the actual use of such techniques for implementing data link control protocols. Designers of data communications software must apply standard design techniques to such protocol implementations, just as designers of compilers and operating systems apply certain basic principles in the implementation of such software.

More research in such standardized implementation techniques is highly desirable. In particular, standard notation for finite state machine descriptions of protocols would be a big step towards obtaining such standardization. Reviewing protocol definitions for DDCMP and SDLC and comparing the different representations of such finite state machines lead quickly to the conclusion that there is a long way to go before such standards will be available.

≡ Terminology ≡

ACK#	procedural states
error control	protocol exceptions
finite state logic	SEQ#
finite state machine	sequence control
formal grammar	startup control
handshaking sequence	timer control
line control	transparency

≡ Review Questions ≡

1. List the aspects of data link control protocol definition.

2. How do finite state machine concepts fit into the implementation of these aspects of a data link control protocol?

25

Testing and Debugging Data Communications Software

**Debugging Problems • Hardware Line Monitors • Modular Testing •
Steps for Testing and Implementation**

Debugging Problems

Much of this book has been dedicated to the development of modular software for data link control protocols. The rewards of good software structure are, of course, greater ease of maintenance and less debugging time. Even if a good design has been used to implement this data communications software, the task of testing and **debugging** can be quite difficult and frustrating for many reasons:

1. Data is transferred in real time, often with character-by-character transfers involving interrupts and processing by interrupt handlers. For high speed lines, the number of asynchronous events (interrupts) occuring in the software can be quite high.

2. Errors occur in hardware outside of the computer system itself, e.g., in cables, modems, and communications lines, not to mention the communications interface itself. Such errors can occur at remote locations, like the site of the other computer system, totally out of reach and the control of the software implementor; pinpointing just where such an error has occurred can be very difficult and time consuming.

3. Difficulties at the remote computer system can create many difficult situations for the communications programmer.

   a. Often it is assumed that someone at the remote computer system can answer questions about what is happening at that system when it is being used for testing. This may not be the case, and the communications programmer is left with intuition and previous experience to help figure out problems which might be occurring at a site hundreds or even thousands of miles away.

   b. No logging facilities for data being transmitted or received (either by software or by a communications hardware line monitor) are available. Even if technical personnel are available at the remote site, it may not be possible to determine just what is being received and/or transmitted.

   c. Ambiguity in the protocol definitions themselves or anomalies (local changes) in specific implementation of the protocols may result in the wrong syntactical or procedural rules being implemented in the software.

The net result of all this is that it is extremely difficult to know what is received or even what is expected at the remote computer system.

It would be ideal if the programmer could test the communications software by communicating with a local computer system which can be examined, controlled and interrogated, but circumstances sometimes make this impossible. Thus, it is best to know what symptoms of errors might arise during the debugging of data link control protocols, and what might cause these symptoms.

Complex protocols are not easy to represent in software, and even if the software designer(s) understood it correctly, the representation in software will likely have some errors in it. If such errors exist, the software will fail in any kind of communications environment which uses the protocol being implemented.

The manipulation of transmit scheduler queues, history lists, and the rescheduling of messages in a full-duplex environment can also yield a source of errors that falls outside of the syntactic rules of the protocol. A simple pointer variable which is not updated can produce strange results when communications software is being tested. For example, a line disconnect could be directed by a remote computer because a duplicate message was being sent again and again as a result of a pointer not being updated correctly. The symptom of being disconnected does not obviously imply the cause: in this case, the remote software took drastic action and the communications programmer has little to go on to find the problem quickly.

Finally, the error detection procedures supported by a protocol must be implemented correctly if any message is to be successfully received or transmitted. Since CRC, LRC and VRC may be implemented in software, errors could exist in the very mechanism which is designed to prevent errors in data which is received.

When debugging, one must learn to expect the unexpected. This seems to be the case in communications software implementations more than in others. If at all possible, a log of sample message traffic from production systems already using the protocol being implemented should be obtained. Reading and studying this log should help to eliminate ambiguities and misunderstandings about the protocol. If such a log is machine-readable, messages can be extracted and processed for testing the data link control protocol modules and the higher level protocol modules without involving the communications line at all. Thus, debugging of these modules can take place "off-line," outside of an environment that involves real-time data transfers, greatly simplifying the debugging of these modules.

It is advisable for the software to have the facility to log all messages sent and received. Such messages should be time-stamped to help determine timing problems which might exist in the software being implemented. This log should be machine-readable and, when necessary, should be capable of being printed in a simple format on a line printer. Although communications line monitors now exist, they are not always available. Even when they are available as a debugging aid, a software-produced log still has value to help compare data received and transmitted by the software to data which actually passed through the interface.

Table 25–1 lists some of the error conditions that might occur when communications software is implemented, along with some possible causes of these errors. This table can be helpful in pinpointing the source of such errors.

TABLE 25–1   Symptoms of Bugs and Possible Causes

Symptom	Possible Causes
Nothing is Received	Wrong SYN character Synchronization hardware is down SYN register not loaded Other computer is down Modems are incompatible Modems not set to same speed Modem in test mode Modem not powered up Cable not connected Bad modem Bad cable Bad phone line "Line" not enabled by other computer
Constant NAKing of transmitted messages	Incorrect LRC, VRC, or CRC Incorrect message format (syntax) Message not valid according to procedural rules
No handshaking	Timer interval(s) not correct Handshake sequence not correct
Timing Out	Timeout interval too small Timer hardware or software not operating correctly Software too slow (design problem) Other system went down
Hardware overruns	Software too slow Interrupts are blocked for receiver interface
Transmitted messages not recognized	Wrong SYN character used for transmit Wrong number of SYNs being transmitted Not waiting for Clear to Send signal from modem Not waiting for data transmission to complete before turning line around
Received buffer too long	Maximum buffer lengths for sending and receiving systems are not the same
Software locked in receive or transmit mode	Line turnaround procedure is incorrect Software "mode" flag is wrong (half-duplex)

Perhaps the most frustrating symptom of a problem in data communications software is that it does nothing, i.e., it loops, never receiving data. In a synchronous protocol environment, the synchronizing procedure often relates to the reason that data is not received: the wrong SYN character was used, it was never loaded, or the synchronizing hardware itself has failed. Without synchronization, of course, no data can possibly be received. When more than one problem exists in the software, e.g., the wrong SYN character was used for transmission and a timer interval is incorrect, it is much more difficult to determine the cause of the error. Often, due to timing differences, the software never seems to do the same thing twice. Each implementation of communications data link control protocols will have its own unique problems which will not necessarily fit into any previous mold of other implementations.

Hardware Line Monitors

There are a variety of **hardware line monitors** available to aid in debugging communications software and in finding problems in production data communications systems. These monitors usually attach to communications ports and "intercept" the data before it gets to the computer communications interface. They provide a wide range of capabilities, like the selection of character codes, protocol, dynamic display of data being received on a screen, and the writing of data characters to tape or other medium for later use and analysis.

Hardware line monitors are another tool to help the communications programmer determine precisely what is being transmitted and received on a given communications line. Some line monitors are quite expensive and may not be available in many installations.

Modular Testing

The modular structure presented in the previous chapter has one distinct advantage (as do most modular implementations): setting up test data in the correct format makes it possible to test each module independently of the others. The "crisp" separation of functions in the communications software allows such **modular testing** because the appropriate data buffers and parameters are passed to the routine being tested. Hence, in a test of the DLCRCV module, formatted "communications" buffers can be passed to the DLCRCV routine without having to come directly from the ICRCV module. If a log of communications traffic in a production implementation of the protocol is available on some computer-readable medium, data buffers can be read from this log (magnetic tape or disk) and passed to DLCRCV for testing in an off-line environment (i.e., without receiving data from the communications interface itself).

Once DLCRCV has been tested in this simulated environment, "raw" data can be passed from test routines to DLCXMT to be processed into transmit buffers. These in turn can be passed to DLCRCV to be sure that DLCXMT produces data consistent with DLCRCV. Hence, much of the complicated testing can be done before a communications link has ever been established with a remote computer. Figure 25–1 illustrates the use of such techniques for testing in the communications environment.

FIGURE 25–1 Modular Software Testing in a Simulated Environment

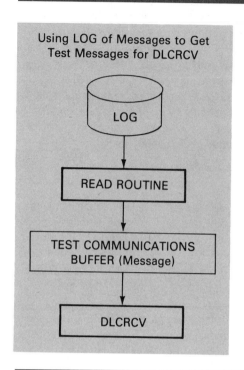

Using LOG of Messages to Get
Test Messages for DLCRCV

LOG

READ ROUTINE

TEST COMMUNICATIONS
BUFFER (Message)

DLCRCV

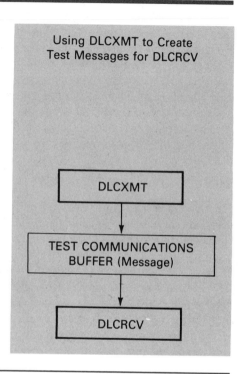

Using DLCXMT to Create
Test Messages for DLCRCV

DLCXMT

TEST COMMUNICATIONS
BUFFER (Message)

DLCRCV

Note that it is important to force as many errors as possible into the system during testing in order to guarantee that the error detection and error recovery routines work. This task can be difficult, for how is a particular kind of error found when it is needed for testing? Not all conditions can be generated from data from a log of communications traffic for the data link control protocol being implemented. Test data must be set up which reflects the conditions to be tested. This is particularly true for testing error conditions. The software must be tested to be sure it detects errors in the format of messages (header errors, missing data terminator, etc.), CRC, LRC, or VRC errors (whichever is appropriate), and invalid conditions which might arise in the data being interpreted according to the syntax of the protocol. Hence, test routines must be developed to force such errors in the test data. By doing this, the programmer can test all error conditions before attempting to test the software on-line with communications to another computer system.

One thing that is almost impossible to test in a simulated environment is the timing of events in the communications software. It is not unusual for the software modules to be thoroughly tested in a modular fashion, only to fail on-line due to timing problems. However, by eliminating as many problems as possible prior to testing on-line, solving the timing problems will be much easier.

FIGURE 25-2   Steps for Testing and Implementing Data
Communications Software

Step	Task(s)
1	Test DLCRCV and DLCXMT Using Simulated Environment * Use data log as source of test buffers to test DLCRCV * Use DLCXMT to generate test buffers to test DLCXMT and DLCRCV
2	Test Error Possibilites * Use test routines to generate error conditions in simulated environment
3	Establish Communications (Startup Sequence) * Use logging facility to determine what is being transmitted and received. * If communications cannot be established, verify the format of the startup message and the site identification (if any). * If possible, determine what was actually received by the other computer system.
4	Receive Data Messages * Use logging facility to check the data link control protocol and higher level protocol format(s) (if any).
5	Process Received Data Messages * Use debugging aids to be sure data is processed correctly by higher level protocols.
6	Process Data Messages for Transmission * Use the logging facility to check that the data to be transmitted is correct according to data link control and higher level protocols. * Use debugging aids to check format of data just prior to transmission.
7	Transmit Data Messages and Receive Acknowledgement * Use logging facility to determine problem if data messages are NAKed.
8	Transmit and Receive a Data File * It is best to send a file to other system, receive the file back, and compare the two files to be sure they are the same.
9	Process Network or Communications Commands * This depends on the environment — if commands to remote system exist, test each one.
10	Test All Error Conditions on Line * Keep a record of all error conditions tested to be sure that all possible error conditions have been tested on-line.
11	Place Software Into Production * In spite of testing, new problems and bugs will seem to arise during early use of software.

Steps for Testing and Implementation

Once the communications software has been designed and coded, you should follow an orderly procedure for testing the software on-line. Figure 25–2 presents in chronological order the steps that have been successful in many implementations. Note that data should be received before you attempt to build and transmit data messages according to the data link control protocol.

By first studying logs of received data, you will fully understand the correct format of messages. Getting acknowledgement from another computer system that startup messages have been successfully transmitted to the other system is the first step, but it is only the tip of the iceberg in implementing the software. If you cannot get past this step, debugging will prove to be a long, long process, for many steps follow this first step.

For obvious reasons, the use of the modular structure for implementing the data link control protocol will greatly simplify this debugging process. Being able to test "off-line" with real messages from an existing implementation will also be of great benefit in shortening the debugging time. [Lane, 1984]

═══ Terminology ═══

debugging   modular testing
hardware line monitor

═══ Review Questions ═══

1. List four reasons that testing and debugging are quite difficult in the implementation of data communications software.

2. Why is it better to attempt to receive data messages than to send them when first testing data communications software online?

3. How can modular testing be done for DLCRCV and DLCXMT?

4. True or false:
   a. After writing communications software, the first thing to do in testing is put it all together and attempt to communicate with another computer.
   b. Failure to load a SYN character into the synchronous hardware will result in data not being received (assume the default SYN character is 000_8).
   c. Real-time data transfer creates many synchronous events in a communications environment which make debugging difficult.

5. In a synchronous communications environment, list five possible causes for data never being received by the software:

_____

_____

_____

_____

_____

Appendix A
Proof of Accuracy of CRC-16

CRC-16 uses the generating polynomial shown below:

$$x^{16} + x^{15} + x^2 + 1 = (x + 1)(x^{15} + x + 1)$$

The remainder of this division yields two eight-bit checking characters. Using this polynomial as an example, it will be demonstrated that this CRC-16 mechanism detects over 99% of all possible errors. This will be proved by breaking error possibilites into several categories. [Martin 1971] An error is represented by a polynomial $E(x)$ added to the transmitted message $M(x)$

Single Bit Errors

A single bit error can be represented by the error polynomial

$$E(x) = x^i$$

$i <= n$, n being the total number of bits in the message. If the generating polynomial has more than one term, x^i cannot be exactly divisible by $G(x)$.

Double Bit Errors

Double bit errors are represented by

$$E(x) = x^i + x^j$$

and if $i < j$,

$$E(x) = x^i (1 + x^{j-i})$$

To detect an error, neither x^i nor $(1 + x^{j-i})$ may be divisible by $G(x)$. Since $G(x)$ has more than three terms, neither is divisible by $G(x)$. Thus, all double bit errors will be detected.

Odd Number of Error Bits

This will be proved by contradiction.

Assertion: If $E(x)$ has an odd number of errors, then it is not divisible by $x + 1$.

Proof: Suppose $E(x)$ is divisible by $(x + 1)$.

Then $$E(x) = (x + 1)Q(x).$$

For $x = 1$ and boolean operations we have

$$E(1) = (1 + 1)Q(1) = 0 * Q(1) = 0$$

Therefore, $E(1) = 0$. But this means that E has an even number of terms, which contradicts the fact that it had an odd number of terms. So if $G(x)$ has $(x + 1)$ as a factor, all odd number of error bits will be detected.

Bursts of Errors

If there is a burst of error bits, define the length of the burst b to be the number of bits having at least the first and last bits in error. For example, if $E(x)$ represents the error pattern 000001101101000, then $E(x)$ represents an error burst of length seven. In all cases of error bursts, we can represent $E(x)$ as

$$E(x) = x^i E_1(x)$$

where $i < n$, the number of bits in the message.

In the previous example,

$$E(x) = x^9 + x^8 + x^6 + x^5 + x^3$$
$$= x^3(x^6 + x^5 + x^3 + x^2 + 1)$$

Now x^i is not divisible by the generating polynomial, since we have already agreed that $G(x)$ will have more than one term. The error represented by $E(x)$ then goes undected if and only if $E_1(x)$ is exactly divisible by $G(x)$. We shall look at various cases on the length b of the error burst represented by $E(x)$.

Case 1. Length of burst $b < g + 1$.

Then all errors are detected, since $E_1(x)$ is not divisible by $G(x)$.

Case 2. Length of burst $b = g + 1$.

In this case, the error goes undetected if and only if $E_1(x) = G(x)$. Now the first and last terms are error bits and will result in 1s. Therefore, $g - 1$ bits remaining must be identical to the middle terms of $G(x)$. The probability of this is

$$(1/2)^{g-1}$$

since each term can take on the value of zero or one only. Thus, for CRC-16, the probability of an undetected error is $(1/2)^{15}$, which is .0000305.

Case 3. Burst $b > g + 1$.

In this case, there are a variety of error patterns divisible by $G(x)$. If $E_1(x)$ is divisible by $G(x)$, we have

$$E_1(x) = Q_1(x)\,G(x)$$

The degree of $Q_1(x)$ must be $(b - 1) - g$, and the number of bits represented by $Q_1(x)$ is $(b - 1) - g + 1$ or $b - g$.

Now the first and last terms of $E_1(x)$ are always 1. Therefore, the first and last terms of $Q_1(x)$ are always 1. Hence, $b - g - 2$ terms of $Q_1(x)$ can alternate in value. This means that there are $2^{(b-g-2)}$ ways that $E_1(x)$ is divisible by $G(x)$.

There are 2^{b-2} combinations of $E_1(x)$. Assuming equal probability, the probability of an error going undetected is

$$\frac{2^{(b-2-g)}}{2^{(b-2)}} = 2^{-g}$$

Again for CRC-16, the probability is $(1/2)^{16}$, which is .0000152.

Note: some error patterns will likely be more prevalent than others, so that in reality, the probability of error is not *exactly* as shown above. The probability of detecting error bursts greater that 16 bits in length is 99.955% utilizing CRC-16 error check characters [McNamara 1982].

Summary of Error Detection of CRC-16

If $G(x)$ has $(x + 1)$ as a factor and one factor with at least three terms, the probability of detecting errors is as follows:

Type of Error	Probability of Detection
Single bit errors	
Two bits in error	
An odd number of bits in error	100%
Error bursts of length $\langle\ g + 1$	
Error bursts of length $= g + 1$	$1 - (1/2)^{g-1}$
Error bursts of length $\rangle\ g + 1$	$1 - (1/2)^{g}$

References

Martin, James. 1970. *Teleprocessing Network Organization.* Englewood Cliffs, New Jersey: Prentice Hall.

McNamara, John E. 1982. Technical Aspects of Data Communications. Second Edition. Bedford, Massachusetts: Digital Press.

Appendix B
Formal Syntax Definition of DDCMP
(Reprinted from Appendix B of DDCMP Specifications Document) [DEC 1978]*

Symbology

In the following formal definition of the protocol grammar, the symbols have the following meanings:

1. ⟨ ⟩ denotes a metalinguistic variable.
2. : = means "is produced by" or "has the value of."
3. ⟨a⟩⟨b⟩ means "a followed by b" or "b concatenated with a."
4. ⟨a⟩!⟨b⟩ means "a OR b" (exclusive OR).
5. Quantities not surrounded by brackets ⟨ ⟩ are constants or literal values.
6. (⟨a⟩*b means "a repeated b times" (⟨a⟩⟨a⟩ — — — ⟨a⟩).
7. ⟨a⟩** means "a occurs from zero to infinity times in succession."
8. null means "the empty set."

Message Syntax

The following definition of the protocol does not include the specific sync sequences and rules when they are used on each link type. . . .

⟨protocol⟩: = ⟨transmission⟩⟨trailer⟩!⟨transmission⟩⟨protocol⟩
⟨transmission⟩: = ⟨msg⟩!⟨syncseq⟩⟨msg⟩

Note that the form ⟨syncseq⟩⟨msg⟩ is required in numerous cases. . . .

⟨syncseq⟩: = ⟨leader⟩⟨sync⟩*m

Where m is a parameter determined by hardware and interchange considerations. (m ⟩ = 1 for asynchronous circuits, m ⟩ = 4 for synchronous circuits.)

Note that ⟨syncseq⟩ is used for inter-message padding as well as for synchronizing.

⟨sync⟩ : = ⟨syn⟩   for synchronous circuits
    : = 10-bit idle line ! ⟨del⟩   for asynchronous circuits
    : = null   for parallel circuits

Where "10-bit idle line" means that the channel is held continuously in the state of the stop element (i.e. Mark, condition Z, 1) for a period not less than 10 bit times.

⟨leader⟩: = (⟨one⟩*j)(⟨sync⟩*k) for synchronous circuits

Where $j + 8k \rangle = 0$ if qsync is set in the previous message. This is a short sync sequence.

Where $j + 8k \rangle = 32$ if qsync is not set in the previous message. This is a long sync sequence.

Either $j = 0$ or $j \rangle = 8$

    : = idle line ! ⟨del⟩** for asynchronous circuits

Where "idle line" means that the channel is held continuously in the state of the stop element (i.e. Mark, condition Z, 1)

    : = null for parallel circuits

⟨trailer⟩: = ⟨one⟩*j   for synchronous circuits, where $j \rangle = 8$
    : = ⟨leader⟩   for asynchronous circuits
    : = mull   for parallel circuits

⟨one⟩: = 1

⟨msg⟩: = ⟨nummsg⟩!⟨unnummsg⟩!⟨maintmsg⟩

⟨nummsg⟩: = ⟨soh⟩⟨header⟩⟨bcc⟩⟨data⟩⟨bcc⟩

⟨unnummsg⟩: = ⟨enq⟩⟨body⟩⟨bcc⟩

⟨maintmsg⟩: = ⟨dle⟩⟨mhdr⟩⟨bcc⟩⟨data⟩⟨bcc⟩

⟨header⟩: = ⟨count⟩⟨qsync⟩⟨select⟩⟨resp⟩⟨num⟩⟨addr⟩

⟨data⟩: = (⟨byte⟩ * value of ⟨count⟩)

⟨bcc⟩: = ⟨byte⟩⟨byte⟩

⟨body⟩: = ⟨ackm⟩!⟨nakm⟩!⟨repm⟩!⟨strtm⟩!⟨stackm⟩

⟨mhdr⟩: = ⟨count⟩⟨qyncl⟩⟨selectl⟩⟨fill⟩⟨fill⟩⟨addr⟩

⟨count⟩: = (⟨bit⟩*14)

⟨select⟩: = ⟨bit⟩

⟨select1⟩: = 1

⟨qsync⟩: = ⟨bit⟩

⟨qsync1⟩: = 1

⟨resp⟩: = ⟨byte⟩

⟨num⟩: = ⟨byte⟩

⟨addr⟩: = ⟨byte⟩

⟨ackm⟩: = ⟨ack⟩⟨fill6⟩⟨qsync⟩⟨select⟩⟨resp⟩⟨fill⟩⟨addr⟩

⟨nakm⟩: = ⟨nak⟩⟨rnak⟩⟨qsync⟩⟨select⟩⟨resp⟩⟨fill⟩⟨addr⟩

⟨repm⟩: = ⟩⟨rep⟩⟨fill6⟩⟨qsync⟩⟨select⟩⟨fill⟩⟨num⟩⟨addr⟩

⟨strtm⟩: = ⟨strt⟩⟨fill6⟩⟨qsync1⟩⟨select1⟩⟨fill⟩⟨fill⟩⟨addr⟩

⟨stackm⟩: = ⟨stack⟩⟨fill6⟩⟨qsyncl⟩⟨select1⟩⟨fill⟩⟨fill⟩⟨addr⟩

⟨rnak⟩: = 000001!000010!000011!001000!001001!010000!010001

⟨byte⟩: = 00000000!00000001!...!11111111

⟨bit⟩: = 0!1

⟨syn⟩: = 10010110

⟨soh⟩: = 10000001

⟨enq⟩: = 00000101

⟨del⟩: = 11111111

⟨fill⟩: = 00000000

⟨fill6⟩: = 000000

⟨dle⟩: = 10010000

⟨ack⟩: = 00000001

⟨nak⟩: = 00000010

⟨rep⟩: = 00000011

⟨strt⟩: = 00000110

⟨stack⟩: = 00000111

STARTUP STATE TABLE

State	Event	New State	Action
any state	User requests halt	HALTED	None — stop timer if running
HALTED	User requests startup	ISTRT	Send STRT-reset variables start timer
	User requests Maintenance Mode	MAINTENANCE	. . . Maintenance Mode
ISTRT	Receive STACK	RUNNING	Send ACK (RESP = 0) stop timer if running
	Receive STRT	ASTRT	Send STACK-start timer
	Timer expires	ISTRT	Sent STRT-start timer
	Receive MAINT message	MAINTENANCE	. . . Maintenance Mode
	Message in error or other message received	ISTRT	Either: Send STRT, start timer; or ignore (do nothing)
ASTRT	Receive ACK (RESP = 0) or Receive Data msg (RESP = 0)	RUNNING	See Data Transfer stop timer
	Receive STACK	Running	Send ACK(RESP = 0) stop timer
	Receive STRT	ASTRT	Send STACK-start timer
	Time expires	ASTRT	Send STACK-start timer
	Receive MAINT message	MAINTENANCE	. . . Maintenance Mode
	Message in error or other message received	ASTRT	Either: Send STACK, start timer; or ignore (do nothing)

State	Event	New State	Action
RUNNING	Receive STRT	HALTED	Notify user of STRT received
	Receive MAINT	MAINTENANCE	. . . Maintenance Mode
	Receive STACK	RUNNING	Send ACK (RESP = R)

RUNNING STATE TABLE

Event	Action
Receive Data Msg (NUM = R + 1) (Also see Receive ACK)	If buffer available, $R \leftarrow R + 1$, give msg to user, set SACK flag; otherwise set SNAK flag, (reason 8. or 16.)
Receive Data Msg	Ignore
Receive message in error	Set SNAK flag, see NAK reasons (See Table 12–4)
Receive REP (NUM = R)	Set SACK flag
Receive REP (NUM not = R)	Set SNAK flag, (reason 3)
Receive ACK, or Data Msg ($A < NUM < = N$)	For all messages ($A < NUM < = RESP$), complete msg to user, $A \leftarrow RESP$ If $T < = A$, then $T \leftarrow A + 1$ If $A < X$, start timer If $A > = X$, stop timer
Receive ACK or Data Msg ($RESP < = A$ or $RESP > N$)	Ignore
Receive NAK ($A < = RESP < = N$)	For all messages ($A < NUM < = RESP$), complete msg to user, $A \leftarrow RESP$ $T \leftarrow A + 1$, stop timer

Event	Action
Receive NAK (RESP ‹ A or RESP › N)	Ignore
Reply timer expires	Set SREP flag
Transmitter is idle and SNAK flag is set	Send NAK with reason value, clear SNAK flag
Transmitter is idle, SNAK flag is clear, SREP flag is set	Send REP, clear SREP flag, * start timer
Transmitter is idle SNAK and SREP flags are clear, $T < N + 1$	MSG(T) is retransmitted, * $X \leftarrow T$, * if timer not running start timer $T \leftarrow T + 1$, clear SACK flag
User requests message to be sent: $T < N + 1$, transmitter is busy, SNAK flag is set, or SREP flag is set	User waits until: $T = N + 1$, transmitter is idle, SNAK flag is clear, and SREP flag is clear
User requests message to be sent, $T = N + 1$, transmitter is idle, SNAK and SREP flags are clear	$NUM \leftarrow N + 1$ Send MSG(NUM) $N \leftarrow NUM$ $T \leftarrow N + 1$, clear SACK flag * $X \leftarrow N$, * if timer not running start timer
Transmitter is idle, SNAK and SREP flags are clear, $T = N + 1$, no user requests waiting, SACK flag is set	Send ACK, clear SACK flag

*If messages are queued for transmission and the timer is started and stopped after actual transmissions of messages are completed rather then [sic] when messages are queued, then ignore the starred (*) actions listed above for the events: Transmitter is idle (SREP set), Transmitter is idle ($T < N + 1$), and User requests message to be sent ($T = N + 1$) and add the following events and actions:

Data message (NUM) transmission completed on link	$X \leftarrow NUM$ If $A < X$ and timer not running, then start timer If $A >= X$, then stop timer
REP message transmission completed on link	start timer

Reference

DEC. 1978. Digital Data Communications Message Protocol — DDCMP Specification Version 4.0 AA-D599A-TC. Mayndard, Massachusettes: Digital Equipment Corporation.

Appendix C
Sample Finite State Machine
Implemented in "C"

```
************************************************************************
* DOCUMENTATION              5/19/81          KEN JONES              *
************************************************************************
```

PROCEDURE NAME: state.c

CALLING PROCEDURE: main.c

ARGUMENTS/PARAMETERS: none

INPUT: external array "buff[ ]"

OUTPUT: printf statements describing the BISYNC data
                          block

UNIX SYSTEM CALLS: return, printf

EXTERNAL VARIABLES: buff[ ], BCNT, BSTATE

RETURN CODES: +4 "bid for line" transmitted (SOH ENQ)
               +3 valid data block received/transmitted
               +2 negative acknowledgement received/transmitted
               +1 positive acknowledgement received/transmitted
               -1 unexpected character received
               -3 communications not established, continue "bid for line"
               -5 severe error — something terrible is wrong
               -11 invalid BISYNC message format of transmission

PURPOSE: validate data blocks according to the Binary Synchronous
               Communication (BISYNC) protocol

DESCRIPTION:

State.c is a finite state machine procedure that scans a data block contained in "buff[ ]" to determine if the data block conforms to BISYNC protocol for message framing. State.c also determines the general data block type from the following list:

1. positive acknowledgement
2. negative acknowledgement
3. normal text data block
4. request "bid for line" to establish communications
5. invalid BISYNC block

State.c knows whether it is validating a transmitted or received data block by using the current contents of "BSTATE". A BSTATE value between 0 and 9 indicates a RECEIVED data block is being validated. A BSTATE value between 10 and 19 indicates a TRANSMITTED data block is being validated. The character count for each block is contained in "BCNT". State.c executes until BCNT becomes zero, a valid data block is found, or an invalid data block is found.

State.c is set up to validate received data blocks excluding the standard timing characters (SYN SYN) normally transmitted before each data block. On the receive side, these two characters are stripped out of the data block by a hardware mechanism and will never be seen by any software logic. On the transmit side, state.c validates the entire data block including the two characters (SYN SYN).

The finite state machine logic involved with this procedure is very simple to follow by reading the source code. There has also been added for future additions a comment card /*** call CRCCALC ***/ in all of the places where a data character should be added to the BCC accumulation character. This will save the programmer the time and research involved to determine which characters are added and which ones are not.

source Listing (state.c)

```
#
 /*
  *
  * state.c
  * BISYNC State Machine
  *
  *
  * Written by Ken Jones
  * April 16, 1981
  *
  */

#include      "globl.h"      /* constant definitions */
#include      "extern.h"     /* index into external data buffer */

state()
{

int      c;         /* current character being processed */
int      sbptr;     /* index into external data buffer */
```

```
sbptr = 0;              /* initialize index into buffer */

while (BCNT > 0) {           /* process all characters */

c = buff[sbptr] & 0377;     /* get next character */

    switch(BSTATE) {     /* 0 - 9 are Receive States */
                         /* 10 - 19 are Transmit States */

        case   0:                       /* look for valid first character */
            if (c = = DLE) {
                BSTATE = 1;     /* could be DLE ACK or DLE STX */
                printf("DLE ");
                }
            else if (c = = NAK) {
                BSTATE = 2;     /* could be NAK PAD */
                printf("NAK ");
                }
            else {
                return(-1);     /* send NAK PAD, invalid first character */
                }
            BCNT — — ;
            break;
        case   1:                       /* look for valid second character */
            if (c = = STX) {            /* did we find DLE STX? */
                BSTATE = 3;     /* change state, look for normal data or DLE */
                printf("STX ");
                }
            else if (c = = ACK) {
                printf("ACK ");
                return(1);      /* ACK message received */
                }
            else {
                return(-1);     /* send NAK PAD, invalid second character */
                }
            BCNT — — ;
            break;
        case  2:                        /* look for PAD character */
            if (c = = PAD) {
                printf("PAD ");
                return(2);      /* NAK message received */
                }
            else {
                return(-1);     /* send NAK PAD, unexpected character */
                }
            break;
        case  3:                        /* look for normal data and DLE */
            if (c = = DLE) {           /* if DLE is found ... */
                BSTATE = 4;     /* change state and look for another DLE */
                printf("DLE ");
```

```c
        BCNT — — ;
        }
    else {
/*** call CRCCALC ***/ /* add normal data character to BCC */
        BCNT — — ;        /* normal data, decrement count */
        }
    break;
case 4:                      /* look for several different things */
    if (c = = DLE) {         /* did we find two DLE characters? */
                             /* treat second DLE as data character */
/*** call CRCCALC ***/ /* add second DLE data character to BCC */
        BSTATE = 3;          /* change state, look for normal data or DLE */
        printf("DLE ");
        }
    else if (c = = ETB) {    /* did we find DLE ETB? */
        BSTATE = 5;          /* change state to look for BCC */
        printf("ETB ");
/*** call CRCCALC ***/ /* add ETB character to BCC */
        }
    else if (c = = SYN) {    /* did we find timing DLE SYN? */
        BSTATE = 3;          /* change state, look for normal data or DLE */
        printf("SYN ");
        }
    else {
        return (-1);         /* send NAK PAD, unexpected character */
        }
    BCNT — — ;
    break;
case 5:                      /* first half of BCC */
        BSTATE = 6;
        printf("BCC1 ");
    BCNT — — ;
    break;
case 6:                      /* second half of BCC */
        printf("BCC2 ");
        return(3);           /* valid data block received */
    break;
case 7:                      /* look for DLE ACK response to our SOH END */
    if (c = = DLE) {
        BSTATE = 8;          /* change state to look for ACK */
        printf("DLE ");
        BCNT — — ;
        }
    else
        return(-3);          /* no DLE ACK found, retransmit SOH ENQ */
    break;
case 8:
    if (c = = ACK) {
        printf("ACK ");
```

```
            printf("OK Communications Established ");
            return(4);            /* send SIGNON */
            }
        else
            return (-3);          /* no DLE ACK found, send SOH ENQ */
        break;

case  10:                         /* look for first SYN character */
        if (c = = SYN) {
            BCNT — — ;
            BSTATE = 11;
            printf("SYN ");
            }
        else
            return(-11);          /* invalid BSC message format */
        break;
case  11:                         /* look for second SYN character */
        if (c = = SYN) {
            BCNT — — ;
            BSTATE = 12;
            printf("SYN ");
            }
        else
            return(-11);          /* invalid BSC message format */
        break;
case  12:                         /* look for several different things */
        if (c = = DLE) {
            BSTATE = 13;          /* could be DLE STX or DLE ACK */
            printf("DLE ");
            }
        else if (c = = NAK) {
            BSTATE = 14;          /* could be NAK PAD */
            printf("NAK ");
            }
        else if (c = = SOH) {
            BSTATE = 15;          /* could be SOH ENQ */
            printf("SOH ");
            }
        else
            return(-11);          /* invalid BSC message format */
        BCNT — — ;
        break;
case  13:                         /* look for several different things */
        if (c = = ACK) {
            printf("ACK ");
            return(1);            /* DLE ACK transmitted */
            }
        else if (c = = STX) {
            BCNT — — ;
```

```
            BSTATE = 16;        /* change state, look for normal data or DLE */
            printf("STX ");
            }
      else
            return(-11);        /* invalid BSC message format */
      break;
case  14:                       /* look for NAK PAD */
      if (c = = PAD) {
            printf("PAD ");
            return(2);          /* NAK PAD transmitted */
            }
      else
            return(-11);        /* invalid BSC message format */
      break;
case  15:                       /* look for SOH ENQ message */
      if (c = = ENQ) {
            printf("ENQ ");
            return(4);          /* SOH ENQ transmitted */
            }
      else
            return(-11);        /* invalid BSC message format */
      break;
case  16:                       /* look for normal data or DLE */
      if (c = = DLE) {
            BSTATE = 17;        /* look for 2nd DLE, STX or ETB */
            printf("DLE ");
            BCNT — — ;
            }
      else {
      /*** call CRCCALC ***/ /* add normal data character to BCC */
            BCNT — — ;         /* normal data, decrement count */
            }
      break;
case  17:                       /* look for several different things */
      if (c = = DLE) {          /* did we find two DLE characters? */
                                /* treat second DLE as data character */
      /*** call CRCCALC ***/ /* add second DLE data character to BCC */
            BSTATE = 16;        /* change state, look for normal data or DLE */
            BCNT — — ;
            }
      else if (c = = SYN) {     /* did we find timing DLE SYN? */
            BSTATE = 16;        /* change state, look for normal data or DLE */
            printf("SYN ");
            BCNT — — ;
            }
      else if (c = = ETB) {     /* did we find DLE ETB? */
            BSTATE = 18;        /* change state to look for BCC */
            printf("ETB ");
      /*** call CRCCALC ***/ /* add ETB character to BCC */
```

```
                    BCNT — — ;
                    }
             else
                    return(-11);          /* invalid BSC message format */
             break;
      case  18:                           /* first half of BCC */
                    BSTATE = 19;
                    printf("BCC1 ");
             BCNT — — ;
             break;
      case  19:                           /* second half of BCC */
                    printf("BCC2 ");
                    return(3);            /* valid data block transmitted */
             break;
      } /* end switch */
sbptr + + ;                              /* increment index into buffer */
} /* end while */
return(-5);                              /* severe error — something terrible is wrong */
} /* end state */
```

Appendix D
Sample Finite State Machine
Implemented in Pascal

PROCEDURE: SEARCH

IMPORTS	EXPORTS	LOCALS	GLOBALS	CALLED BY	CALLS
ARRAY2	NONE	STATE2	COL	INTERPRET	CALCCOUNT
INTEGER		N	DONE		CVSTR
		TABLE	NXTCHR		DEPOSIT
		TEMPUF			EVALBCB
					EVALMSG
					EVALRCB
					EVALSCB
					EVALSRCB
					EVALTYPE
					REASON
					WRITEIT

PURPOSE: DETERMINES IF THE CURRENT STATE TABLE CHARACTER
MATCHES THE LIST OF CHARACTERS THAT CAN HAVE VARI-
ABLE VALUES. IF A MATCH OCCURS THE PROPER ROUTINE IS
CALLED TO EVALUATE THE CHARACTER OR AN IMMEDIATE
ACTION IS TAKEN.

PROCEDURE SEARCH (TABLE: ARRAY2; VAR STAT2: INTEGER);
    VAR

```
      TEMPBUF:   SMSTR;
      N:   INTEGER;
BEGIN
   N: = TABLE [STATE2,COL,1];
   IF (N = OTH) OR (N = DLE2) THEN BEGIN
            DONE: = 1;
            CVSTR(NXTCHR,TEMPBUF);
            DEPOSIT (TEMPBUF)
         END
   ELSE IF N = BCC THEN WRITEIT ('BCC ')
      ELSE IF N = BCB THEN EVALBCB (NXTCHR)
         ELSE IF N = SRCB THEN EVALSRCB (NXTCHR)
            ELSE IF N = SCB THEN EVALSCB (NXTCHR)
               ELSE IF N = TYPE2 THEN EVALTYPE (NXTCHR)
                  ELSE IF N = CNT THEN CALCCOUNT
                     ELSE IF N = ADDR THEN WRITEIT ('ADDR')
                        ELSE IF N = DATA THEN EVALMSG
                           ELSE IF N = MSG THEN WRITEIT ('MSG#')
                              ELSE IF N = NUM THEN WRITEIT ('MSG#')
                                 ELSE IF N = REAS THEN REASON (NXTCHR)
                                 ELSE IF N = NXT THEN BEGIN
                                 STATE2: = STATE2 + 1;
                                 COL: = 1
                              END
END;
```

PROCEDURE: INTERPRET

IMPORTS	EXPORTS	LOCALS	GLOBALS	CALLED BY	CALLS
ARRAY2	INTEGER	BUFFER	ATTEMPTS	EVALUATE	NEXTCHR
INTEGER		STATE	COL		SEARCH
LGSTR		STATETABLE	DONE		WRITECHR
			FBCOUNT		
			MARKER		
			MESSAGE		
			MSGNUM		
			NXTCHR		

PURPOSE: INTERPRETS A SINGLE MESSAGE BUFFER USING THE STATE TABLE PASSED TO THE ROUTINE.

METHOD: CONTAINS NESTED REPEAT STATEMENTS. THE INNER LOOP CALLS THE SEARCH ROUTINE TO DETERMINE IF THE CHARACTER IS A CONTROL CHARACTER THAT REQUIRES EVALUATION. IF IT DOES NOT REQUIRE EVALUATION THE INNER LOOP THEN TRIES TO MATCH THE CURRENT CHARACTER TO THE STATE TABLE CHARACTERS IN THE CURRENT STATE. IF NO MATCH OCCURS AN ERROR STATEMENT IS PRINTED AND THE PROCEDURE TERMINATES. THE OUTER LOOP SEQUENTIALLY READS CHARACTERS FROM THE DATA FIELD UNTIL THE DATA MESSAGE IS EVALUATED OR AN ERROR OCCURS

CODES: DONE FLAG IS USED TO CONVEY THE STATUS OF EACH CHARACTER EVALUATION:

0 — EVALUATION IN PROGRESS.
1 — NORMAL TERMINATION, ADVANCE TO NEXT CHARACTER AND STATE.
2 — TERMINATION, BUFFER EVALUATION COMPLETE BUT MAINTAIN CURRENT STATE AND MESSAGE NUMBER.
3 — TERMINATION, BUFFER EVALUATED, TERMINAL SIGN-ON OR SIGN-OFF FOUND.

THE STATE ALSO ACTS AS A CODE TO CONVEY THE STATUS OF THE BUFFER EVALUATION.

0 — 100   — EVALUATION IN PROGRESS.
101 — 111 — EVALUATION COMPLETE.

```
PROCEDURE INTERPRET
        (STATETABLE: ARRAY2; BUFFER: LGSTR; VAR STATE: INTEGER);

   BEGIN
     FBCOUNT: = 1;
     MARKER: = 1;
     STATE: = 1;
     ATTEMPTS: = ATTEMPTS + 1;
     REPEAT
       COL: = 1;
       NXTCHR: = NEXTCHR(BUFFER);
       DONE: = 0;
       REPEAT
         IF NXTCHR = BLANK THEN BEGIN
```

```
              DONE: = 2;
              MSGNUM: = 22;
              STATE: = 111
           END
           ELSE BEGIN
              SEARCH (STATETABLE, STATE);
              IF DONE = 0 THEN
                IF NXTCHR = STATETABLE [STATE, COL, 1] THEN
                   BEGIN
                      DONE: = 1;
                      WRITECHR(NXTCHR);
                   END
                   ELSE BEGIN
                      COL: = COL + 1;
                      IF COL = 4 THEN DONE: = 1
                      END
           END
      UNTIL DONE < > 0;
      IF DONE < > 2 THEN BEGIN
         MSGNUM: = STATETABLE [STATE,4,2];
         STATE: = STATETABLE [STATE,COL,2]
      END;
      IF (COL = 4) OR (DONE = 3) THEN STATE: = 111
   UNTIL STATE > 100;
   WRITELN (MESSAGE [MSGNUM])
END;
```

Appendix E
Programming Project: ASYNCHRONOUS TERMINAL/LINE DRIVER — MLDRV

Design, Implement, and thoroughly test multiline asynchronous terminal/line driver **MLDRV**. The driver must control N (where $N \geq 2$) asynchronous interfaces or N lines on a multiline asynchronous interface (depending on your laboratory equipment) using re-entrant code. Each line must be represented by a line control block (LCB) similar to the one shown in Figure 18-2. Program structure should be such that another interface or support for more lines on a multiline interface is added by adding LCBs and setting appropriate line definitions, i.e., without changes to executable instructions in MLDRV.

The following entry points must be provided in MLDRV:

MLINIT — Saves system interrupt vectors and other information (system-dependent, sets up MLDRV interrupt vectors or equivalent) and initializes any parameters necessary.

MLCLEAR — Resets the asynchronous interface(s) (turns off interrupt enable and/or clears device) and restores the system information saved by MLINIT. MLCLEAR must be called before exiting the test program.

MLENABLE — Enables the line associated with the LINE specified. If multiple asynchronous interfaces are being programmed, then line numbers must be associated with a specific interface. If a multiline interface is being programmed, then the line number is the number of the line in the interface. Interrupts for the receiver should be enabled for line being enabled.

Calling sequence for MLENABLE is:

CALL MLENABLE(LINE,EFLAG)

where
LINE is the line number (0-N) being enabled and on return

EFLAG = 1 if line enable is okay
        -1 if LINE is invalid
        -2 if LINE already enabled

Option for MLENABLE: If line characteristics are programmable, then the calling sequence for MLENABLE must provide the parameters SPEED, PARITY, and CLEN:

CALL MLENABLE(LINE,EFLAG,SPEED, PARITY,CLEN)

where

SPEED = 1 if speed is   110 bps
      = 2 if speed is   300 bps
      = 3 if speed is   600 bps
      = 4 if speed is 1200 bps
      = 5 if speed is 2400 bps
      = 6 if speed is 4800 bps
      = 7 if speed is 9600 bps

PARITY = 0 if parity is not enabled
       = 1 if parity is odd
       = 2 if parity is even

CLEN = 7 if character length is 7
     = 8 if character length is 8

and in addition to the previous values for EFLAG,

EFLAG = -3 invalid SPEED requested
      = -4 invalid PARITY requested
      = -5 invalid CLEN requested

MLDSAB — Disables LINE. Interrupts for the receiver should be disabled for LINE.

Calling sequence is:

CALL MLDSAB(LINE,EFLAG)

where LINE is the line number (0-N) and on return

EFLAG = 1 if the line was disabled
      = -1 if LINE is invalid (< 0 or $> N$)
      = -2 if line specified by LINE was not enabled

MLWRITE — Used to output data to a line. The calling program must control all carriage returns and line feeds for terminal mode to allow the user to format the CRT screen in whatever manner desired. Messages or buffers for terminal mode must be in ASCII. If a length parameter (WLEN below) is not present, the NULL

(000) character terminates output. It is the calling program's responsibility to insert this NULL character if no length parameter is provided.

Calling Sequence is:

CALL MLWRITE(LINE,EFLAG,WBUFFER,{WLEN})

where

LINE is the line number (0-N)

WBUFFER is a buffer containing the characters to be sent to the terminal or line. The number of characters transmitted is either the number specified in WLEN if this parameter is present, or the number of characters in the buffer before a NULL character is detected if WLEN is omitted.

and on return

EFLAG is event flag to indicate status or result of the requested operation:

EFLAG = 0 write operation started, but is not finished
      = 1 Operation completed
      = -1 Invalid LINE ($<$0 or $>$7)
      = -2 LINE busy
      = -3 Invalid WLEN ($<$0)

MLREAD — used to read data from a terminal or line. Input can be in terminal mode or line mode (specified by the MODE parameter). If input is in terminal mode, characters received may be either echoed or not echoed, depending on the value in the MODE parameter.

Calling sequence is:

CALL MLREAD(LINE,MODE,EFLAG,RBUFFER,RLEN)

where

LINE is line number (0-N)

MODE — specifies line mode or terminal mode:

MODE = 0 $>$ Block Mode
     = 1 $>$ Terminal Mode with ECHO Enabled
     = 2 $>$ Terminal Mode with ECHO Disabled

RBUFFER is data area to be used to store the characters being entered. (Size of RBUFFER must be at least greater than or equal to the length specified in RLEN).

RLEN is an integer variable specifying the maximum number of characters to be read in terminal mode (MODE = 1 or 2) or the exact number of characters to be read in block mode (MODE = 0). RLEN should dynamically carry the number of characters currently in the user buffer when in line mode. RLEN should be set to the actual length of the data read on operation complete (carriage return or exact number of characters input) in terminal mode.

Note: EFLAG will be set to 1 when exactly the number of characters specified in RLEN has been read when input is in line mode or, in terminal mode, when the specified number has been read without a carriage return being detected.

EFLAG Return Codes/Event Flag Values for MLREAD

EFLAG = -1   MLINIT was never done.

   = -2   Last event on line or terminal was not complete before next operation attempted.

   = -3   Length parameter has value less than 1.

   = 0   Requested read operation was started, but is not yet complete.

   = 1   Requested read operation is complete. (On MLREAD, RLEN contains the number of characters read).

   = 11   ATTENTION signal (^C) was entered when in terminal mode on a read from terminal using MLREAD.

Special Control Characters on Input in Terminal Mode

DEL   key (177 octal) — Results in the previous character being deleted from the screen as well as from the buffer in memory. If the cursor is at the beginning of the current field, DEL is ignored. (BACKSPACE)

^U   (025 octal) — Blanks out the current field and moves the cursor to the beginning of the current field. (ERASE FIELD)

^C   (003 octal) — Aborts the current operation requested on input and sets the event flag to 11 (decimal). This is useful to force a terminal back into "command mode." (ATTENTION)

Bell Ringing on Input (Terminal Mode):

Type-ahead may be accomplished on the terminal, i.e. input can be accepted (but not echoed) into an echo buffer until a MLREAD request from a user's control program is issued for a specific terminal or line. If the echo (or ring) buffer fills up before an input request is issued, "ring the bell" when in terminal mode for each character lost. The echo buffer length should be easy to change by changing a size "variable" and reassembling or recompiling MLDRV. Its value should be set to at least 12 bytes in length for this assignment.

Test Program — MLTEST

You must implement a test program **MLTEST** to test the various capabilities of MLDRV. MLTEST should provide for:

1. The selection of a master input line/terminal to enter data to be written to multiple lines/terminals (including possibly this master terminal).
2. The selection of 2 or more output lines/terminals to display a message entered using the master line/terminal.
3. The selection of the mode for a particular test:
   a. Block mode
   b. Terminal mode with Echo enabled
   c. Terminal mode with Echo disabled
4. The selection of the type of write to use for a test:
   a. Exact count — WLEN provided
   b. Implicit count — WLEN omitted and WBUFFER contains NULL Character at the end of the data.
5. Overlapped output to terminals/lines using event flags to check the progress of MLWRITE while driving two or more terminals concurrently.
6. A way to end each specific test (e.g., entering *END on master input terminal).
7. A way to select a new test.
8. A way to stop the execution of MLTEST.
9. The checking of error possibilities, i.e., forcing "bad calls" to MLREAD, MLWRITE, etc. to guarantee that error checks work.

Device (Register/Vector) Addresses

Controlling asynchronous interfaces is very machine-dependent. Your instructor will give you the following information (if applicable) for each line to be controlled:

LINE	Device/Register Address	Interrupt Vector Address
0	_____	_____
1	_____	_____
.		
.		
.		
N	_____	_____

Appendix F
Programming Project: SHDP Protocol Using Asynchronous Communications

Goal

To use the block mode of the multiline asynchronous communications project in Appendix E to implement the simple half-duplex protocol (SHDP) defined in Chapter 10.

Protocol

Use the protocol definition presented for SHDP in Figure 10-1 and the finite state diagram for SHDP from Figure 10-10 and Assignment 1 of Chapter 10.

Minimimum Requirement

The minimum requirement is to be able to send a file from the Computer A to Computer B in your laboratory and display the received output on the CRT on Computer B. Error checking using CRC-16 (or the optional LRC and VRC) must be demonstrated (and hence your test program must be able to "force" errors). The direction of transfer should also be able to be reversed, i.e., from Computer B to Computer A.

Final Test

Send a file TEST from Computer A to Computer B and store it as file TESTB. Then send this file (TESTB) back from Computer B to Computer A and store as TESTA. Then compare the orginal file file TEST to the file TESTA on Computer A. The files must be identical.

The Simple Half-Duplex Protocol (SHDP) is defined in Chapter 10. Using the definition, provide support for:

System Start-up:

Upon starting communications software on each system, the following is the startup sequence:

Computer System A   ——————————⟩   Computer System B
⟨startmsg⟩

⟨—————————
⟨ackmsg⟩

——————————⟩   "Communications
⟨ackmsg⟩   Established"
                                    message printed

"Communications   ⟨—————————
Established"   ⟨ackmsg⟩
message printed

Handshake/Timeout Sequence:

Computer System A   ——————————⟩   Computer System B
⟨ackmsg⟩

⟨—————————
⟨ackmsg⟩

Computer System A — Wait 1 second before sending handshake ACK after receiving previous ACK from Computer System B.

Wait 1 second for receiver to go active after enabling receiver for ACK or other message. If receiver times out without going active during this 1 second interval, print "Receiver Timeout" on the terminal and send NAK. If NAK is received, print "NAK received" on terminal, and send ACK immediately.

Computer System B — Upon receiving an ACK, send ACK immediately. Wait 3 seconds before timing out in receive, i.e., after receiver is enabled. If receiver times out, print "Receiver Timeout" on terminal and send a NAK.

File Transfer Request

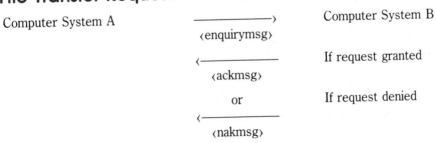

Computer System A   ——————————⟩   Computer System B
⟨enquirymsg⟩

⟨—————————   If request granted
⟨ackmsg⟩

or   If request denied

⟨—————————
⟨nakmsg⟩

If NAK received on ENQ, must continue sending ENQ until ACK is received before data transfer can begin.

Computer System B can send ENQ to Computer System A if line is "idle" to send file the opposite direction, i.e., systems above are symmetric on file transfer request.

File Transfer

Once ACK is received (permission to send granted) in response to file transfer request (ENQ), data transfer can begin. Recall that the format of data messages is as follows:

$$STX \langle data \rangle \ ETX \ BCC$$

The maximum length of ⟨data⟩ is 252, which makes maximum length of a message 256. This data field consists of "printable" ASCII characters (i.e., ASCII characters greater than or equal to 040_8).

Computer System A

———————⟩
Data Message

Computer System B

⟨———————
ACK

If OK

or

⟨———————
NAK

If error.

Message is retransmitted when an error is detected. Data message error possibilities include CRC errors (or VRC/LRC errors if option A below is selected for the project), message format errors, and a message being too long. Report each with appropriate message on the computer system's terminal and send a NAK.

End of Data Transmission

Normal end of transmission is indicated by the use of an EOT (end of transmission) message. The line then goes back to handshake mode upon receipt of an EOT. A message should be printed on the CRT terminal of the receiving computer indicating "End of Transmission" on data transfer.

Aborting Data Transfer

Either station can abort transmission by sending an abort message (ESC) instead of an ACK or a Data Message (receiver and transmitter respectively). Message should be printed on CRT stating "Data Transfer Aborted." The line then returns to handshake mode.

Receiver Busy

The sending of a WACK message (DLE) instead of an ACK by the Receiver of data is a pause in data flow. The system receiving the WACK responds by sending ACK. Pause continues as long as WACK is sent as the response to a previously-sent data message. When ACK is sent back to system which is sending data, transmission of data messages can resume. (This WACK is used to control data flow when writing data to devices, etc.). A message indicating this WACK condition exists should be printed on the terminal of the system sending data.

Command Handler

A command handler COMSHDP must be included in the SHDP protocol support. It must provide for:

1. Starting communications (initiate startup sequence)
2. Terminating communications
3. Beginning data transmission from a specific disk file
4. Beginning data reception to a specific disk file
5. Aborting data transfer
6. Forcing timeout errors
7. Forcing CRC (or VRC/LRC if option 1 selected) errors
8. Forcing the receiver busy condition (send WACK) during data transfer
9. Forcing sequence errors if option 2 below is selected
10. Stopping the SHDP system and returning to the operating system

Note: since there is no file-naming facility in the data link control protocol SHDP, before a file is sent from system A to system B, a "Receive File" command should be entered on system B to specify the disk file name to be used to store the data being received. Then a "Transmit File" command can be entered on system A to specify the name of the file to send. If no receive file has been entered on system B, the ENQ message should be NAKed until this "Receive File" command is entered or ESC is received from the other system. This process should be reversed to send data from system B to system A. The output file being used to receive data can be automatically closed on the receipt of an EOT or an ESC message.

The state of each system should be maintained, indicating if the system is in handshake state, receive data state, transmitting data state, etc., as indicated in Figure 10-10.

Options

1. Use VRC even or odd parity for each data character and LRC for the entire message (including STX and ETX) instead of the CRC-16 as the BCC character.

2. Implement the project for SHDP, including the sequence checking added in Assignment 1 of Chapter 10.

3. Implement the project using synchronous communications. It will be necessary to implement a synchronous communications interface driver using techniques similar to those used to implement block mode for MLDRV.

Appendix G
Programming Project: A "Mini" DDCMP Data Link Control Protocol

Purpose

To design and implement the DDCMP data link control protocol defined in Appendix B using synchronous communications which will "talk" via the a synchronous communications interface to another computer system running the same software.

Goals

1. To send startup sequence to System A and receive the Start acknowledgement (STACK).
2. To perform proper communications handshake sequence when the line is idle.
3. To send one or more data files from System A to System B and vice versa.
4. To send and receive (and process) NAK messages and REP messages.
5. To provide timer support for receiver timeout.
6. To force REP message request and errors which will test error recovery procedures.

Minimum Test

1. Send an ASCII data file TEST from System A to System B and store it as TESTB on System B.
2. Receive the file TESTB stored in 1 back from System A and store it as TESTA. Then compare the two files (via a source compare program if available) to be sure they are identical.

Refer to Chapter 12, particularly Figures 12-15 through 12-17, for sample message traffic. Appendix B provides formal syntax definition for DDCMP and state tables for the procedural rules of DDCMP. More specific information on DDCMP can be obtained from the DDCMP Specification [DEC 1978].

Protocol Overview:

1. STARTUP: System startup uses the sequence shown in Figure 12-14.
2. HANDSHAKE: Handshake consists of ACK-ACK sequences between stations when there is no data to transmit.
3. REP: The protocol should support the use of the REP message illustrated in Figure 12-17 to force a reply to a previously-sent message particularly if implemented in full-duplex.
4. NAK: NAK messages are used to indicate when errors have been detected. The reasons for NAK shown in Appendix B are to be supported.
5. Data Message: Data message traffic should be supported in half-duplex such as shown in Figure 12-15.

Options

1. Implement DDCMP project using half-duplex.
2. Implement DDCMP project using full-duplex.

Dictionary

ACK   Character used for acknowledging the successful receipt of a message.

ACK number   The number of the last successfully received message.

ACK#   *See* ACK number.

ACK0   The acknowledgement sequence used to acknowledge "even numbered" messages in the BSC protocol.

ACK1   The acknowledgement sequence used to acknowledge "odd numbered" messages in the BSC protocol.

acoustical coupling   Placing a telephone handset into cups so that it may transmit and receive data using audible tones on a voice-grade line.

acoustical modem   A modem which uses acoustical coupling; *compare* direct connect.

Advanced Research Projects Agency   Government agency within the Department of Defense which supported the development of ARPANET; *see* ARPANET.

American Standard Code for Information Interchange   *See* ASCII.

amplitude modulation   Modulation of an otherwise continuous carrier signal by changing amplitude.

analog signal   A signal which is continuous in nature (smooth transitions to different levels).

answer modem   A modem which signals when the telephone is ringing and provides for the answering of the ringing telephone and the carrier signal used for modulation; an answer modem can use frequencies which are different from an originate modem to provide full-duplex capability; *compare to* originate modem.

application layer   The highest layer in the ISO Open System Interconnection model.

ARC   The name (trademark) of Datapoint Corporation's local area network (Attached Resource Processor), which uses token passing.

ARPA   *See* Advanced Research Projects Agency.

ARPANET   A network funded by the Advanced Research Projects Agency, which provided most of the basic research for modern networks.

ASCII   American Standard Code for Information Interchange; a seven-bit computer code usually used with an additional high order parity bit.

ASR 33   An early terminal manufactured by Teletype Corporation.

asynchronous communications   Communications which uses START and STOP conditions to frame each character.

asynchronous serial interface   An interface which provides for asynchronous communications.

asynchronous transmission   *See* asynchronous communications.

attenuation   The loss of power as a signal travels over a distance on a communications medium.

Backus Naur Form   A notation, commonly used to define programming languages and protocol grammars. An example of this notation is given in Appendix B. *Abbreviated* BNF.

bandwidth   The difference between the highest frequency and the lowest frequency transmitted on a communications medium, measured in cyles per second (hertz).

baseband signalling   Signalling which usually uses a bandwidth of no more than 50 Mhz; *compare to* broadband signalling.

batch environment   A computing environment using an operating system which executes a collection of programs called a job. Each program within the job is executed before the next progam can begin execution.

baud   The number of times a signal changes state per second.

Baudot code   An early five-bit data code used for transmitting and receiving data.

BCB   *See* Block Control Byte.

BCC   Block Check Character; another name for CRC or LRC error check characters.

Binary Synchronous Communications   An IBM character-oriented synchronous protocol; *abbreviated* BSC, BISYNC.

BISYNC   *See* Binary Synchronous Communications.

bit   A binary digit.

bit time   The time required to transmit or receive one bit.

bit-oriented protocol   A protocol which does not recognize character boundaries during transmission.

bits per second   A measure of transmission or receiving of data; is not always equivalent to baud; *abbreviated* bps; *compare to* baud.

block check character   Another name for CRC or LRC error check characters; *abbreviated* BCC.

block control byte   A control byte in the HASP multileaving protocol which provides for message sequencing.

block transmission   Transmission of a group of data characters as a single transmission.

BNF   *See* Backus-Naur Form.

boot   The intial loading of an operating system into a computer, usually from disk or diskette.

bps   *See* bits per second.

break condition   A condition on an asynchronous line, which is forced by holding the line in a zero (space) condition for longer than the duration of the START, the data character and the STOP condition; the resulting framing error often is used as an attention signal.

broadband signalling   Signalling which uses bandwidths of 300 MHz or greater and allows multiple signals to coexist on the transmission medium; *compare to* baseband signalling.

BSC   *See* Binary Synchronous Communications.

buffer pool   A collection of buffers used as needed as transmission or receiver buffers and as device buffers in communications software.

bus   1) conductor used for the transmission of signals or energy; 2) in a computer, a single path or multiple parallel paths for power or data signals to which several devices may be connected at the same time.

byte-count-oriented protocol   A protocol having a header which contains a field specifying the exact length of the data field in data messages.

carrier detect   A control signal provided by a modem indicating that a carrier signal has been detected on the communications medium.

Carrier Sense Multiple Access with Collision Detection   A multiple access protocol used in local area networks in which collisions may occur and recovery from such collisions is provided; *abbreviated* CSMA/CD.

carrier sense   The capability which allows a node to listen before transmitting to determine if a channel is free.

carrier signal   A continuous signal on a communications medium which can be modulated and demodulated.

CCITT International Alphabet Number 2   Another name for Baudot code.

CCITT Recommendation X.21   General purpose interface between Data Terminal Equipment (DTE) and Data Circuit-Terminating Equipment (DCE) for synchronous operation on public data networks.

CCITT Recommendation X.25   Standard packet switching protocol defined by CCITT allowing for the interface to packet switched public data networks.

CD   *See* Carrier Detect.

centralized control   Control in a network in which a single node controls when other nodes may transmit data.

channel allocation   How a channel is allocated (efficiently) to nodes in a local area network.

channel control   How a channel in a local area network is controlled; uses two techniques—centralized or distributed.

character string   A collection of characters which represents a duplicate string of characters or a series of nonduplicate characters.

character-oriented protocol   A protocol which uses special control characters to delineate message fields and requires that all messages be scanned when received for these special control characters.

circular list of receiver buffers   A circular list implemented for receiver buffers in which each buffer has a pointer to the next and in which the "last" buffer points back to the first. A status field indicates if a given buffer is available for processing by a particular communications task.

clear to send   A control signal set by a modem, which indicates that it is okay to transmit data; in half-duplex, it is set after a terminal or computer (software) sets request to send.

clock   A means of timing intervals or events in a computer system; timing can be done either by a hardware clock or by timer software which makes use of a hardware clock; *see also* hardware clock, software clock.

cognitive level   Level in human communication which involves basic understanding and knowledge.

collision   The transmission of data by two or more stations at the same time on the same channel, which results in a loss of data.

collision detect   The capability of communications hardware to detect when a collision has occurred, which is possible because collisions cause a change in the electrical signal level on a channel.

compression   A technique of reducing the number of characters required to be transmitted by representing duplicate characters with one- or two-character control sequences or by having different lengths for characters. In the latter case, the most common characters are represented by shorter bit patterns.

concurrent execution   The execution of two or more programs in an interleaved manner by one CPU.

conditioned   The addition of certain hardware equipment to a leased voice-grade line to provide certain minimum values of line characteristics required for data transmission; *see also* equalization.

configure   To set certain values in software which represent the environment required for data communications (e.g., parity, line speed, etc.)

contention techniques   Techniques which anticipate the collision of data transmission on a network channel and require no polling.

control bits   Bits in a status word or status register which represent a control signal on a standard interface.

control block   A data structure which represents an event, a communications line/interface, or the execution of a task in an operating system or in communications software.

control message   A message defined by a protocol, which is used to specify the status of transmission or control data transmission (e.g., an ACK or NAK message).

control registers   Device registers which are used to control a device or to determine the status of a device.

CRC   *See* cyclic redundancy check character.

CRC-12   A cyclic redundancy check character which uses the polynomial $x^{12} + x^{11} + x^3 + x^2 + x + 1$.

CRC-16   A cyclic redundancy check character which uses the polynomial $x^{16} + x^{15} + x^2 + 1$.

CRC-CCITT   A cyclic redundancy check character which uses the polynomial $x^{16} + x^{12} + x^5 + 1$.

cross talk   Undesirable detection of a signal from one communications channel on another channel.

CRT   A cathode ray tube used as a display in an interactive terminal.

cryptography   The enciphering of stored or transmitted data so that it is scrambled in such a way that anyone trying to understand the information is unlikely to be able to unscramble the data; data must be deciphered by the receiving station or other program before it can be used; provides a means of data security in a network environment.

crystal clock   *See* line clock.

CSMA/CD   *See* carrier sense multiple access with collision detect.

CTS   *See* clear to send.

cyclic redundancy check   Used to compute an error check character, a technique which employs polynomial division to compute the value of the check character; *abbreviated* CRC.

data code conversion   The translation of data from one into another data code (e.g., from ASCII data codes into EBCDIC data codes.)

data codes   The bit patterns used to represent control characters and display characters.

data communications   The exchange of data messages from one point to another using communications channels; *see* data transmission.

data compression   *See* compression.

data link control layer   *See* data link layer.

data link control protocol   A protocol used to control message traffic in the data link layer of the ISO OSI model.

data link control receive monitor   The software module which provides the data link control protocol rules when data is being received.

data link control task   An independent software task in data communications software which provides either the receive or transmit rules of a data link control protocol.

data link control transmit monitor   The software module which provides the data link control protocol rules when data is being transmitted.

data link layer   The second layer of the ISO OSI model for describing networks, it controls message traffic on the physical communications medium.

data message   A message type in a data link control protocol, which contains a block of data (as opposed to a control message, which contains no data.)

data set   1) An early name for a modem, not commonly used today; *see* modem; 2) a collection of data records logically related to one another (a file).

data set change   A control signal set by a communications interface, which indicates that the carrier signal has changed, the clear to send condition has changed, or the data set ready signal has changed; can cause an interrupt if the interface is set to generate interrupts on data set change.

data set ready   A control signal from the modem, which indicates that the modem is powered up and ready for use.

data terminal ready   A control signal set by a terminal or computer interface, which prepares a modem to be connected to a communications channel (e.g., to answer a ringing phone.)

data transfer   *See* data transmission.

data transmission   The sending of data from one station to be received by another station.

DDCMP   *See* Digital Data Communications Message Protocol.

debugging   The process of testing for, finding, and correcting errors in a computer program.

decibels   Power level measurement unit; a unit for measuring the relative strength of a signal parameter such as power, voltage, etc.

DECNET   The network architecture of Digital Equipment Corporation; *also called* DNA.

decompression   The expanding of data back to its original length and form after it has been compressed; *see* compression.

delay distortion   Type of distortion resulting from the difference it takes in time for different frequencies to travel over a communications channel.

demodulation   The process of recreating the original signal from a modulated carrier signal; the process of converting an analog signal representation back to a digital form; *see* modulation.

device handler   A software module which controls a specific device attached to a computer; usually includes the interrupt handler and may be a part of the operating system.

dibit   Two bits represented by a single signal state (often using phase modulation); *see also* phase modulation, baud.

digital   *See* digital signal.

Digital Data Communications Message Protocol   A byte-count-oriented data link control protocol used in DECNET; *abbreviated* DDCMP; *see also* DECNET, Digital Network Architecture.

Digital Network Architecture   The network architecture of Digital Equipment Corporation; *abbreviated* DNA.

digital signal   A signal using two discrete states; *compare to* analog signal.

direct connect modem   A type of modem which attaches directly to a telephone line, usually using a modular phone plug; *compare to* acoustical coupler, acoustical modem.

direct memory access   A hardware feature which allows a device control unit to directly read or write data to memory without software intervention; *compare to* direct program control.

direct program control   A type of device control which requires that every character read from or written to a device control unit be processed by software; *compare to* direct memory access.

distortion   An unwanted change of a signal from its true form, resulting from the characteristics and transmission capabilities of the communications medium itself.

distributed   *See* distributed processing.

distributed processing   An environment making use of more than one processor distributed geographically, i.e., not located at the same physical site.

DLC   An abbreviation for data link control; *see* data link control.

DLCRCV   The name used in this book to describe the software module which provides the data link control protocol rules for receiving data; *see* data link control receive monitor.

DLCXMT   The name used in this book to describe the software module which provides the data link control protocol rules for transmitting data; *see* data link control receive monitor.

DLE   A character in a particular data code which provides "data link escape"; used in the BSC protocol to provide transparency.

DMA   *See* direct memory access.

DNA   *See* Digital Network Architecture.

downline loading   The process of sending data to a remote computer; the data is software which will eventually be run on this remote computer.

DSR   *See* data set ready.

DTR   *See* data terminal ready.

dumb terminal   An interactive terminal which can be used to access a timesharing computer; a terminal which provides no local processing and is used to enter and display data using a computer via a communications medium.

duplicate blanks   The occurrence of two or more blanks in data to be transmitted, which are often compressed to improve the throughput of a communications line; the most commonly compressed characters; *see* compression.

EBCDIC   An eight-bit data code used in IBM systems, providing 256 different bit patterns; extended binary coded decimal interchange code.

echo   1) the reflection of a signal; 2) the process of displaying on the CRT or hardcopy unit of a terminal a character entered on a keyboard.

EIA   An abbreviation for the Electronics Industry Association.

EIA interface   A interface which uses a standardized set of signal characteristics and hardware protocols (voltages, currents, etc.) defined by the Electronics Industry Association.

EIA RS-232 interface   *See* RS-232 interface.

emulation   1) the process of using software and hardware to permit one computer to run the programs designed for another without change; 2) the process of using software and communications interfaces to allow a computer to function as a remote terminal to another computer, usually referred to as terminal emulation; *see* terminal emulator.

end of text   a character defined in a protocol, which is used to identify the end of data in a data message; in BSC, also indicates that there are no more data blocks to send; *abbreviated* ETX.

end of transmission   A character defined in a protocol, which is used to identify the end of a message transmission which may contain a number of data blocks; used primarily in BSC protocol; *abbreviated* EOT.

end of transmission block   A character which is used to identify the end of data in a data message; in BSC, indicates a block check character will follow; *abbreviated* ETB.

end-to-end   A description of a type of conversation between similar programs on source and destination machines in a computer network; contrast to intermediate conversations between neighboring nodes which are at lower layers in a network architecture; also called *host-to-host*, peer-to-peer.

end user   An application program or process in a communications network; *also called* application entities in the ISO OSI model description.

ENQ   *See* enquiry.

enquiry   A character which is primarily used to bid for control of a line in point-to-point communications using the BSC protocol; *abbreviated* ENQ.

envelope   A term used to describe the header and trailer defined by a protocol and placed by a particular OSI layer around data to be sent to a lower layer.

EOT   *See* end of transmission.

equalization   Compensating for distortion present on a communications channel by boosting frequencies which lose power and delaying frequencies which do not suffer delay; *see also* equalizer.

equalizer   A device which compensates for distortion present on a communications channel; *see* equalization.

error control   The portion of protocol rules which defines error detection and error recovery procedures.

error detection   Recognition by LRC, VRC, or CRC techniques that data has been erroneously changed from its original form; *see also* LRC, VRC, and CRC.

error recovery   Depending on the protocol rules for error control, the procedures used to correct a received message or inform a sender of an error in a message so that it can be retransmitted.

ESC   The "escape" character used as a control character in protocols, terminal control and other environments; in ASCII is 33_8 and in EBCDIC is 27_{16}.

ETB   *See* end of transmission block.

Ethernet   A local area network standard developed by and supported by Digital Equipment Corporation, Xerox Corporation, and Intel Corporation. It uses a CSMA/CD protocol.

ETX   *See* end of text.

even parity   1) The setting of a parity bit in a character (VRC) so that the sum of the 1 bits in the character including this bit is even; 2) the setting of a parity bit in a particular position in an LRC character so that the sum of the 1 bits in the corresponding position of all characters in a block of characters is even; *compare to* odd parity.

event control block   A variable or location used to designate that a particular event required by one or more task in an operating system and/or communications software system has occurred; *also called* event flag.

event flag   *See* event control block.

event-driven   A software structure which uses the completion of events to control what tasks can run and/or be given control of the CPU.

Extended Binary Coded Decimal Interchange Code   *See* EBCDIC.

external clocking   A term often used to describe nonmodem clocking; clocks located outside of a modem; because of confusion in the use of the term, it is better to use the terms "modem clocking" and "nonmodem clocking"; *see also* modem clocking, nonmodem clocking.

FCS   *See* function control sequence.

FDM   *See* frequency division multiplexing.

FDX   *See* full-duplex.

FEP   *See* front-end processor.

fiber optics   The use of an optical fiber for the transmission of data by means of a light beam.

FIFO   1) Abbreviation for first-in/first-out; 2) a hardware feature which provides for the temporary holding of data characters received from multiple lines on a multiline asynchronous communications interface; *also called* silo.

FIFO buffer   A data area used temporarily to store data characters received from an asynchronous interface using direct program control; *also called* ring buffer.

FIFO circular buffer   *See* FIFO buffer, ring buffer.

FIFO full alarm   A hardware signal on a multiline asynchronous interface which indicates that the hardware FIFO has an overrun condition, i.e., a data character was lost from some line.

FIFO full alarm enable   The process of setting a multiline asynchronous interface so that the FIFO full alarm will generate a hardware interrupt if a FIFO overrun occurs.

FIFO overrun   A condition which results when a character is received from a line and fills the hardware FIFO is already full; on an asynchronous multiline interface; *see* FIFO full alarm.

file lockout   Provided by a file system or operating system, the capability which prevents other programs or tasks from accessing a file, usually during update of a file.

finite state automata   *See* finite state machine.

finite state logic   Programming logic which relies on techniques using the representation of state diagrams via data structures to define states, a set of rules, state transitions, and actions; by changing the data structure (state diagram) driving the software, the same program logic "interpreting" the various state diagrams will result in the implementation of different rules; in communications software, finite state logic is used to implement both the syntactic and procedural rules of protocols; *see* state diagram.

finite state machine   A software module which is driven by data structures (state control blocks) representing states and a set of rules whereby the response (state transitions and actions) of the module is well defined; *see also* finite state logic, state control block.

First In/First Out   An ordering in which the first data element to arrive is the first data element to leave; *see* FIFO.

first level interrupt handler   An interrupt handler which receives control on some computers and which must determine what device or channel caused the interrupt and then invoke the proper second level interrupt handler; *abbreviated* FLIH; *also called* first level interrupt processor.

FLAG   The bit pattern used in bit-oriented protocols to delineate the beginning and end of a message. Data between FLAGs is modified during transmission so that it will not be confused with a FLAG character, and then it is converted back to its original form by the receiving bit-oriented hardware; used in SDLC and HDLC protocols.

FLIH   *See* first level interrupt handler.

formal grammar   A syntax description of a computer language or protocol, usually written with BNF notation; *see* BNF, Backus-Naur form.

frame   1) a group of bits considered as a unit; 2) a slot in a slotted ring; see slotted ring; 3) a block of storage used in paging into which a user page is placed by a paging operating system.

framing   1) The process of identifying the beginning and end of a data character using START and STOP conditions in asynchronous communications; 2) the process of identifying the beginning (and possibly the end) of a block of characters (message) in synchronous communications.

framing error   An error occurring in asynchronous communications, which is detected by the hardware and is caused by a STOP condition not appearing at the end of a data character when expected; is often forced by a break condition to generate an attention signal to a remote computer; *see* break condition.

frequency   The number of cycles per second of a signal.

frequency division multiplexing   The process of allowing data to co-exist on a communications medium as different frequency bandwiths representing the flow of information for different terminals or computers.

frequency modulation   Modulation of an otherwise continuous carrier signal by changing frequency.

front-end processor   A communications processor which interfaces a host computer to a network and removes the communications workload from the host computer; *abbreviated* FEP.

full-duplex   Communications in two directions simultaneously on a communications channel; *abbreviated* FDX.

full-duplex with local echo   A mode of operating an interactive terminal in which data transmission can occur simultaneously in both directions, but characters are echoed locally by the terminal itself rather than by the software on the remote computer.

function control sequence   A set of control bytes used in the (HASP) multileaving protocol to control the suspension of data transfer for up to seven streams of data; *abbreviated* FCS.

gateway   A device (computer) which converts messages in a protocol in one network to the correct format for the same or a different protocol in another network.

generating polynomial   The polynomial used as the divisor in computing a CRC error check character.

GHz   *See* gigahertz.

gigahertz   1 billion cycles per second.

hackers   Persons who attempt to penetrate the security of a computer, usually from a remote location.

half-duplex   Communications capability in two directions on a communications channel, which can occur alternately, i.e., not simultaneously; *abbreviated* HDX.

handshake   *See* handshaking sequence.

handshaking sequence   The procedural rules of a data link control protocol which specify the message traffic between stations when there is no data to transmit.

hardcopy unit   A unit which can produce printed output and can serve as the display for an interactive terminal (hardcopy terminal).

hardware clock   A hardware device that provides some type of timing capability by either interrupting at a regular interval or interrupting at the expiration of a variable interval; used by software to time various events in operating systems and/or data communications software.

hardware line monitor   A device which can intercept data being transmitted or received on a communications line and which provides the ability to display (and perhaps store) this data; used for determining problems which might occur during debugging of communications software or in a production environment.

hardwired   A controller or device which is not programmable; early communications controllers were hardwired, but today's controllers are driven by software, i.e., programmable.

HASP multileaving protocol   Developed by IBM's Houston Automatic Spooling group for use in a batch environment, a protocol which provided for data transfer alternately on a communications line and for data for multiple devices in a single transmission buffer.

HDLC   *See* high-level data link control protocol.

HDX   *See* half-duplex.

header   A group of bits containing control information which is placed at the beginning of a message according to a particular protocol; *see* also envelope.

hertz   A measure of frequency; cycles per second.

high-level data link control protocol   A bit-oriented protocol similar to SDLC; an HDLC standard is defined by CCITT and ISO.

higher level protocol   A protocol in a data communications system or network which is above the data link control layer (protocol).

history list   A FIFO group of messages which have been transmitted but not yet acknowledged by the receiving station; required for full-duplex data link control protocols so that messages received in error can be retransmitted.

Hollerith code   A punched card code used for 80-column cards, which defined 256 different valid punches.

host   A general-purpose mainframe computer in a computer network, often providing centralized control of communications in the network.

host-to-host layer   A layer which provides a conversation between similar programs on source and destination machines in a computer network; contrast to intermediate conversations between neighboring nodes which are at lower layers in a network architecture; *see also* end-to-end, peer-to-peer.

I/O   Abbreviation for input/output.

I/O page   The portion of a PDP-11's or LSI-11's address space which is used to address device registers which control I/O.

IBM 2780   An early IBM batch terminal which used the BSC protocol.

IBM 3705   The IBM communications front-end processor used to control communications to and from a host computer; used to provide communications for an SNA network.

IC   The abbreviation used in the book to designate software modules which control (communications) interfaces in the implementation of data communications software using a modular structure.

ICRCV   The name used in this book to describe the software module which provides the (communications) interface control when receiving data; see interface control receive monitor.

ICXMT   The name used in this book to describe the software module which provides the (communications) interface control when transmitting data; *see* interface control transmit monitor.

idle time   The time during which a computer system's CPU is doing no useful work.

idling of SYNs   The automatic sending of SYN characters by a synchronous communications hardware interface when the software does not provide data at the time it is required during synchronous transmission.

IMP   *See* interface message processor.

information transfer message   A type of message in the SDLC protocol which contains data.

initialization routine   A software module which initializes a (communications) device to ready it for use by the communications software.

interactive terminal   A computer terminal with a keyboard and some type of display, used to interact with a computer system.

interface control receive monitor   The software module which provides communications interface control when receiving data; named *ICRCV* in this book.

interface control task   A task in data communications software which controls a communications interface when sending or receiving data.

interface control transmit monitor   The software module which provides communications interface control when transmitting data; named *ICXMT* in this book.

Interface Message Processors   The ARPANET nodes which control message traffic.

International Standards Organization   An international organization whose constituents are the national standards organizations of member countries, which defines standards for the world; abbreviated ISO; the ISO has defined standards for data communications, most notably, the ISO model for Open System Interconnection.

interrupt   The temporary stopping of a current program's execution via a hardware signal to execute some higher priority program (interrupt handler).

interrupt enable bit   A bit in a PDP-11 or LSI-11 device register which when set causes a device to generate an interrupt when an I/O operation is complete or an error has occurred.

interrupt handler   A program which receives control when an interrupt occurs and does the processing necessary to service the interrupt; *also called* interrupt service routine.

interrupt service routine   *See* interrupt handler.

interrupt vector   A memory location or collection of memory locations containing information which is used to invoke an interrupt handler when an interrupt occurs; contains the address of the interrupt handler and other information used in the process of transferring control of the CPU to the interrupt handler.

interrupt-driven   A software structure which uses the interrupts to determine what tasks can run and/or be given control of the CPU.

interval timer   A hardware timer which can be set with a variable interval which is decremented at a specific time interval and generates an interrupt when the counter is decremented to 0.

ISO   *See* International Standards Organization.

jam   A short burst of noise emitted by a node on a multiple access channel, used to ensure that other nodes (by means of a CSMA/CD protocol) have detected that a collision has occurred.

JCL   Job control language; the "language" used to provide control information for jobs executing in a batch mode, particularly in an IBM environment.

job   A collection of one or more steps to be executed in sequence, i.e., one after another, in a batch environment.

LAN   *See* local area network.

language   1) A set of words and rules for building sentences that is used for communicating; 2) a level in human communication concerned with how information is formulated into words and sentences.

layered structure   A structure which isolates functions required in a computer network or computer communications software and which defines the interface between these layers.

LCB   *See* line control block.

LCD   A liquid crystal display used as the display unit of some computers or computer terminals, particularly portable battery-operated ones because of the small amount of current required to drive the display.

line clock   A hardware clock which interrupts on a fixed interval, usually at a rate of 60 times per second.

line control   The part of the procedural rules of a protocol which determine what station has control of a communications line at a particular instant in time.

line control block   A data structure used to represent the activity of a specific communications line for software controlling a multiline asynchronous communications interface.

Line Parameter Register   The part of a communications interface used to set the characteristics to be used for communications, e.g., character length, CRC enable, etc.

line throughput   The number of characters transmitted on a line per second; data compression can improve the effective throughput of a line by sending fewer characters, which represent the original data to be transmitted, and expanding the data at the receiving station.

linked list   A data structure in which each element "points" to the next element; in assembler language and some high-level languages, each element contains the address of the next element; in high level languages, an index or subscript is used to point to the next element.

links   The communications path or circuit between nodes in a computer network.

Local Area Network   A data communications network that spans a physically limited geographic area (less than 10 km), is implemented using some type of switching capability and high bandwidth communications on a relatively inexpensive medium such as coaxial cable, and is owned by the user (as opposed to using communications facilities like those provided by a public utility); most implementations use a processor at each node which can easily share resources in the local area network and allow for expansion by the addition of processors; *abbreviated* LAN.

logical line number   *See* logical unit.

logical unit   A means of referring to a communications line or a device by using a number which is mapped to the physical line or device via software; allows changing the logical to physical mapping and assignment of devices and lines just prior to or during program execution.

longitudinal redundancy check   A method of generating an error check character for detecting errors in a data block by computing the parity in a particular bit position across the entire data block and setting the corresponding bit in the check character so that when the 1 bits are added in a particular position, including that in the check character, the sum of the 1 bits is either even or odd, depending on whether the parity is to be even or odd; abbreviated LRC.

low-level protocol   A data link control protocol; a protocol below the network layer.

LRC   *See* longitudinal redundancy check.

maintenance message   A message type in a data link control protocol which provides some maintenance function defined in the protocol.

mark   1) The presence of a signal; in telegraphy it represents a condition when current is flowing; 2) equivalent to a binary 1 condition on an asynchronous communication line.

mark parity   Parity in which the parity bit is always set to 1.

master/slave   Terms used to refer to the central control station and secondary remote stations in a network which relies on centralized network control.

mathematical compression algorithms   Algorithms used in more sophisticated implementations of data compression, which assign different length character representations to different characters, depending on their probability of occurrence as a data character; characters with high probability of occurrence are assigned shorter bit patterns to provide for higher line throughput.

message types   The type of message in a data link control protocol, specifically one of three—control, data, or maintenance.

microwave   1) Radio transmission which uses very short wave lengths, i.e., ultra-high frequency waveforms; 2) a microwave system is a broadband facility which provides line-of-site radio communications and which requires that repeater stations be placed every 40 km or so because of the curvature of the earth.

modem   A modulator/demodulator which is used to convert digital signals to analog for transmission and convert analog signals back to digital when received.

modem clocking   In synchronous communications, the providing of a data clocking signal by the modem (as opposed to the communications interface); compare to nonmodem clocking or external clocking.

modem turnaround time   The amount of time required by a modem to go from receive mode to transmit mode; the amount of time between the setting of request to send by a communications interface (software) and the setting of clear to send by a modem.

modular software structure   A software structure which uses modules or routines which are relatively short in length and which isolates functions provided by the software to specific modules.

modular testing   Testing software by testing each module on its own, usually by simulating the environment in which it will eventually run by routines designed specifically for testing such modules.

modulation   The modification of an otherwise continuous carrier signal based on the instantaneous value of a discrete (digital) signal.

multidrop line   The connection of a single communications line to more than two stations; *also called* multipoint line; compare to point-to-point line.

multileaving transmission block   A data message transmitted using the HASP multileaving protocol; *see* HASP multileaving protocol.

multiline asynchronous interface   A single device which connects a number of asynchronous communications lines to a computer.

multiple access   The capability of a communications medium or channel to be accessed by more than one node in a network by using a listen-before-transmitting mechanism.

multiplexing   A division of a data communications facility into two or more channels; *see* time division multiplexing, frequency division multiplexing.

multipoint line   *See* multidrop line.

multiprogramming   A capability of an operating system to execute more than one program residing in shared memory of a single CPU by using concurrent (inter-leaved) program execution and representing the execution of a program via some type of data structure (task control block); *see also* concurrent execution, inter-rupt-driven, event-driven.

multistream modem   A modem which provides multiple data streams of slower speed by dividing a communications channel using time division multiplexing; multiple interfaces can be attached to such a modem and the data transmission appears identical to that using multiple single stream modems; *also called* split steam modems.

NAK   The character or message used to indicate that an error has been detected in a communications system; a negative acknowledgement.

native mode   The mode of operating an interactive terminal without emulating the characteristics of another terminal type.

Network Control Program   The name of the software used to control the IBM 3705 communications controller.

network layer   The third layer of the ISO OSI model, whose primary purpose is to provide the routing necessary to move information through the "pipe" defined by the transport layer.

network topology   The selection of the number of nodes, how they are connected (the links), and the location of the nodes.

Nine Thousand Remote protocol   A simple character-oriented, full-duplex protocol used by Univac Corporation for data communications from a host to and from a Nine Thousand Remote terminal.

node   In a network location containing computer, switching and/or terminal equipment connected by one or more communications links, which transmits and receives data on these links.

noise   Unwanted electronic signals which exist on a communications medium; noise can generate errors during data transmission.

nonmodem clocking   In synchronous communications, the providing of a data clocking signal outside of the modem, i.e., in the communications interface; also called external clocking; *compare to* modem clocking; *see also* external clocking.

nonsequenced message   A message in SDLC which provides certain commands and responses between primary and secondary stations; *compare to* information transfer and supervisory messages of SDLC.

nontransparent   Transmission in which not all data character bit patterns may be transmitted because they might be confused with control characters of a protocol.

NTR   *See* Nine Thousand Remote protocol.

null modem   A device or cable wiring which eliminates the need for a modem in asynchronous transmission over short distances; generally connects receive to transmit, transmit to receive, and signal ground to signal ground (see Figure 7-6).

odd parity   1) The setting of a parity bit in a character (VRC) so that the sum of the 1 bits in the character including this bit is odd; 2) the setting of a parity bit in a particular position in an LRC character so that the sum of the 1 bits in the corresponding position of all characters in a block of characters is odd; *compare to* even parity.

Open Systems Interconnection   The name of the model defined by the International Standards Organization for comparing and defining computer network architectures; *abbreviated* OSI.

open wires   Bare copper wires attached to ceramic insulators used for many years for data transmission, particularly for telegraph.

originate modem   A modem used to originate a call, as opposed to answer an incoming call; *compare to* answer modem.

OSI model   A model defined by the International Standards Organization containing seven layers used for comparing and defining computer network architectures; *see* Open Systems Interconnection.

overrun condition   A hardware condition which occurs when the next data character to be received arrives before the previous character is processed by software; a data character is lost.

packet   A collection of bits which is treated as a unit for routing purposes within a computer network.

parity bit   A bit added to a data character so that the sum of the number of 1 bits is either even or odd; *see* even parity, odd parity.

PC   *See* program counter.

peer-to-peer   *See* end-to-end.

phase modulation   Modulation in which the phase of an otherwise continuous carrier signal is modified (shifted) based on the data value to be transmitted.

physical layer   The lowest layer of the ISO model for network architectures; the physical medium itself, on which "raw" data bits are transmitted.

physical line number   The hardware line number used in a multiline asynchronous interface to identify a specific communications line attached to a computer via the interface.

point-to-point line   The connection of a single communications line between two stations; compare to multidrop line.

poll   *See* polling.

polling   1) A technique of device control in which a device is continuously or periodically checked by software to determine if an I/O operation has completed; compare to interrupt-driven; 2) a technique used in protocols to provide centralized control of a communications channel in which a secondary station cannot transmit unless selected (polled) to do so by the master station.

polling LAN protocol   A local area network protocol which uses polling; *see also* slotted ring, token passing.

polling technique   *See* polling.

posted   The process of informing a task of the completion of an event; posting an event; for example, a received data buffer may be posted by a lower level protocol to a higher level protocol for use by the higher level protocol once it is validated by the lower level protocol.

presentation layer   The sixth layer of the ISO model for network architectures, which deals with the representation of data being transferred from one end user to another.

primary station   The station which controls the communications channel in a network using centralized control; *see also* secondary station, primary/secondary, master/slave.

primary/secondary   *See* master/slave.

priority-driven dispatcher   A program module in a multiprogramming operating system and/or a data communications system which decides which independent task (process) will next get control of the CPU, based on the priority of the task; *compare to* round robin.

procedural rules   The semantics or rules defining the meaning of messages to be transmitted and received using a protocol.

procedural states   The states describing the procedural rules of a protocol; each state is characterized by one or more states, the action to be performed upon the occurrence of an event (receiving a certain message, timeout, etc.), and the next state.

processor status word   A hardware word in a computer containing certain status information about a computer; on the PDP-11 contains condition codes and processor priority as well as processor mode.

program counter   The hardware register within a computer (CPU) which contains the address of the next instruction to be executed.

protocol   The rules for operating a data communications system or for transmitting and receiving data.

protocol exceptions   Any rule defined by a protocol which is not included in the rules for error control, line control, startup control, transparency, framing, sequence control and timeout control; *also called* special cases.

PS   *See* processor status word.

pseudosimultaneous, bidirectional transmission   A type of transmission introduced in the 1960s with the HASP multileaving protocol, which allowed data transfer to alternate directions between stations and did not require one station to send all its data messages to another station before the other station could begin transmitting data.

queue structure   A structure which is a collection of data normally ordered in a FIFO manner; used in data communications to pass messages from one independent task to another in a modular software implementation.

RCB   *See* record control byte.

receiver   1) The part of a communications hardware interface which receives data; 2) the software modules which control the receiving of data in a data communications system.

receiver active   A status bit or control condition which indicates that the receiver of a hardware interface is active and receiving data; in synchronous communications indicates a SYN or FLAG sequence has been detected, depending on the protocol.

Receiver Buffer Register   A data register in a communications interface used to transfer a character received from a communications line to the internal memory of a computer.

Receiver Control/Status Register   A register used to control and to determine the status of an asynchronous or a synchronous data communications hardware interface.

Receiver Data Register   *Same as* Receiver Buffer Register.

receiver interrupt handler   The interrupt handler which processes data received via an asynchronous or a synchronous data commmunications hardware interface.

Receiver Ready   A status condition or signal indicating that the receiver of an asynchronous or a synchronous data communications interface has received a character which must be processed by the receiver software.

receiver status register   *See* Receiver Control/Status Register.

receiver task   An independent task in data communications software which provides a receiving function, either controlling the hardware interface in receive mode or providing the protocol rules for interpreting data which is received.

receiver timeout service routine   The module in data communications software which gets control upon the occurrence of a receiver timeout condition.

receiver timer interval   The length of time which the software will wait before indicating a receiver timeout error has occurred.

record   A group of data items processed as a unit; in a multileaving protocol, a collection of data destined for a specific device.

record control byte   A control byte which identifies the beginning of a record in a multileaving protocol; *see also* HASP multileaving protocol.

remote batch entry   *See* remote job entry.

remote job entry   The submission of batch jobs via a remote terminal, usually using cards or card images, and receiving the output from the job on line printers attached to the remote terminal; also called remote batch entry.

REP   A control message in DDCMP which is used to force a response from another station which has been sent data messages.

repeater A device used to restore or retransmit signals because of distortion or because of limitations of distance (e.g., microwave line-of-sight).

request to send A signal or condition set by a terminal or computer software that informs the modem that the terminal or computer wishes to transmit; transmission cannot begin until clear to send is set by the modem.

reverse interrupt A two-character control message (see Table 12-2) used in the BSC protocol, which, like ACK0, ACK1, and WACK, is a positive acknowledgement but is also a request that the transmitting station terminate the current transmission because the receiving station has a high priority message to send to the other station and therefore needs to turn the line around, i.e., transmit data the other direction; *abbreviated* RVI.

ring *See* ring indicator.

ring buffer A circular data buffer used to temporarily hold data characters received by a receiver interrupt handler until they are requested by an applications or a systems program.

ring buffer overflow A condition in an asynchronous multiline interrupt handler which occurs if the software ring buffer for a line is full when another character is received for that line.

ring indicator A signal or condition set by a modem, informing a terminal or computer that a ringing signal is being received on a communications channel (telephone line); terminal or computer software must set data terminal ready interface lead in order to have modem answer the incoming call.

RJE *See* remote job entry.

round robin A dispatching technique in which independent tasks or processes are given control of the CPU on a FIFO basis; true round-robin dispatching gives CPU control to a task for a limited amount of CPU time, called a *time slice; compare* to priority-driven dispatcher.

round-robin driver program A dispatching program used in a simple communications system which dispatches communications tasks using a round-robin technique.

RS-232 interface A specification adopted by the Electronics Industry Association which defines the number of wires that are used to connect a modem to a terminal or computer communications interface, the electrical signals that are sent along these wires, and the signal levels that are used; it also defines the particular type of connector (25 pin) that is used on the cable; similar to CCITT V24 specification.

RS-232 serial interface *See* RS-232 interface.

RTS *See* request to send.

RVI *See* reverse interrupt.

satellite transmission Microwave transmission from an earth station to a satellite orbiting the earth. It is retransmitted by a transponder using a different frequency to another earth station.

SCB *See* string control byte.

scheduler list A FIFO list of messages formatted and stored by the transmitter data link control module (DLCXMT), which are waiting for transmission by the interface control module (ICXMT) in a modular communications software design.

SDLC   *See* synchronous data link control.

second level interrupt handler   An interrupt handler which receives control from a first level interrupt handler and services the device or event which caused the interrupt; *abbreviated* SLIH; *compare to* first level interrupt handler.

secondary station   In a network using centralized control, a station which can only transmit when polled by the primary station; *see also* primary station, primary/secondary, master/slave.

security   The safeguarding of data, programs, and equipment, particularly in a network, from unauthorized access or change.

select bit   A bit in the header of a DDCMP message used to poll secondary stations and to indicate last message transmitted from a secondary station.

semantics   The rules which define the meaning of messages received and transmitted using a data communications protocol; *also called* procedural rules; *compare to* syntax.

SEQ#   Used in software, a variable which contains the message number of the last message transmitted.

sequence control   The part of a protocol definition which deals with the numbering of messages and the detection of duplicate received messages or lost messages.

session   The connecting of two end users by the session layer of a network architecture.

session layer   The fifth layer of the ISO model for network architectures, which deals with setting up connections between two users and preserving the integrity of data exchanges between these users.

Shannon's law   A law which specifies the maximum speed of a communications channel based on its bandwidth and signal-to-noise ratio.

signal-to-noise ratio   The relative power of a signal to the noise in a channel, usually measured in decibels.

simplex   Communications capability in one direction only on a communications channel.

sine wave   Continuously varying, repeating signal characterized by amplitude, frequency, and phase.

SLIH   *See* second level interrupt handler.

slot   An area in a slotted ring used for local area networks, into which a node can place data for transmission if the slot is empty.

slotted ring   A local area network protocol used in a ring network, which provides distributed control of the communications channel by providing a ring with frames into which data can be placed if the frame is empty; the slotted ring is constantly transmitted around the ring.

SNA   *See* Systems Network Architecture.

software clock   A clocking capability provided by software controlling a hardware clock.

software methodology   The techniques used to design and implement computer sofware.

SOH   *See* start of header.

space   1) The absence of a signal; in telegraphy represents a condition when current is not flowing; 2) equivalent to a binary 0 condition on an asynchronous communications line.

space parity   A parity bit which is always set to 0.

split stream modems   See multistream modems.

square wave   A wave form which represents a digital signal; see digital signal.

SRCB   *See* sub-record control byte.

STACK   The control message used in the DDCMP protocol to acknowledge a START message; part of the startup sequence defined by DDCMP.

star   See star configuration.

star configuration   A network topology that results from nodes being connected only to a primary central node; there are no interconnections between nodes except through the central node.

START condition   The condition used in asynchronous communications to recognize the beginning of a data character; *also called* a space or space bit.

start of header   The character which identifies the beginning of an optional header in a data message of the BSC protocol; *abbreviated* SOH.

start of text   The character which identifies the beginning of the text or data area in a data message of the BSC protocol; *abbreviated* STX.

START/STOP transmission   Another name for *asynchronous communications;* see asynchronous communications.

startup   A name for a message used in some protocols during start of transmission; *see also* startup control.

startup control   The part of the procedural rules of a protocol which specifies the message traffic required to initiate communications between two stations.

state control block   A data structure used to represent a state in a state diagram; for a given state, the data structure must contain the input characters or events which are valid for the state, the action to be performed upon the recognition of a valid character or event, and the next state.

state diagram   A diagram illustrating state transitions, which has nodes or circles representing states and lines (arrows) representing events; provides a graphic way to represent state transitions; see also finite state logic, finite state machine.

status bits   Bits in a control register for a device which indicate the status of the device.

status word   A word containing hardware status, either for the CPU or a device.

STOP condition   The condition used in asynchronous communications to signal the end of a data charcter; *also called* mark *or* mark bit.

store and forward   The process of receiving data messages containing address information about the destination, storing the messages temporarily, and later transmitting them to the destination (or perhaps an intermediate station on the way to the destination.)

string control byte   A control byte which identifies the beginning of character strings within a record; provides for compression of duplicate charcters; *see also* HASP multileaving protocol; *abbreviated* SRCB.

strip SYN   A mode in a synchronous interface in which characters which match the

SYN character currently in the SYN register are not passed on to the processor for processing by software, i.e., they are thrown away.

STRT   The name of the startup message in the DDCMP protocol.

stuffing   Inserting bits or characters into a data stream to avoid having data confused with control or delimiter characters.

STX   *See* start of text.

sub-record control byte   A control byte which provides additional information about a data record in a multileaving protocol; *see also* HASP multileaving protocol; *abbreviated* SCB.

supervisory message   A type of message in SDLC which is primarily used to control data message traffic; includes Receiver Ready, Receiver Not Ready, and Reject messages.

SYN   *See* synchronization character, synchronizing character.

synchronization character   The bit pattern used to identify the beginning of a message in character-oriented and byte-count-oriented protocols; *also called* synchronizing character; *abbreviated* SYN.

synchronizing character   *See* synchronization character.

synchronous communications   Data communications in which the receiving and the transmitting stations are synchronized during the sending of a block of data (as opposed to a single data character in asynchronous communications); compare to asynchronous communications; *also called* synchronous transmission.

synchronous communications hardware interface   An interface on a computer which supports one or more types of synchronous communications.

Synchronous Data Link Control   The name of the data link control protocol used by IBM in its System Network Architecture; *abbreviated* SDLC.

synchronous transmission   *See* synchronous communications.

syntax   The set of rules needed to construct valid expressions of sentences in a language.

syntax of protocol   Rules which specify the syntax of messages in a protocol; *see* syntax.

Systems Network Architecture   The name of a computer network architecture designed, implemented and supported by IBM Corporation.

TDM   *See* time division multiplexing.

terminal   A device for data input and output which contains a keyboard or some other means of entering information and a display (CRT, LCD, LED, or harcopy) for displaying information entered and system responses and messages.

terminal emulation   The process of using software to make a computer system react as an interactive terminal; additional features not found on standard terminals (such read from disk and transmit) are often included in terminal emulators.

terminal emulator   A software package which allows a computer to emulate a terminal; *see* terminal emulation.

terminal mode   A mode of operation of an asynchronous communications line driver used to control a terminal, requiring special sequences to properly display data on a CRT or hardcopy terminal.

time division   A dividing of an interval of time so that it can be assigned to a specific terminal wishing to transmit data during that subinterval.

time division multiplexing   The process of using a round-robin allocation of fixed intervals of time for transmitting data from several lines over one high speed line.

timeout control   The part of the procedural rules of a protocol which controls time-out intervals and recovery procedures for timeout.

timer control   Control provided by software to time various intervals in data communications, particularly for handshake sequences.

timesharing systems   Systems which use terminals with a CRT, hardcopy or other display to interact with a computer in such a way that users of a terminal appear to be the sole user of a system.

token   The data element in a token passing network which provides the possessor of the token with the permission to transmit data in a local area network.

token passing   A distributed control protocol used in local area networks; *see* token.

trailer   The part of a data communications message which follows after the header or the data, depending on the message type; the right half of an "envelope" placed around a data message passed from a higher level protocol.

transition   Using finite state logic, the movement from one state to another caused by an input character or event logic; *see* finite state logic.

transmission   The sending of data using some communications medium.

transmit data register   A data register in a communications interface into which the next data character to be transmitted is placed.

Transmit Line Number   The control information in a transmitter control register of a multiline asynchronous interface, which specifies the line needing transmit service.

transmit scanner   The part of a multiline asynchronous interface which looks at each line to see if a line needs transmit service.

transmit status register   A data register used to provide status information about an asynchronous or synchronous communications interface's transmitter.

transmitter   1) The hardware portion of a communications interface, which controls data transmission; 2) the software portion of data communications software that deals with data transmission and control.

Transmitter Break Control Register   A register which provides for the transmitting of a break character on a multiline interface.

Transmitter Buffer Register   *Same as* transmit data register.

Transmitter Control/Status Register   A device register on a communications interface, which provides both control bits and status information for the transmitter part of the interface.

transmitter interrupt handler   The interrupt handler which processes interrupts resulting from an error condition relating to data transmission or from a line needing service on output.

Transmitter Line Control Register   The register in a multiline interface used to enable or disable the transmitter side of a particular line.

Transmitter Ready   The condition which indicates a line is ready to accept the next data character to be transmitted.

transmitter task   An independent task in data communications software, which provides a transmitting function, either controlling the hardware interface in transmit mode or providing the protocol rules for transmitting data.

transparency   The part of a communications protocol which defines how the protocol provides for the transmission of any bit pattern as a data character, even if it is the same as a control character.

transponder   A device used in satellites to receive a data communications signal at one frequency and retransmit the signal at a different frequency.

transport layer   The fourth layer of the ISO OSI model, whose primary function is the creation of a transport pipe for transmitting data to the destination machine.

TTY   An abbreviation for the early teletype terminal, still in use today as the device name for an interactive (console) terminal, particularly on minicomputers and microcomputers.

turnaround time   *See* modem turnaround time.

turnkey   A computer system with software which is set up to meet a user's needs and requires only that the "key be turned" in order for it to work; in theory, a turnkey system requires no changes and seldom can be changed to meet a user's needs.

twisted wire pair cables   Two insulated wires twisted together to form a pair on which a communications signal can be sent.

UART   *See* universal asynchronous receiver transmitter.

UNIBUS   The name of the patented architectural I/O design of the PDP-11 and LSI-11 family of computers manufactured by Digital Equipement Corporation.

universal asynchronous receiver/transmitter   An asynchronous communications interface commonly used on microcomputers; *abbreviated* UART.

universal synchronous/asynchronous receiver transmitter   A communications interface commonly used on microcomputers, which provides either asynchronous or synchronous communications; *abbreviated* USART.

USART   *See* universal synchronous/asynchronous receiver transmitter.

vertical redundancy check   An error check technique which uses a parity bit appended to the high-order position of a data character and set so that the sum of the one bits in the character including the parity bit is either even (even parity) or odd (odd parity); *abbreviated* VRC.

voice-grade   A term used to describe a typical dial-up line with a bandwidth of 3000 Hz.

VRC   *See* vertical redundancy check.

WACK   The name of the character sequence in the BSC protocol which acknowledges a data message but tells the transmitting station to wait before sending the next data message.

wait-a-bit   The condition of telling a transmitting station to wait before sending the next data message by sending a WACK message as an acknowledgement to a data message; *see* WACK.

WAN   *See* wide are network.

wide area network   A network which is not limited to a geographic area within a range of 10 Km, as a local area network is; a wide area network often uses common carrier facilities for data communications; *compare to* local area network.

X.21 An interface standard of CCITT, which specifies physical layer requirements.

X.25   An interface standard of CCITT which provides for three levels of protocol definition: 1) the physical layer (*see* X.21); 2) the data link control layer (*see* high level data link control protocol); and the network layer using packet switching.

XOFF A character used in asynchronous transmission to suspend data transmission; XOFF is equivalent to ˆS (023_8) ; the station receiving data transmits XOFF (in full-duplex) when data transmission by the other station is to be suspended, and transmits XON when data transmission is to resume; *see also* XON.

XON A character used in asynchronous transmission to resume data transmission after an XOFF has been sent previously; XON is equivalent to ˆQ (021_8) ; *see also* XOFF.

XON/XOFF The name of a simple protocol rule in asynchronous communications, used to suspend and resume data transmission; *see* XON, XOFF.

Bibliography

CHEONG, V. E., and R. A. HIRSCHHEIM. 1983. *Local Area Networks: Issues, Products, and Developments.* Chichester, Great Britain: John Wiley & Sons.

Convergent Technologies. "Convergent Technologies: A Major Success, A Well-Kept Secret." *Business Microworld* (December 1983): 11–12.

CORR, F. P., and D. H. NEAL. 1979. "SNA and Emerging International Standards." *IBM Systems Journal* 18 (no. 2). IBM Corporation.

CYPSER, R. J. 1978. *Communications Architecture for Distributed Systems.* Reading, Mass.: Addison-Wesley.

Datapoint. 1983. "The Datapoint ARC Local Area Network Milestones and Fact Sheet." San Antonio, Tex.: Datapoint Corporation.

DAVIES, D. W., and D. L. A. BARBER, W. L. PRICE, and C. M. SOLOMONIDES. 1979. *Computer Networks and Their Protocols.* Chichester, Great Britain: John Wiley & Sons.

DEC. 1978. *Digital Data Communications Message Protocol — DDCMP Specification Version 4.0 AA-D599A-TC.* Maynard, Mass.: Digital Equipment Corporation.

———. *KG11 Reference Manual.* Maynard, Mass.: Digital Equipment Corporation.

———. 1982. *Introduction to Local Area Networks.* Maynard, Mass.: Digital Equipment Corporation.

DEITEL, HARVEY M. 1984. *An Introduction to Operating Systems.* Reading, Mass.: Addison-Wesley.

Digital Research, Inc. 1983. *Display Manager Productivity Tool Programmer's Guide for the CP/M-86 Family of Operating Systems.* Pacific Grove, Calif.: Digital Research, Inc.

DONNAN, R. A. and J. R. KERSEY. 1974. "Synchronous Data Link Control: A Perspective." *IBM Systems Journal* 13 (no. 2). IBM Corporation.

FALK, GILBERT. 1983. "The Structure and Function of Network Protocols." In *Computer Communications:* Vol. 1, *Principles.* Edited by Wushow Chou. Englewood Cliffs, N.J.: Prentice-Hall.

GESALMAN, PAUL W. 1982. "Table Driven Implementation of Multiple Data Communication Protocols." Master's Project Report, West Virginia University.

GRAUBE, MARIS, and MICHAEL C. MULDER. "Local Area Networks." *Computer* (October 1984): 242–47.

GREEN, P. E. 1979. "An Introduction to Network Architectures and Protocols." *IBM Systems Journal* 18 (no. 2). IBM Corporation.

GRIES, DAVID. 1971. *Compiler Construction for Digital Computers.* New York: John Wiley & Sons.

HABERMANN, A. N. 1976. *Introduction to Operating System Design.* Chicago: Science Research Associates.

HOUSLEY, TREVOR. 1979. *Data Communications and Teleprocessing Systems.* Englewood Cliffs, N.J.: Prentice-Hall.

IBM. n.d. "System/370 Reference Summary. GX20-1850-4." White Plains, N.Y.: IBM Corporation.

————. 1971. *The Hasp System.* Hawthorne, N.Y.: IBM Corporation.

————. 1974. *IBM Synchronous Data Link Control General Information: Form GA27-3093.* White Plains, N.Y.: IBM Corporation.

————. 1981. *Systems Network Architecture — Concepts and Products: Form GC30-3072.* White Plains, N.Y.: IBM Corporation.

ISO. 1982. *Draft International Standard ISO/DIS 7498: Information Processing Systems — Open Systems Interconnection — Basic Reference Model.* Reprinted in Meijer & Peeters 1982. International Standards Organization.

————. *Data Communication. High-level Data Link Control Procedure — Frame Level.* International Standards Organization.

JONES, JAMES KENNETH, II. 1981. "Implementing Hasp Multileaving Data Communications Protocol Using Finite State Logic." Master's Project Report, West Virginia University.

LANE, MALCOLM G. 1984. "Data Communications Hardware and Software." In *Advances in Data Communications Management.* Edited by Jacob Slonim, E. A. Unger, and P. S. Fisher. Vol. 2. Chichester, Great Britain: John Wiley & Sons.

————. 1984. "Data Communications Protocols." In *Advances in Data Communications Management.* Edited by Jacob Slonim, E. A. Unger, and P. S. Fisher. Vol. 2. Chichester, Great Britain: John Wiley & Sons.

————. 1975. "Hasp Remote Workstation Enhancements". *Proceedings of SHARE XLIV,* Los Angeles: 248–60.

LANE, MALCOLM G., and JAMES D. MOONEY. 1983. "A Text Processing System for IBM OS6-Produced Documents on the VAX 11/780 under VMS." United States Department of Energy (for Morgantown [West Virginia] Energy Technology Center).

LOOMIS, MARY E. S. 1983. *Data Communications.* Englewood Cliffs, N.J.: Prentice-Hall.

McNAMARA, JOHN E. 1982. *Technical Aspects of Data Communication.* 2d ed. Bedford, Mass.: Digital Press.

MARTIN, JAMES. 1970. *Teleprocessing Network Organization.* Englewood Cliffs, N.J.: Prentice-Hall.

————. 1981. *Computer Networks and Distributed Processing: Software, Techniques, and Architecture.* Englewood Cliffs, N.J.: Prentice-Hall.

MEIJER, ANTON, and PAUL PEETERS. 1982. *Computer Network Architecture.* Rockville, Md.: Computer Science Press.

NYQUIST, H. 1924. "Certain Factors Affecting Telegraph Speed." *Transactions A.I.E.E.*

————. 1928. "Certain Topics in Telegraph Transmission Theory." *Transactions A.T.E.E.*

OSBORNE, MARK CRAIG. 1983. "An Asynchronous Communications Terminal Emulator." Master's Project Report, West Virginia University.

SIPPL, CHARLES J., and CHARLES P. SIPPL. 1972. *Computer Dictionary.* Indianapolis: Howard W. Sams & Co.

SHANNON, CLAUDE E. "Mathematical Theory of Communication." *Bell System Technical Journal* (July and October 1948).

SHERMAN, KENNETH. 1981. *Data Communications: A Users Guide.* Reston, Va.: Reston.

STALLINGS, WILLIAM. "Local Networks." *ACM Computing Surveys* (March 1984).

TANENBAUM, ANDREW S. 1981. *Computer Networks.* Englewood Cliffs, N.J.: Prentice-Hall.

THURBER, K. J., and FREEMAN, H. A. October 1979. "Architecture Considerations for Local Area Computer Networks." *Proceedings of the First International Conference on Distributed Computing Systems:* 131–42.

WECKER, STUART. September 1979. "Computer Network Architectures." *Computer* 12 (no. 9). Long Beach, Calif.: IEEE Computer Society.

Answers to Selected Review Questions

Chapter 1

1. receiver, transmitter, and medium   **2.** protocol   **3.** (c)

Chapter 2

1. distortion   **2. a.** False   **b.** False   **c.** True   **d.** True   **3.** frequency division and time division   **4.** transponder   **5.** Shannon's Law   **6. a.** simultaneous two-directional transfer   **b.** one-way transfer   **c.** two-directional alternating transfer

Chapter 3

1. using a multiplexer and using a concentrator   **2.** short haul modems   **3. a.** False   **b.** True   **c.** True   **4.** speed, number of bits per character, parity, duplex   **5. a.** character-by-character   **b.** block transfer

Chapter 4

1. a. 7-bit   **b.** 5-bit   **c.** 8-bit   **2.** ASCII   **3. a.** True   **b.** False   **c.** True   **d.** False   **e.** False   **f.** False   **4.** longitudinal redundancy check (LRC) and vertical redundancy check (VRC)

Chapter 5

1. START and STOP conditions   **2.** break   **3.** STOP bit or condition   **4.** interrupt facility, clock, bus interface   **5.** START/STOP transmission   **6. a.** False   **b.** True

Chapter 6

1. block of data by a synchronizing bit pattern (and possibly a header) and a trailer   **2.** SYN character or FLAG   **3.** character in asynchronous transmission and a message for synchronous transmission

Chapter 7

1. amplitude, frequency, phase (shift)   **2.** dibits   **3.** RS-232 interface   **4.** receive on one end to transmit on the other   **5.** transmit digital signals using an analog signal

Chapter 8

1. Open System Interconnection (OSI), ● International Standards Organization ● physical ● data link ● network ● transport ● session ● presentation ● application   **2.** to provide a standard basis for designing and comparing network architectures   **3.** provides conversation between similar programs on the source and destination machines in a network (as opposed to intermediate neighbor machines)   **4.** data link   **5.** ARPANET   **6.** Systems Network Architecture (SNA)   **7.** Digital Network Architecture (DNA)   **8.** presentation   **9.** transport

Chapter 9

1. error control and sequence control   **2.** control messages and data messages   **3.** to detect when a message or connection has been lost and to provide timing for handshake sequences   **4.** transparency   **5.** character-oriented, byte-count-oriented, and bit-oriented

Chapter 10

1. provides precise definition of syntax of messages   **2.** data characters. messages or events (e.g., timeouts)   **3.** data state in BSC protocol when the received character is not a control character for BSC

Chapter 11

1. Data compression   **2.** (HASP) multileaving protocol   **3.** mathematical algorithms

Chapter 12

2. variable length   **3.** to frame a message ● hardware inserts 0s after 5 consecutive 1 bits in data stream; receiving hardware removes these extra 0s   **5.** block check character ● LRC ● or CRC check characters   **6.** all control characters must be preceded by a DLE character and any DLE in data stream must have a DLE inserted before it before transmission   **8.** DDCMP

Chapter 13

2. b, c   **5.** broadband: 300 MHz or greater; baseband: usually no more than 50Mhz   **7.** contention techniques   **8.** CSMA/CD

Chapter 14

2. event driven   **3.** round robin or priority-driven   **4.** the receiver task and the transmitter task   **5.** form (data messages)

Chapter 15

3. a. must be saved for preserving integrity of interrupted program   **b.** must be saved in order to return to interrupted program   **c.** used by hardware to determine where the interrupt service routine is located in memory   **d.** represent events which are pending or have occurred in an interrupt-driven environment   **e.** can be started and thereafter serviced by interrupt service routines which receive control upon the triggering of an interrupt by a device

Chapter 16

1. using table translate techniques or by using XOR, SHIFT, and AND instructions   **2.** hardware because of its speed   **3.** in mark parity, parity bit is always 1; in space parity, parity bit is always 0

Chapter 17

3. RCV-FLAG is set by an interrupt handler which can automatically get control in the middle of the loop

Chapter 18

1. transmitter control/status register ● receiver control/status register ● line parameter register ● transmitter buffer register ● transmitter line control register ● transmitter break control register ● receiver buffer register   **2.** speed differences of lines do not permit data characters to be taken from a FIFO in first-in/first-out order   **3.** a data character arrives from a line when the FIFO buffer is full   **6.** a holding buffer for characters received by hardware and stored by receiver interrupt handle, which have not yet been "read" by a user program

Chapter 19

2. characters will appear garbled on screen   **4.** 7 and 8   **5.** even ● odd ● none ● mark ● space   **6.** nothing may appear or garbled characters may appear   **7.** XOFF and XON charcters are used to suspend and resume data transmission

Chapter 20

1. signals computer software that telephone is ringing (detected by auto-answer modem)   **2.** device initialization ● determining transmitter/receiver status ● controlling or setting up transmitter/receiver ● performing data reads (receive) and writes (transmit)   **3.** transmitter hardware which has not been given data to send by software when it is needed will automatically transmit a SYN character   **4.** generally no, because modem has not turned line around to transmit; data will most likely be lost

Chapter 21

1. syntactic and procedural   **2.** represents a particular state, events which might occur, action to perform on occurrence of event, and next state to move to when event occurs

Chapter 22

1. DLCXMT: c, f; DLCRCV: a, i, j; ICXMT: b, h; ICRCV: d, e, g

Chapter 23

1. to implement timeout control and provide handshake sequence   **2.** by setting a counter and decrementing it on every interrupt checking for the interval in the counter being 0   **3.** handshaking sequence   **4.** time from the setting of request to send by terminal or computer software until clear to send is set by the modem

Chapter 24

1. timeout control ● startup control ● sequence control ● error control ● line control ● transparency ● exceptions or special cases

Chapter 25

2. can study format of data and control messages received before building and transmitting such messages   **4. a.** False   **b.** True (if two NULL characters in a row are not in data stream, nothing will be received; if they are in data stream, incorrect message format will be the result) **c.** True   **5.** SYN register not loaded ● Wrong SYN character ● Modems not the same speed ● Bad cable ● Other computer down or line not started

INDEX

(Also Refer to Dictionary pp. 355-379)